Romanticism
Comes of Age

Published by Barfield Press

Books by Owen Barfield:

Poetic Diction: A Study in Meaning
Romanticism Comes of Age
This Ever Diverse Pair
Saving the Appearances: A Study in Idolatry
Worlds Apart: A Dialogue of the 1960's
Unancestral Voice
Speaker's Meaning
What Coleridge Thought
The Rediscovery of Meaning, and Other Essays
History, Guilt and Habit
Owen Barfield on C. S. Lewis
Night Operation
Eager Spring
The Rose on the Ash-Heap

Translations:

The Case for Anthroposophy

Forthcoming new editions:

The Silver Trumpet
Orpheus: A Poetic Drama
English People
Short stories
Poetry

www.owenbarfield.org

Owen Barfield

Romanticism Comes of Age

Barfield Press
OXFORD, ENGLAND

Copyright © 2012 Owen Barfield Literary Estate

All images are privately owned.

The right of Owen Barfield to be identified as the author of this work has been asserted in accordance with the Copyright, Designs and Patents Act 1988.

All rights reserved. No part of this publication may be reproduced, stored in a retrieval system, or transmitted in any form or by any means, electronic, mechanical, photocopying, recording or otherwise without permission in writing from the Owen Barfield Literary Estate.

Series Editor: Dr. Jane Hipolito

Published by Barfield Press UK, Oxford, England

First published by Anthroposophical Publishing Co., London, 1944
New and augmented edition, Rudolf Steiner Press, London, 1966;
   Wesleyan University Press, Middletown, CT, 1967
This third edition, Barfield Press, Oxford, 2012

A catalogue record for this book is available from the British Library.

Romanticism Comes of Age by Owen Barfield
ISBN 978 0 9569423 1 9

Printed on paper with Sustainable Forestry Initiative (SFI) accreditation.

Produced on behalf of
the Owen Barfield Literary Estate.

The Literary Estate promotes and safeguards the works
and intellectual legacy of Arthur Owen Barfield.

O˙B

www.owenbarfield.org

To my many friends in

the Anthroposophical Movement,

I humbly and gratefully dedicate this book.

(See pages 12 and 29.)

CONTENTS

with date of first publication

Introduction to the 1944 edition	1
Introduction to the 1966 edition	15
From East to West — 1930	35
Thinking and Thought — 1927	60
Speech, Reason and Imagination — 1927	83
Of the Consciousness Soul — 1928	102
The Form of *Hamlet* — 1931	124
Of the Intellectual Soul — 1929	148
The Inspiration of the *Divine Comedy* — 1934	167
Coleridge's "I and Thou" — 1931	191
The Philosophy of Samuel Taylor Coleridge — 1932	201
Goethe and the Twentieth Century — 1949	223
The Time-Philosophy of Rudolf Steiner — 1955	246
The Fall in Man and Nature — 1959	270
Man, Thought and Nature — 1962	290
Rudolf Steiner's Concept of Mind — 1961	310

INTRODUCTION TO THE 1944 EDITION

THE ESSAYS OF which this book is comprised were written at irregular intervals during a period between twelve and eighteen years ago. With one exception (here called "Coleridge's 'I and Thou'"), which was contributed as a book review to *The Criterion*, they appeared in article form in a periodical published under the auspices of the Anthroposophical Society in Great Britain. They are here gathered together in the form of a book, to which I am asked to write an Introduction. On re-reading them at this distance of time I see that the area of the subject-matter over which they directly or allusively range must appear wide, its communications tortuous and its boundaries ill-defined. I seem to have chosen a continent, instead of a country, for a rather haphazard walking-tour. A map on the scale required is accordingly out of the question and the best service I can do for any patient reader who may desire to read this book as a connected whole is to show him my diary and lend him my Baedekers.

In other words I have decided to try and give some account of the circumstances which led to their being written. I will not be so insincere as to express personal regret at the autobiographical stain which this will necessarily involve (it is a necessity which rarely arises and which few of us really regret when it does), but neither do I propose to indulge in any personal reminiscences merely for the fun of the thing.

I was brought up without religious beliefs and with somewhat of a bias against them. On the emotional side I was taught not to be flippant about things which others revere, but was not taught to be reverent myself. Thus, when I first began to think about such things as literature, art and religion, my mind was *tabula rasa* as far as any preconceived notions went. There was nothing I held fast to, but on the other hand nothing which personal experience, as distinct from contemporary fashion, had taught me to reject as humbug. As time went on, I began to abhor the vacuum in myself which did not at all fit with the promptings either of my emotional or of my moral nature, but I did not see that I could do anything about it.

The first serious thing that happened to my mind was (at the age of about twenty-one) a sudden and rapid increase in the intensity with which I experienced lyric poetry. This was a fact. It was something I could not successfully convict myself of believing because I wanted to believe it. It was something that kept on actually happening to me — not nearly as often as I should have liked, but still often enough — and in the intellectual vacuum created by my skepticism on all subjects pertaining to the origin and spiritual nature of man it was a conspicuous object to which I was not sorry to turn my attention. I began instinctively to investigate it and the method I adopted, so far from drying up the sources of delight, seemed rather to enhance it. I attribute this to the fact that I kept my attention on the experience itself and was not attracted by rhetorical explanations which led away from it.

INTRODUCTION TO THE 1944 EDITION

What impressed me particularly was the power with which not so much whole poems as particular combinations of words worked on my mind. It seemed that there was some magic in it; and a magic which not only gave me pleasure, but also reacted on and expanded the meanings of the individual words concerned. From the purely literary point of view this was dangerous and might have led (perhaps it did) to preciosity or pedantry. If it did not, it was partly because I had enough general love of literature to balance it and partly because I was not content to stop short at the magical experience but felt a strong impulse to penetrate into it and to reach what, if anything, lay behind it. This kept me from merely wallowing.

The second fact which made a tremendous impression on me was the way in which my intense experience of poetry reacted on my apprehension of the outer world. The face of nature, the objects of art, the events of history and human intercourse betrayed significances hitherto unknown as the result of precisely these poetic or imaginative combinations of words to which I have referred. I found I knew things about them which I had not known before.

Thus, without any particular exertion or theorising on my part I had had two things strongly impressed on me, firstly that the poetic or imaginative use of words enhances their meanings and secondly that those enhanced meanings may reveal hitherto unapprehended parts of reality. All this seemed to promise a way out of the vacuum and I began to pursue my investigations more systematically. In the first place the second of the two propositions just mentioned might be (and I was thoroughly conditioned to believe it was) an illusion. What I have just now called a revelation might be merely an emotion of my own. I was lucky enough in those days to be master of my own time. So, like Mr. Brooke in *Middlemarch*, I "went into all that a good deal."

Naturally it was the Romantic poets who supplied in the richest measure the kind of imaginative treatment of language and life in which I had become interested. But Romanticism had a philosophy as well as a literature and this philosophy was the natural starting point of my enquiries. I pondered much on Wordsworth's *Prefaces* and on Coleridge and his sources. But I did not specialise unduly. I went on to read a good deal of general philosophy and among other things was led by my enthusiasm on the trail to renew a rather sketchy acquaintance with Greek and to peruse all the later Platonic Dialogues, besides as much of Aristotle as I supposed relevant (which included the whole of the undeservedly neglected *De Anima*).

Actually it was the point at which philosophy borders on psychology which interested me most and I pursued my studies to some extent into the latter realm, limiting them however to psychology proper, that is to the study of the *psyche* starting from psychic data. To begin, as so much contemporary psychology did, from physiological facts or theories appeared to me to be preposterous. Above all, it was *genetic* psychology in which I was interested.

INTRODUCTION TO THE 1944 EDITION

To avoid giving a false impression, I ought to add that I cannot claim to be expert or even widely read in any of these subjects. I inspected much, dipped into a good deal, but my actual reading was intensive rather than extensive and the quantity was not large. It was all grouped round the particular line of investigation I was pursuing. I was looking out all the time for ideas which (*a*) would fit in with the experiences I have referred to and (*b*) were not contradicted either by the rest of my own experience or by scientifically ascertained facts. The incidence, when it occurred, that they ran counter to widely, or even almost universally, held scientific *theories*, was a matter of less moment. It was a drawback, but a less serious one and it weighed with me less and less as time went on. The habit of distinguishing sharply between facts and theories is, I think, a good one to acquire in a scientific age.

I came out of all this with a fairly well-considered theory of poetry, or rather of poetic *diction*, as a means of cognition, which I embodied in a book that met with fairly wide approval and is, I have reason to believe, still consulted by those concerned with the subject. At the same time the attention which I had been giving to the semantic aspect of language (that is, the study of meaning and changes of meaning) had thrown a flood of light for me on the history and evolution of human consciousness, which I distinguished sharply from the history of *thought*.

I now began to look about me and consider what to do next, and the first thing I realised (for up to now I had been too absorbed and busy to do so) was that nobody else appeared any longer to take Romanticism very seriously. It seemed to have been attacked on all sides and defended (though I remember a valiant attempt of Mr. Middleton Murry's in his *Adelphi*) with little spirit. The Humanists had been levelling its towers and pinnacles, while the psychoanalysts were busy tunnelling beneath its walls. The comrade whom it grieved me most to lose was busy moving back all his formidable artillery into the ancient citadel of naïve realism and patriarchal theology —— where, by the way, his arrival has since been made known to the enemy by a series of revealing explosions near the latter's Base. A fourth, and by far the largest, group had simply disappeared over the horizon altogether, marching to the deafening tune that no proposition concerning the human spirit even merited the privilege of refutation unless it was derived wholly and solely from contempt of the rottenness of twentieth-century society. Altogether things were in a bad way.

I understood, or thought I understood, the reactions of this last group pretty well, though I could not make common cause with them. As to the outward symptoms of the rottenness, it seemed to me more important to look round for a remedy and inculcate its adoption than to go on depicting them in sardonic verses which, whatever their merits might be, were a tremendous bother to read because they would neither parse nor scan. As to the underlying spiritual causes, I believed and still believe them to be near enough to the heart of my own matter to justify me in proceeding with it.

Now at a fairly early stage in the process which I have attempted to record I came into contact with the writings of Rudolf Steiner. I began, after some hesitation, to study his spiritual science, or anthroposophy (a name which, after twenty years' experience, I am not confident that the mother tongue will ever manage to assimilate), seriously and steadily; and this went on side by side, and in close interaction, with the other studies I have mentioned. As time went on, three things in particular struck me most forcibly about anthroposophy. The first was that many of the statements and ideas which I found there produced an effect very similar to the combination of words to which I have already alluded. As in the one case, so in the other, this effect was independent of belief. Something happened: one felt wiser. This was a fact. The question as to what exactly one believed about the fact came after. The second was that, so far as concerned the particular subject in which I was immersed at the time, Steiner had obviously forgotten volumes more than I had ever dreamed of. It is difficult to lay my finger on what convinced me of this. As far as I know there is no special treatise on Semantics or Semasiology among his works. Rather it was a matter of stray remarks and casual allusions which showed that some of my own most daring and (as I thought) original conclusions were *his* premises —— just as, when you meet a man for the first time, without knowing his background, it is not some long harangue, but the casual way in which he uses a particular word in a particular context, that reveals quite suddenly the extent of his knowledge of a subject with which you are yourself well-acquainted.

So much for my own particular subject; and when it came to psychology (the adjoining region on which, as I have said, I had also been led to trespass), it was quickly apparent to me that Steiner's teaching of the three 'souls' (Sentient Soul, Intellectual Soul and Consciousness Soul), at once delicate and profound, accurate and inexhaustible, resembled anything else I had read on the subject about as much as I suppose a modern textbook on electricity and magnetism resembles an adventurous eighteenth-century essay on the vagaries of lightning and the curious results which may be observed when amber is rubbed on silk.

The third was, that anthroposophy included and transcended not only my own poor stammering theory of poetry as knowledge, but the whole Romantic philosophy. It was nothing less than Romanticism grown up.

Let me expand this last a little. The adjective *romantic*, as Mr. Pearsall Smith pointed out long ago, was originally applied in a pejorative sense to persons like Don Quixote whose heads were supposed to be filled with the old Romances, of which they had absorbed too many. By a further development it was employed to characterise aspects of Nature of a kind among which these 'Romances' were usually set. To the eyes of those who had stocked their minds with the events of romance and incidentally with the scenes among which they were usually set — uncouth mountains and blasted heaths — such scenes came to possess a significance to which other eyes remained opaque. Thus, the word denoted on the one hand the pure workings of fancy and on the other (by way of ridicule) the effect of these on man's observation of Nature. But the ridicule died away after the *Lyrical Ballads* had shown what could be done by choosing to be

INTRODUCTION TO THE 1944 EDITION

romantic in earnest. "It was agreed," wrote Coleridge afterwards:–

> that my endeavours should be directed to persons and characters supernatural, or at least romantic; yet so as to transfer from our inward nature a human interest and a semblance of truth sufficient to procure for these shadows of imagination that willing suspension of disbelief for the moment, which constitutes poetic faith. Mr. Wordsworth, on the other hand, was to propose to himself as his object, to give the charm of novelty to things of every day, and to excite a feeling analogous to the supernatural, by awakening the mind's attention to the lethargy of custom, and directing it to the loveliness and the wonders of the world before us ...

Nor did either of them ever lose sight, as their successors have sometimes done, of the duplex nature of the process by which, for the romantic, the spiritual significance of nature is revealed —— first the purely subjective experience artificially induced and then the reaction of this upon nature. Coleridge's oft-quoted

> We receive but what we give
> And in our life alone does Nature live

is matched by many passages in the *Prelude* which stress the importance of the productions of fancy for the opening of man's eyes to the true spirit of nature.

This is not the place to expound Steiner's theory of knowledge or to dilate on the "supersensible" cognition to which it naturally leads, and to which he has pointed the way in numerous books. All I wish to stress is that the "intuition" in which it culminates is to be reached by way of two preliminary stages, the first of which he terms "imagination" and the second "inspiration." In imaginative cognition, Steiner taught, one acquires a sort of picture-consciousness, a vigilant dreaming, in which the spiritual facts of life and creation come before the soul in the form of pictures. This is however purely subjective and it is of its essence that it should be recognised as such. It is only at the second stage, that of inspiration, that the *perceptive* faculty itself is enhanced in a way that has objective value for cognition.

From Steiner too I learned that a serious attempt to obtain exact results with the help of a perceptive faculty developed through controlled imagination had been made more than a hundred years ago, and by no means without success, by that uncrowned king of Romantics, Goethe. For a fuller account of this, with my other grounds for affirming that anthroposophy is 'Romanticism come of age,' I refer the reader to the first of the essays which follow.

Here was food indeed for thought —— enough, it might have seemed, to draw in anyone in my peculiar position, whatever the nature of the teachings erected by Steiner on these foundations might prove to be. But what could I say when I came to grasp (as I quickly did) how this very method of knowledge had confirmed for him, as a fact of experience, the historical tradition of the Incarnation of Christ and how those teachings, with their startling width of scope, were rooted at all points in that Event? When, thanks to him, the impossible superstition (as I had hitherto judged it) from which the disintegrating spiritual life and the tottering civilisation of Europe had drawn their spiritual strength, became for me an obvious fact? To cut a long story short, I gave in. I acknowledged Rudolf Steiner with reverence as *il maestro di color che sanno* —— the master of those who know. Not without reluctance; for had I not already a single page of notes headed *Evolution of Consciousness* —— germ of the *magnum opus* with which I myself had proposed one day to startle the world? Others in like case were sacrificing careers and cash in order that they might devote their whole lives to his movement. I at least joined it.

It was clear that all I had to do now was to point all this out to the lettered world. I began trying to do so. But at this point things began to go wrong. A very few experiments were enough to show that even those who shared my interest in literature, even those who were prepared to lend at least a sympathetic ear to my own observations on the subjects of poetry and semantics, were not in the least interested in the news about Rudolf Steiner which I was so anxious to bring them. They simply would not listen. I gave up the experiment and made one last attempt to convey my message in a different form and on a more ambitious scale, linking it up closely and, as I thought, sympathetically with psychoanalysis and the rottenness and theology and much else. Again I failed entirely, and it began to be borne in on me that I had not the abilities which such a task required at such a time. Shortly after this I lost the inestimable privilege of leisure and as a result was able, as far as the lettered world was concerned, to advance cautiously from inaudibility to silence.

By way of contrast with this dismal tale, I found that those who shared my devotion to Steiner *were* most anxious to hear all the news I could bring, both from my adventures in the realm of English language and literature and from my other studies, to them and through them to a wider circle which they were then, as now, seeking to approach. *Their* acknowledgements were almost embarrassing and my only regret is that I have not repaid better and more copiously the liberal hospitality which they extended to the products of my pen. What I did do with the material I had collected is — most of it — contained in the following pages, some of the articles having been written during the period which I have just been describing and others a year or so after its close. Whatever their value may be, it is certain that without the encouragement I have mentioned they would never have been written. To my many friends in the Anthroposophical Movement therefore I humbly and gratefully dedicate this book.

I feel that one more word is called for on the subject of certain allusions to Germany and the German spirit which will be found in it. These essays were as it happens all written before 1933. I have never underrated the evil significance of the Nazi movement and the hold which it has taken of the German people as a whole. At a time when a good many of those who are very sure they do not *now* underrate it were finding excuses for Hitler, and some of my own friends were advancing the view that practically any concession or betrayal was preferable to war, I held and expressed the opposite opinion with vehemence. As far as I am able to understand it, the political Reich is and always has been not so much a nation as a septic disease of Europe —— all the more so because it is *not* perfectly distinguishable from the spiritual Germany to which occasional reference is made in these essays, but is a recognisable distortion thereof. *Corruptio optimi pessima*. Those who best understand what the German spirit stands for in the whole concern of the human spirit will not be the least vigilant against the portent of its aberration. There is warrant for this. The existence of the British Expeditionary Force in 1914 was admittedly due to the foresight and exertion of the late Lord Haldane, wearer of ancient hats, who used to refer to Germany as his spiritual home. ("Here he comes," said the facetious Edward VII once at a garden party, "in the hat which he inherited from Goethe!") When the passion and misery of this war are beginning to recede, and the irrepressible leader-writer has forgotten what he was thinking and saying in 1937 and as generously as he forgot between 1930 and 1937 what he had been thinking and saying in 1919, let us hope — if the disease does begin to spread again — that there will still be someone about in an old hat inherited from Goethe.

Meanwhile there are few attitudes I dislike and distrust more than the complacent humility which declares that, because "we" are all tarred with the same brush, any measures taken against Germany in the name of justice must needs be sheer hypocrisy. Perhaps some day this stupid and vicious "hypocrisy-lie" will be properly nailed. It was the main plank of the excusers and appeasers of 1934–1938 and has, in my opinion, played a large part in landing Europe where it is today. I, for one, shall not be in the forefront of those who after this War will cry out against the severity of any measures taken against that unhappy country, provided only that, whether preventive or retributive, they are honestly aimed at protecting Europe against a recurrence of the appalling events of the last ten years. Moreover I believe it to be a practical necessity that such measures should take absolute precedence of any grandiose scheme for "re-education" or reconciliation. But all this in my view in no way destroys the positive significance of the spiritual Germany in its pure act, which is all I was concerned with —— and which I think the ruined janizaries of National Socialism can hardly obliterate, though they might succeed in driving it elsewhere. On the contrary I firmly believe that the question whether our own Commonwealth is to stand for something more in the history of human consciousness or is to become a hollow political shell and go the way of Nineveh and Tyre,[a] will depend very largely on the candour with which the spirit of this Island learns to open its arms to that spirit and its gifts. There is nothing in this book on that or any other subject which I wish unsaid or would not say again today.

OWEN BARFIELD
May 1944

Editor's Note

a. This is very likely a reference to a passage in Rudyard Kipling's 'Recessional' (1897): 'Lo, all our pomp of yesterday / Is one with Nineveh and Tyre!' Nineveh, the capital city of ancient Assyria, was destroyed by the Medes and Babylonians in 612 B.C. Tyre was the capital city of ancient Phoenicia; it was captured by Alexander the Great in 332 B.C. and destroyed by the Muslims in A.D. 1296.

INTRODUCTION
TO THE 1966 EDITION

THE HANDFUL OF books I have written and published during my life have been spread over a very long period of time, more than forty years in fact. With two exceptions, which are not material and are both out of print, in each one of these books I have made clear in one way or another the paramount debt I owe to Rudolf Steiner. Among my sympathetic readers, who seem to have grown a little more numerous lately, there are a number who have expressed surprise at this emphasis and asked me to explain it.

In the nature of the case a brief explanation could be no sort of explanation at all, and it occurs to me that the following essays, apart from any wider significance they may possess, may afford the best answer I can give to the kind of question sometimes put to me by thoughtful people who have more than a nodding acquaintance with one or two of my books but little or no acquaintance with Steiner.

They extend over practically the same long period, during which they were contributed from time to time, after having in some cases been first delivered in lecture form, to periodicals published by or in association with the Anthroposophical Society in Great Britain, namely *Anthroposophy* (a quarterly publication discontinued many years ago), *Anthroposophical Movement*, a current quarterly publication intended primarily for members of the society referred to above, and the current annual, *The*

Golden Blade. With the exception of the last five essays, none of which is earlier than 1949, they were collected and published in 1944, in the first edition of this book, by the Rudolf Steiner Press under its then name of Anthroposophical Publishing Company. "The Philosophy of Samuel Taylor Coleridge", to which I shall refer again, was however given as a lecture at the Goetheanum, Dornach, Switzerland, the headquarters of the international Anthroposophical Society, in 1932 on the occasion of the centenary of Goethe's death; it made its first appearance in print in *Romanticism Comes of Age*. Two essays included in the first edition, "Coleridge's 'I and Thou'" and "The Inspiration of the *Divine Comedy*", are omitted from the present one. The former was a book review reprinted from T. S. Eliot's *New Criterion* and the latter now seems to me to fall rather outside the intended scope of the collection. The concluding essay, "Rudolf Steiner's Concept of Mind", is reprinted here by kind permission of Messrs. Hodder and Stoughton from *The Faithful Thinker*, a volume of essays by various writers on Steiner, his work and the posthumous development of his work, which appeared, on the centenary of his birth, in 1961. Like the books I have referred to, these essays were written not only over a long period of time but at widely irregular intervals during that period. This is the principal ground of a fear I have that the whole collection may lack something of the unity proper to a book. In the Introduction to the first edition, which itself appeared no less than twelve years after the latest of the essays it contained, I wrote:

INTRODUCTION TO THE 1966 EDITION

On re-reading them at this distance of time I see that the area of the subject-matter over which they directly or allusively range must appear wide, its communications tortuous and its boundaries ill-defined. I seem to have chosen a continent instead of a country, for a rather haphazard walking-tour. A map on the scale required is accordingly out of the question and the best service I can do for any patient reader who may desire to read this book as a connected whole is to show him my diary and lend him my Baedekers.

With the double object then of bonding the separate blocks of which the volume is composed into something like a solid building and of assuaging curiosity where it exists, I go on now to say a little about the way I came to be a follower of Rudolf Steiner and how it was that these essays came to be written.

Relevantly to that account, the first serious thing that happened to my mind was (at the age of about twenty-one) a sudden and rapid increase in the intensity with which I experienced lyric poetry. This was a fact. It was something I could not successfully convict myself, though I tried hard to do so, of believing because I wanted to believe it. It was something that kept on actually happening to me — not nearly as often as I should have liked, but still often enough — and in the intellectual vacuum created by my scepticism on all subjects pertaining to the origin and spiritual nature of man (I had been brought up as an agnostic) it was a conspicuous object to which I was not sorry to turn my attention. I began instinctively to investigate it, and the method I adopted, so far from drying up the sources of delight, seemed rather to refresh them. I attribute this to the fact that I kept my attention fixed on the experience itself and was not attracted by theoretical explanations that led away from it

What impressed me particularly was the power with which not so much whole poems as particular combinations of words worked on my mind. It seemed there was some magic in it; and a magic which not only gave me pleasure but also reacted on and expanded the meanings of the individual words concerned. From the purely literary point of view this was dangerous and might have led (perhaps it did) to preciosity and pedantry. If it did not, it was partly because I had enough general love of literature to balance it and partly because I was not content to stop short at the 'magical' experience but felt a strong impulse to penetrate into it and to reach what, if anything, lay behind it. This kept me from merely wallowing.

The second fact that made a tremendous impression on me was the way in which almost any intense experience of poetry reacted on my experience of the outer world. The face of nature, the objects of art, the events of history and human intercourse betrayed significances hitherto unknown as the result of precisely these poetic or imaginative combinations of words to which I have referred. I found I knew (there was no other word for it) things about them which I had not known before.

Thus, without any particular exertion or theorising on my part, I had had two things strongly impressed on me, firstly that the poetic or imaginative use of words enhances their meanings and secondly that those enhanced meanings may reveal hitherto unapprehended parts or aspects of reality. All this seemed to promise a way out of the vacuum and I began to pursue my investigations more systematically. In the first place the second of the two propositions just mentioned might be (and I was thoroughly conditioned to believe that it was) an illusion. What I have just now called revelation might be merely an emotion of my own.

Naturally it was the English Romantic poets, underpinned by Shakespeare, who supplied in the richest measure the kind of imaginative treatment of language and life in which I had become interested. But Romanticism had a philosophy as well as a literature and this philosophy was the natural starting point of my enquiries. I pondered much on Wordsworth's *Prefaces* —— more on Coleridge and, to the slight extent that I was then equipped for it, his sources. But I did not specialise unduly. I had leisure in those early days and I went on to read a good deal of general philosophy and among other things was led by my enthusiasm on the trail to renew a rather sketchy acquaintance with Greek and to peruse all the later Platonic Dialogues, besides as much of Aristotle as I supposed relevant (which included the whole of the undeservedly neglected *De Anima*).

Actually it was the point at which philosophy borders on psychology which interested me (as incidentally it interested Coleridge) most, and I pursued my studies to some extent into the latter realm, limiting them however to 'psychology' proper, that is to the study of the psyche starting from psychic data. To begin, as so much contemporary psychology did, from physiological facts and theories appeared to me to be, in the literal sense, 'preposterous'. Besides, I had already done plenty of thinking along those lines and had found that, instead of penetrating the experience, they simply looked away from it. One must either ignore *them* or ignore the experience; and I was determined to remain empirical. Above all it was *genetic* psychology in which I was interested.

I came out of all this with a fairly well considered theory of poetry as a means of cognition, which I embodied in the book called *Poetic Diction*. At the same time the attention I had been giving to the semantic aspect of language (I use the word in its older and wider sense, connoting the historical as well as the analytical study of meanings) had thrown a flood of light for me on the history and evolution of human consciousness, which I found I must distinguish sharply from the history of *thought*. It was this that led to my writing *History in English Words*, on the invitation of Messrs. Methuen, who published the first edition in 1926. *Poetic Diction* was first published by Faber and Faber in 1928, but the two books were composed more or less contemporaneously, for *Poetic Diction*, in its original form, was my Thesis for the degree of B.Litt. and I had begun working on it as early as 1922.

The British literary élite have not, during my time, been notorious for mental vigilance or philosophical depth. Vogue, rather than personal investigation, has all too obviously been their criterion for valuing new — or old — ideas. This was not true of W. B. Yeats, who however declined or was unable to look below the fitness of an idea for the special kind of lyric he was determined to write. As to the professional critics, perhaps it would be going too far to say, with Coleridge, that their "intellectual claims to the guardianship of the Muses seem, for the greater part, analogous to the physical qualifications which adapt their oriental brethren for the superintendence of the Harem". At all events it was unfortunate for me that all this I have described was going on at a time when Romanticism in general was under a growing cloud and everybody who was anybody was losing interest in it. Directly and indirectly, for I had to make a living, I suppose it was mainly for this reason that, beyond the contributions I have mentioned, I produced nothing more of significance in the present context until *Saving the Appearances* appeared in 1957 —— except for a few short papers, like "Poetic Diction and Legal Fiction", which found a home long after it was written in Max Black's anthology *The Importance of Language.*

It was a year or two before my first book was published that I first came into contact with the writings of Rudolf Steiner. I began, after some hesitation, to study his spiritual science, or anthroposophy, seriously and steadily; and this went on side by side, and in close interaction, with the other studies I have mentioned. As time went on, three things in particular struck me most about anthroposophy. The first was, that many of the statements and ideas which I found there produced an effect very similar to the combinations of words to which I have already alluded. As in the one case, so in the other, this effect was independent of belief. Something happened: one felt wiser. This was a fact. The question as to what exactly one believed about the fact came after. The second was that, so far as concerned the particular subject in which I was immersed at the time, that is the histories of verbal meanings and their bearing on the evolution of human consciousness, Steiner had obviously forgotten volumes more than I had ever dreamed. It is difficult to lay my finger on what convinced me of this. As far as I know there is no special treatise on semantics or semasiology among his works. Rather it was a matter of stray remarks and casual allusions which showed that some of my most daring and (as I thought) original conclusions were *his* premises —— just as, when you meet a man for the first time, without knowing his background, it is not some long harangue but the casual way in which he selects or uses a particular word in a particular context that reveals quite suddenly the extent of his knowledge of a subject with which you count yourself well acquainted.

So much for my own particular subject; and when it came to psychology (the adjoining region on which, as I have said, I had been led to trespass), it was quickly apparent to me that Steiner's teaching of the three 'souls' (sentient soul, intellectual soul and consciousness soul), at once delicate and profound, accurate and inexhaustible, resembled anything else I had read on the subject — on the subject of the psyche *itself* as distinct from physiologically or clinically based causal hypotheses — about as much as I suppose a modern textbook on electricity and magnetism resembles an adventurous eighteenth-century essay on the vagaries of lightning and the curious results which may be observed when amber is rubbed on silk.

The third was, that anthroposophy included and transcended not only my own poor stammering theory of poetry as knowledge, but the whole Romantic philosophy. It was nothing less than Romanticism grown up.

Let me expand this last a little. The adjective *romantic*, as Mr. Pearsall Smith pointed out long ago, was originally applied in a pejorative sense to persons like Don Quixote whose heads were supposed to be filled with the old Romances, of which they had absorbed too many. By a further development it was employed to characterise aspects of nature of a kind among which these 'Romances' were usually set. To the eyes of those who had stocked their memories with the events of romance and incidentally with the scenes among which they were usually set — uncouth mountains and blasted heaths and so forth — such scenes came to possess a significance to which other eyes remained opaque. Thus, the word denoted on the one hand the pure workings of fancy and on the other (by way of ridicule) the effect of these on man's perceptive feeling for Nature. But the ridicule died away after the *Lyrical Ballads* had shown what could be done by choosing to be romantic in earnest. "It was agreed," wrote Coleridge afterwards:

> ... that my endeavours should be directed to persons and characters supernatural, or at least romantic; yet so as to transfer from our inward nature a human interest and a semblance of truth sufficient to procure for these shadows of imagination that willing suspension of disbelief for the

moment, which constitutes poetic faith. Mr. Wordsworth, on the other hand, was to propose to himself as his object, to give the charm of novelty to things of every day, and to excite a feeling analogous to the supernatural, by awakening the mind's attention to the lethargy of custom, and directing it to the loveliness and the wonders of the world before us....

Nor did either of them ever lose sight, as their successors have sometimes done, of the duplex nature of the process by which, for the romantic, the spiritual significance of nature is revealed: first the purely subjective experience, artificially induced, and then the reaction of this upon nature. Coleridge's oft-quoted:

> We receive but what we give
> And in our life alone does Nature live

is matched by many passages in Wordsworth's *Prelude* which stress the importance of the products of fancy for the opening of man's eyes to the true spirit of nature.

This is not the place to expound Steiner's theory of knowledge or to dilate on the 'supersensuous' cognition to which it naturally leads, and to which he has pointed the way in numerous books and lectures. Such an exposition, highly condensed, will be found in the concluding essay of this volume. All I wish to stress here and now is that the 'Intuition', in which his method culminates, is to be reached by way of two preliminary stages, the first of which he terms Imagination and the second Inspiration. Any number of critics, following Schelling and Coleridge, have dealt with imagination as an ultimate mental activity

INTRODUCTION TO THE 1966 EDITION 25

that opposes, and transmutes into a kind of aesthetic or mystical contemplation, that absolute dichotomy between perceiving subject and perceived object on which our practical everyday experience (Coleridge's 'lethargy of custom') is necessarily based. Only Steiner, as far as I know, has clearly apprehended this activity as part, and but the first part, of a long, sober process of cognition that may end in a man's actually overcoming the dichotomy —— sober, but involving a plus of self-consciousness amounting to a mutation, since it presupposes no less than a crossing of the stark threshold between knowing and being. In imaginative cognition, he taught, one acquires a sort of picture-consciousness, a vigilant dreaming, in which the spiritual facts of life and creation come before the soul in the form of pictures.

This 'cognition' is however mainly subjective ('a semblance of truth') and it is of its essence that it should be recognised as such. It is only at the second of the three stages, that of Inspiration, that the *perceptive* faculty itself is enhanced in a way that begins to have objective value for cognition.

From Steiner, too, I learned for the first time that a serious attempt to obtain exact results with the help of a perceptive faculty developed through controlled imagination had been made more than a hundred years earlier, and by no means without success, by that uncrowned king of Romantics, Goethe. For a fuller account of this I refer the reader to the first of the essays that follow, since the later one, "Goethe and the Twentieth Century", which appeared in *The Golden Blade* in the year of the bicentenary of the poet's birth, does not deal at all with his scientific writings. This was because they were being separately covered by another contributor; and I was glad to have the opportunity of supplementing the deficiency with a broadcast talk on *Goethe and Evolution*, which I gave in the BBC Third Programme series on Goethe in the same year, and in which I again pointed to Steiner as the indispensable authority on the whole subject of Goethe as scientist.

It has been the deepest of disappointments to me to find that, when one refers to Steiner, people do not listen. Or rather I have not merely been disappointed, I have been shocked and puzzled to have it borne in on me over and over again that even those who are prepared to lend a very sympathetic ear indeed to *my own* observations, whether on language and poetry or on the wider issue of the whole evolution of human consciousness, are not in the least interested in the news about Steiner which it has been one of my main objects in life to set before the educated public with all the earnestness and sobriety at my disposal.

This raises, for me at least, a question very much bigger than my own particular failure up to now —— which could certainly be my own particular fault. One may resolutely dismiss from one's mind sensational phrases like 'conspiracy of silence', when they enter it, as they sometimes do, unbidden. One is left with the unanswered question: how does it come about that this most responsible of minds so often evokes unwonted irresponsibility in others? As an example that will serve *a fortiori* for all the rest, even the late C. S. Lewis, who was meticulous, if ever a man was, about passing on hearsay judgments, who would never, for instance, express an opinion even on a minor but all too prolix poet of the sixteenth century without first having read the great bulk of what the man himself had actually written —— that even he, on more than one occasion, broke his rule in the case of Steiner?

But I am not thinking so much of positive denigration. I am thinking of that combination of a refusal to investigate with a readiness to dismiss, which can alone account for the absence of at least a *reference* to Steiner from a hundred Indexes where one would expect, simply because of his obvious and extreme relevance, to find it as a matter of course: in good books, for example, by otherwise thoughtful and open-minded men concerning the relation between Eastern and Western thought in religion and philosophy and evincing a wide acquaintance with the best that has been thought and said on the subject in our time.

I have sometimes tried to attribute the boycott to Steiner's occasional use of the detested word 'occult': for instance, in the title of the principal source-book of anthroposophy: *Occult Science: an Outline*. But after all the men I have in mind are not children, to be frightened with bogies, and an hour or two's receptive reading would be enough to reveal that, in the context, the word signifies no more than what a more conventionally phrased cosmogony would determine as 'non-phenomenal', 'noumenal', 'transcendental'. Yet, for some reason, it seems almost useless to point this out. It will be the same after you have finished as before you began. *Uttered*, the term 'occult' will signify 'concealed' (from the senses, because by definition not accessible to the senses, because by definition noumenal): *heard*, it will still signify 'secret' (because witchery)!

And it is the same with the vocabulary of spiritual science as a whole, which is commonly taken 'literally' even by those well-equipped to know better; though the notion that the verbal imagery which the mere use of language involves does not necessarily refer only to yet other images (*phaenomena*), is not even a particularly new one. It is almost exactly a hundred and fifty years now since Coleridge, for instance, was writing in his *Biographia Literaria*: "... all the organs of sense are framed for a corresponding world of sense; and we have it. All the organs of spirit are framed for a correspondent world of spirit: though the latter organs are not developed in all alike." It does seem as if not only the imagination, but the understanding also of the twentieth century is so prone to the 'lethargy of custom' that the conclusions of positivism remain concealed (or perhaps 'occult' is the word) as habit, even where its premises have been explicitly abandoned as theory.

That future historians of Western thought will interpret the appearance of Romantic philosophy towards the close of the eighteenth century as foreshadowing the advent of Rudolf Steiner towards the close of the nineteenth I have no sort of doubt. For the account I am now rendering, however, the point is that the climate of opinion in which I have been writing has been one of hostility to the one and indifference, based on total ignorance, to the other. Now against this depressing liability there is one corresponding asset which it is most agreeable to record. If the literary, let alone the philosophical, élite were not in the least interested in my news of Steiner, a tiny public, who already shared my estimate of his spiritual stature and world-historical significance, *were* most anxious to hear all the news I could bring them, both from my adventures in the realm of English language and literature and from my other studies. *Their* acknowledgments were almost embarrassing and my only regret is that I have not repaid more satisfactorily the liberal hospitality they extended to the occasional products of my pen. Whatever the value of the ensuing essays may be, it is certain that without that sustaining encouragement neither they, nor very probably (since it was they, above all, that kept my literary 'hand' in) the last three books I have published would ever have been written. It is to my many friends in the anthroposophical movement, therefore, that I humbly and gratefully dedicate this one.

So much in explanation. But I do not feel this Introduction would be complete without a passing reference to changes that have occurred since the first edition appeared twenty-two years ago. For in this matter of Romanticism there *has* been quite a noticeable change in the climate of literary, and in some measure of philosophical, opinion. To mention C. Day Lewis's *The Poetic Image*, Graham Hough's *Image and Experience* and Donald Davie's *Articulate Energy* in this connection is no doubt to select somewhat arbitrarily, but an Introduction cannot be a bibliography. In any case it is in the Western hemisphere that Romanticism is now being re-examined most energetically. Indeed, in the field of American literary criticism, the change I have remarked had begun still earlier, only I was not aware of it at the time. In England, as far as I recall, only Mr. Middleton Murry had been insisting on treating the Romantic Movement as no mere literary and aesthetic fashion but a permanent step forward in the evolution of human consciousness; and there had been very few to listen to him. In America, when Professor Arthur O. Lovejoy, in his Wellesley lectures on *The Great Chain of Being* delivered in 1933, described the Romantic Movement as evincing a change in the way of thinking of European man, he was only the first of a gathering host. Or I may still not be dating the change far enough back. What I do know is that in America, since that time, there has been something like a spate of critical work of high quality[1] in which the same underlying idea finds expression.

No doubt various developments in other domains have contributed, and particularly the growing appeal of existentialism, whether as a philosophy or as an attitude to life, and the increasing popular interest in anything to do with 'depth-psychology'. The current absorption in, almost obsession with, the topics of symbolism and myth

---

[1] Perhaps the example most likely to be known to English readers is Mr. M. H. Abrams' paperback *The Mirror and the Lamp*, in which, among much else of value, he relates the distinction he has drawn between the symbolist-abstract aesthetic on the one hand and the Romantic on the other to two contrasted images of man as 'heterocosm' and man as microcosm.

is also highly compatible with a willingness to look again at the principles developed and expressed in somewhat different terms by the Romantic philosophers and critics. There is, for instance, a wide circle of readers for whom it is a commonplace in the appraisal of Romanticism that the 'organicism', which (contrasted with 'mechanism') has long been such an indispensable weapon in the armoury of aesthetics, is relevant in the interpretation as well of nature as of art —— potentially relevant therefore to science as well as to the humanities. It is in this connection that the distinction has been drawn between a 'positive' Romanticism on the one hand and on the other, that 'negative' Romanticism, which (according to Mr. Morse Peckham writing in 1951 in *Publications of the Modern Language Association*) "causes isolation and despair because it offers no cosmic explanations".

It is true that the 'cosmic explanations', when they *are* forthcoming, tend to entail a spineless relativism; that a somewhat tortuous preoccupation with symbolism often discloses at the heart of the metaphysical labyrinth the old, rather boyish notion of a 'God' gradually coming into being; while an equally sophisticated preoccupation with myth may explode at any moment into the wilful crudities of the 'God is dead' theology, which is attracting so much attention as I write. There is perhaps room, then, for a modest attempt to unite positive and negative romanticism, modern symbol and ancient myth, imagination and inspiration in a single structure firmly bedded in the dimension of history, to show that, when so united, they may become an instrument for the kind of action required to be taken in our present predicament, and in fact to insist that the question: "Where do we go from here?" and the question: "How did we get here?" cannot fruitfully be considered in isolation from one another.

Compared with other disciplines perhaps the most unique feature of spiritual science is the fact that in it these two questions are always inseparably linked. Studying and practising it, we find the whole past history of man still present in him as latent faculty, so that by truly illuminating the former he awakens the latter, but so also that only by awakening the latter can he truly illuminate the former.

And here, if I may still pursue the metaphor of my title, I would say that a young man may be considered as fully come of age only when he has discovered two things: firstly his identity and secondly his vocation. And I would add that the young man called the Romantic Impulse appears to have gone a long way since most of these essays were written towards discovering his identity, but that I see little sign as yet of his having discovered his vocation.

Such alternative ideas and movements as I have just now referred to may or may not endure, but the impulses that beget them are, I surmise, deep and, though they may change their names, will not quickly expend their force. It is an open question whether the still deeper spiritual impulse, which was the original drive underlying the Romantic Movement in Europe, will steer its way into the light of full consciousness or be shattered on Charybdis or swallowed by Scylla. I have tried to make clear in what follows why I do not believe it can win through unless it is prepared to come to terms with the findings of spiritual science.

It is an open question, but there are hints here and there, and one in particular, which a prophet might find healthful and of good augury. Pending resort to the proffered chart and compass, which it has so far declined to handle, Romanticism in the English-speaking world is becoming increasingly aware that it has a star to steer by in the steadfast and inextinguishable nucleus of truth and energy that *still* somehow radiates from the intense mind of Samuel Taylor Coleridge and flashes through his scattered utterances. There is noticeable throughout the body of criticism I have referred to an increasing preoccupation with Coleridge and an increasing effort to penetrate his thought. "Interest in the theory of imagination," wrote Professor Kathleen Coburn a few years ago, "is now almost synonymous with interest in Coleridge." If this is so, we owe it in no small measure to the recent work of a few devoted scholars and above all to Miss Coburn herself. Access to a vast body of hitherto unpublished writings, as well as renewed access to some that had long been out of print, has steadily improved during the last few decades and will continue to improve still further, as she progresses with her five volume edition of the *Notebooks* and Professor Earl Grigson completes his *Collected Letters*, of which the first four volumes have already appeared. It will be total, when the *Collected Coleridge*, which Miss Coburn is editing from the University of Toronto, is finally concluded; but that I gather is still a long way in the future.

This reawakening interest in Coleridge's thought is moreover not confined to the literary world, as witness for example a carefully documented article by Professor Craig Miller on "Coleridge's Concept of Nature" in the New York *Journal of the History of Ideas* in the spring of 1964. Altogether the scholarly work that has been done in this field and the fullness of thought that has been given to it in many quarters make me rather ashamed of the inchoate and skeletal lecture on *The Philosophy of Samuel Taylor Coleridge* which I delivered in 1932. I have left it in its place here partly because, though there are plentiful allusions to him elsewhere in the book, a collection of this nature without one essay actually *on* STC would be too much like Hamlet without the Prince; partly also as a kind of 'trailer' for the amends I hope to make before long in the shape of a full-length book on Coleridge, wherein the whole issue of the 'dynamic' philosophy will be taken up on lines not hitherto, as far as I know, attempted.

OWEN BARFIELD
Cambridge, Massachusetts
February 1966

FROM EAST TO WEST
first published 1930

READERS OF CARLYLE'S *French Revolution* will remember the opening chapters, in which he describes ironically the glories of what he calls 'Victorious Analysis'. In this phrase, characteristically repeated many times, he endeavours to sum up a state of mind which descended on intellectual Europe in the course of the seventeenth and eighteenth centuries, and which he presents as one of the deeper causes of the Revolution itself. Universal and exclusive homage to common sense and to the inductive method of reasoning, this was at the root of the matter. And it was in the form of a reaction against this mood and this sense of values that the movement which I am now to consider first appeared.

With this preface I shall be less uneasy in naming it the Romantic Movement, or Romantic Revival. I begin by considering it in its purely literary aspect —— but only after making it clear that it was not a purely literary movement. As a literary movement, then, the Romantic Revival seems to me to have fallen into two fairly distinct halves. On the one hand the pursuit of what I will call pure Romance and the attaching to this of high human value. Strangeness and distance, these are the essence of this pure Romance. It is the cult of 'far away and long ago'. It is the mood of

From a paper read before the Lotus Club, Oxford University, 1929.

> Will no one tell me what she sings?
> Perchance the plaintive numbers flow
> For old unhappy far-off things
> And battles long ago.

"Over the hills and far away," said Mr. Chesterton, an excellent modern exponent of pure romance, "is the finest line in English poetry." The other half of the movement is metaphysical. It comes forward with a new theory of poetry, which it sees for the first time more as a religion than as a pastime. It makes much use of such words as *genius, imagination, creative,* filling them with a meaning which Dr. Johnson could hardly even have understood —— much less approved.

It is with this half of the movement, and its subsequent history, that I am principally concerned. And it is this half of it which also leads us out of literature and into other departments of life. I mentioned the new use of the word *creative*. It is significant that the application of this epithet to human beings — poets and artists — aroused in the first place some hostility on religious grounds. It was regarded in some quarters as blasphemy. And it was, of course, just this sort of piety, or pietism, which convinced Shelley of the 'necessity of atheism' —— by which he really meant a new religion that would allow men to be free.

I doubt whether anyone, who considers it, will deny that the Romantic Movement is closely connected with an enhanced sense of *human freedom*. We have only to take such representative figures as Shelley, Beethoven, Byron, Wordsworth, and think of all that the French Revolution and the hopes it aroused meant to their inner life. I particularly say their *inner* life. If they dreamed of the *rights of man* it was because they had already felt the *powers of man* —— in themselves.

To this dim inward sense of powers, and, therefore, of rights, hitherto unsuspected, I would draw your attention. Looking at the history of the seventeenth and eighteenth centuries one seems to feel it growing in the darkness, this mysterious impulse, behind the outer shell of customary thought, customary routine, customary religion, until at the time of the Romantic Revival it cracks that shell and bursts through. It cracks the shell in many places. And I would like to remind you once more of the two especially large cracks which we have already noticed. First — hovering as it were between the two parts of the literary movement (the purely Romantic part and the Metaphysical) — a new conception is born, which we may sum up in the word *Beauty*. Beauty for its own sake is a new object of human devotion. In the eighteenth century we hear of elegance, and adornment and so forth, in speaking of works of art, but not much of *beauty*. Among the English Romantics I should put John Keats as in a sense epitomising the conception of literature as beauty.

Secondly there is, as we have seen, the conception of human *freedom* and connected with it, I suppose, a new, or at least renewed attitude to the problem of *goodness*. And Shelley here takes the place of Keats as the principal exponent.

And now there enters in a tragic element, a tragic element of which I shall have much to say. For the point is that a third large crack ought also to have appeared in the rind of 'Victorious Analysis'. This did not take place, and here, too, there is a person who for me at least has come to symbolise the intercepting finger of tragedy. He is, however, a much less distinguished person than Keats or Shelley, indeed a nameless person.

Readers of Coleridge's *Biographia Literaria* will remember how he begins in the thirteenth chapter to give a philosophical account of the *Nature of Imagination*. After about two pages, however, the chapter breaks off, and for the remainder is substituted a note to the effect that "thus far had the work been transcribed for the press when I received the following letter from a friend whose poetical judgment I have had ample reason to estimate and revere…" Coleridge subsequently describes this letter, which prevented or excused him from finishing the chapter, as 'very judicious'.[1] It is this disembodied, 'very judicious', friend of Coleridge's who symbolises for me the tragic destiny of the Romantic Movement in this country. For it is perfectly plain to me that beside the two large cracks, or rather beside the new-fledged ideas which issued from them, there should have been a third. To make Romanticism into a self-sufficient organic being, able to stand on its own legs and face the rest of the world, there ought to have been added to the new concept, beauty, to the renewed conception of freedom, a new idea also of the nature of *truth*.

---

[1] Later in his life he disclosed that the 'friend' was an invention and he had composed the judicious letter himself.

We find in abundance an instinctive *conviction*, and courageous *assertions*, that Poetry, that Imagination, as it is now understood, bears some special relation to Truth. We need only go to Shelley's *Defence of Poetry* or to Keats' *Letters* for these. But there they stop short. "Poetry," said Shelley in the former work, "is the breath and finer spirit of all knowledge. It is the impassioned expression on the face of science." "I am certain of nothing," wrote Keats, "but the holiness of the heart's affections and the truth of imagination." The point is that he did not in actual fact (whatever he might have done if he had lived) concern himself with the question: '*In what way* is Imagination true?' The point is that no satisfactory *critique* of Romance ever arose. It was never grounded satisfactorily in reality. And as a result the modern reader or critic is apt to feel, as he approaches even some of its noblest and completest productions, 'Yes, it is all very fine, very exciting, very noble —— but as a philosophy of life, it really will not do!'

In the legend of Parsifal tragic consequences follow the failure of the hero to ask the crucial question at the crucial moment. The question he should have asked when he saw the Holy Grail was 'Of what is it served?' The same question should have been asked by the Romantic Movement, when it saw the visionary Grail of the human imagination. But it was not asked — not at any rate in this country — except by Coleridge who, as we saw, was at the mercy of his judicious friend. And in the state of Romanticism, as it exists today, we see the tragic consequences that followed. The charm faded. The mirror cracked from side to side. Just as Coleridge, who had indeed had a vision of imagination as the vessel by which divinity passes down into humanity —— just as he fell back from *this* kind of imagination into the fantastic dreams of the opium-slave; so the metaphysic of Romanticism has gradually fallen sick, lost faith in itself. Imagination is still accepted, but it is accepted for the most part as a kind of conscious make-believe or personal masquerade. Modern aesthetic theory — as far as I am acquainted with it — has rejected Coleridge in favour of Croce. The few writers who are interested at all in the philosophy of poetry today drink of the Crocean spring either at the fountainhead or indirectly and in a slightly filtered form through some such native feed-pipe as Mr. I. A. Richards.

We have seen then that, as a result of what is commonly called the Romantic Movement, a new conception arose of the faculty of imagination. This was conceived not as mere idle fancy, but as being actually in some way a vehicle of truth or knowledge. But it was not asked *how*. And consequently Romanticism, without roots, is dying.

What then is the really characteristic thing about this 'creative imagination' for which the Romantics claimed so much? How does it differ from any other human faculty and experience? I think the true *differentia* of imagination is that the subject should be somehow merged or resolved into the object. Talent may copy Nature, but genius claims to 'create' after the fashion of Nature herself. Nature 'takes the pen from its hand and writes': and there are many phrases of the same nature. Thus, Coleridge called imagination *organic*. It was 'the repetition in the finite mind of the eternal act of creation in the infinite

I AM'. I think it was Lamb who spoke of the soul being 'resolved into the element which it contemplates', and the same feeling confronts us in the *Adonais*:

> He is a portion of that loveliness
> Which once he made more lovely.

In a word, imagination involves a certain disappearance of the sense of 'I' and 'Not I'. It stands before the object and feels 'I am that'.

Now in the East this resolution of the subjective-objective duality, the 'I am that' or *Tat tvam Asi*, is a very ancient maxim indeed. The West may resolve the duality in *theory*, and there are passages in Kant's *Critique of Pure Reason* which suggest that he had done so. The Eastern sages, however, exhorted their disciples to make 'I am that' a personal experience. With them it was not the abstract conception of a Transcendental Unity of Apperception but a single and highly concrete proposition ('I am that'). And in the Greek expression γνῶθι σέαυτον or 'Know thyself!' we really find the same principle embodied. This was no exhortation to introspection, but rather, in modern jargon, an exhortation to make the unconscious conscious. If 'I' in my true self — that is, if you choose, in my unconscious self — am *that* (the apparently objective), then it is only by knowing *that* and by knowing it *imaginatively* that I can 'know myself'.

We begin in this way to see the Romantic conception of imagination, not as something entirely new, but rather as the emergence in the West, and of course in an altered form, of an experience which the East had cultivated for ages. The passage from East to West has always been a curiously fertilising process. "Time and again," said the late Sir Walter Raleigh, "when East meets West, the spirit of Romance has been born."

And this leads us directly to another episode, a subsidiary one — a kind of underplot — in the tragedy of which I am speaking. There is a difference between passing from East to West or from West to East and *jumping* from one to the other. When towards the close of the last century Madame Blavatsky arrived in London and drew around her a circle of romantics and would-be romantics, including, for example, William Butler Yeats, it is a psychological *jump* from West to East with which we are concerned. And the modern Theosophical Society which arose from her inspiration is based, essentially, not on a naturally developing theory of imagination, a theory with its roots deep in Western soil, but on revelations given by mysterious beings whom Blavatsky styled her 'Masters'. I am not seeking to ridicule her claim; I am merely stating that this was, as far as I know, the point from which she started.

And now, like Aristotle, I have to draw your attention to the fact that between two extremes is to be found the mean. That, just as geographically Central Europe stands between the Eastern and the Western elements of civilisation, such too is her cultural position. It seems to be her true function to hold the balance, so to say, between Eastern and Western thought, to prevent, if possible, just such a flighty *jumping* as I have indicated, and turn it into a sober *passing*.

What is the position of Germany with respect to the Romantic Movement? It is, I think, a typical difference between the two nations that, whereas the English will do a thing half instinctively, and only really wake up to what they have done when it is all over, the Germans are much more conscious of their activity. They strive to be fully conscious of and to theorise about a thing actually while they are doing it. It was so with the Industrial Revolution. It was so with the Romantic Movement. Not only did the new ideas cause a great deal more general excitement on the Continent, but the Germans came much nearer to evolving what I have called a *critique* of Romance than anyone in this country.

Schiller, for example, is not content with extolling freedom and seeking beauty; he must have a full-dress epistolary discussion on freedom with Kant, opposing the latter's notion of a categorical imperative. Or again he seeks to show in his excellent *Letters on the Æsthetic Education of the Human Race* how moral freedom and the sense of beauty are closely and necessarily connected, how the passage from a compulsory morality to a free morality must lie through the appreciation of the beautiful.

There is moreover the group of Romantic philosophers, Fichte, Schlegel, Schelling, about whom I am not competent to speak. But above all there is Goethe. Goethe was a kind of prophet of Romanticism. From Goethe's hand, besides all the productions of his powerful imagination, we have abundance of critical work showing a harmonious and complete understanding of what they *meant*. He not only sought for beauty, freedom and truth; he knew that he was seeking them —— knew, moreover, the bonds of necessity which unite them. And he could say what he knew. It is typical of Goethe's completeness that he worked as a scientist no less than as a poet. Much is written in England of a more or less sentimental nature, as the case may be, of the discrepancy between poetry and science. It really makes one ashamed how few people here are aware that Goethe can so much as put in a *prima facie claim* to have resolved that discrepancy. Whereas in fact the claim can be substantiated.

In the first place a few words are necesary as to the state of natural science as Goethe found it. It was, as we have seen, completely under the thumb of 'Victorious Analysis'. Many philosophers have divined two opposing principles of human cognition — that faculty which analyses and distinguishes ideas and sense-phenomena one from another, and that again which unites them, which re-discovers the unity in their multiplicity. *Verstand* and *Vernunft*, or, as Locke called them, Judgment and Wit. In Goethe's time natural science had almost lost the use of the second faculty. Knowledge was a matter of making finer and yet finer sensible distinctions. In botany, for instance, it was the method of Linnaeus which held the field. Some slight variation from type being observed for the first time, the question was not asked, how did this varied form come into being out of the type? But the new variation was eagerly marked down and named as a new 'species'. Species multiplied in this way until they were as the sands of the sea.

Into this state of intellectual disintegration Goethe brought his own scientific method, which is really none other than the method of imagination. You may remember that in that thirteenth chapter of the *Biographia Literaria*, to which I have aheady referred, Coleridge invented a new word 'esemplastic'. The derivation is from the three Greek words — εἰς ἓν πλάττειν — 'to mould into one'. Now Goethe with his method of the 'exact percipient fancy', as it is often translated, really transferred the esemplastic imagination from literature and art to science. His method differs from the ordinary method of induction in that the observer, when he reaches a certain point (the 'prime phenomenon'), stops there and endeavours rather to sink himself in contemplation *in* that phenomenon than to form further thoughts *about* it. It implies a certain — if one may use the word — *chastity* of thought, a willingness not to go beyond a certain point. The blue of the sky, said Goethe, *is* the theory. To go further and weave a web of abstract ideas remote from anything we can perceive with our senses in order to 'explain' this blue —— that is to darken counsel. But more of this later. Meanwhile we must note that it was by this method that Goethe discovered that morphological principle which is now laid down on almost the first page of many botanical textbooks —— the principle that all the parts of a plant can be regarded as metamorphoses of the leaf. It was by this method that he discovered — not only that there was, but that there *must* be (please note) — a bone in the human skeleton hitherto unknown to science —— the *os intermaxillare*.

Thus in Central Europe we see Romanticism actually rising to the great question *"In what way is imagination true?"* and demonstrating that it had begun to find an answer. We see poetry approaching science with outstretched arms. Yet still they do not embrace. Still the tragedy remained unresolved. The scientific world took the most obvious and elementary of Goethe's discoveries into itself. Those which demanded a little effort, which demanded some understanding of his *method* if they were to be comprehended, it left alone. This was the case with the Goethean theory of colour, of which comparatively few people have even heard.[2] Yet the prevailing Newtonian theory is in reality not a theory of colour at all, but only of the conditions under which colour is possible. Similarly the Darwinians have, with their historical investigations, made 'species' look silly and unreal enough — but they have not presented science with any way of getting at the unity which underlies these innumerable variations — other than the trivial subterfuge of imagining a very remote time when they did not yet exist. Once upon a time....

* * * * *

We come, somewhat late in the day, to the real hero of my tragedy. In the sixties of the last century there was born in Central Europe (to be precise somewhere near the borders of Austria and Hungary) a man called Rudolf

---

[2] It is no longer quite the case today (1966), if my information is correct that Goethe's theory has been resorted to and applied in developing the process of colour-reproduction in print.

Steiner. He tells us in his autobiography how, from earliest childhood, he felt a longing to overcome the apparent lack of connection between inner and outer experience, the subjective and the objective worlds. At the age of twelve he was reading Kant's *Critique of Pure Reason* secretly, during school lessons, having bound it up in the covers of a textbook for that purpose. At some time during his twenties Steiner was called to Weimar to co-operate in producing the *National-Literatur* edition of Goethe's complete works. His task was to edit Goethe's voluminous scientific writings, and he particularly emphasises the way in which this event in his life, occurring at this time, coloured and helped to determine the whole of his intellectual life.

More and more convinced, as the work proceeded, of the importance of Goethe's outlook and method, and yet convinced at the same time of the incapacity of his contemporaries to understand it owing to their deeply ingrained habits of thought (owing, in fact, to 'Victorious Analysis'), he felt impelled to turn aside from his editorial work and produce — what is, I believe, his first published book: the short *Principles of a Theory of Knowledge implicit in Goethe's Outlook.* (Grundlinien einer Erkenntnistheorie der Goetheschen Weltanschauung.)

It is particularly important to notice that this was Steiner's first work, and to understand that his own epistemological method and his own outlook were developed organically and uninterruptedly out of Goethe's.

I should have wished to say very much of this little book, but space compels me to be content with the following brief remarks. In it Steiner exemplifies and defines more closely these *Urphänomene* — the 'prime phenomena', such as the blue of the sky — behind which it is really meaningless to try and penetrate. These are the true 'laws of nature'. They are apodeictic. And to seek either for objective 'causes' or for subjective formal principles of apprehension which compel us to 'accept' these laws is to depart from nature and knowledge into the realm of fancy. Corresponding to these prime phenomena, or laws of nature, which are the first principles of the inorganic world, we have in the organic world the Type. Having found the type in his imaginative experience, it is the business of the natural scientist to pause, to contemplate, to sink himself *into* it in such a way that he can redevelop the individual from it by his own activity. The point is that these *Urphänomene* are *neither objective nor subjective*. They come into existence *as* types, or *as* laws, only as they are intuited by human beings. And until they have so come into being, the object itself is incomplete. Knowledge in fact, so far from being a mental copy of events and processes outside the human being, inserts the human being right *into* these processes, of whose development it is itself the last stage.

Readers of Aristotle's *De Anima* will realise the parallel here between the Goethe-Steiner system and Aristotle's conception of the reality ($\varepsilon\tilde{\iota}\delta o\varsigma$) which only exists potentially ($\delta v v \alpha \mu \varepsilon \tilde{\iota}$) until it is known, and when it is known has its full existence actually ($\dot{\varepsilon}v\varepsilon\rho\gamma\varepsilon\iota\alpha$).

Now in a science proceeding on this method the function of the thing we call *experiment* would also be different from what it is in a science proceeding on purely inductive lines. Here the purpose of experiment is not simply to provide data, from which explanatory hypotheses can then be evolved, but rather to clear away the accidents and leave the prime phenomenon visible in its naked purity. It might be compared to the drawing of figures by a geometrician. The figures are not there for him to learn from, but only to make his own thoughts clear to himself. "Experiment," says Steiner, "is the mediator between subject and object."

The remainder of Steiner's life, after he had finished the appointed work on Goethe, is the history of the further development of this method of knowledge, derived or developed from Goethe, and the application of its fruits in his own case to many different departments of life. I want to make the point once more that Steiner's method of knowledge is, in its essence, *systematic imagination*. The truth of imagination is apodeictic, not empirical, and he makes accordingly no less a claim for the results of his spiritual investigation. For imagination is not a *reasoning about*, it is a *Schauung*, a *seeing*, and indeed a *being*, the object. Systematic imagination is, in fact, clairvoyance.

I have spent some time in insisting that ideas of this kind are not easily grasped by contemporary Western thought, which is still to a large extent under the thumb of 'Victorious Analysis'. We have seen, however, that the same ideas are in some sense native to the East. Out of these two facts arises the sequel to the minor tragic episode of which I spoke a little way back.

Steiner had much to say; he was obliged to speak to those who would listen. And when he was asked by the Theosophical Society to co-operate with them and to act as the General Secretary of the German Section, he did not refuse. I venture to call this event tragic, because I do not suppose on the one hand that he could wisely have refused, while on the other there is no doubt that this temporary connection with the Theosophical Society has caused considerable unnecessary prejudice against himself and his work — especially in this country — and will stand in the way of his speedy recognition. It is important to note that, in agreeing to work with the Theosophical Society, Steiner reserved from the first the right to complete freedom in his choice of expression and activity. On the same day that the inaugural meeting of the German Section of the Theosophical Society was held, with himself as General Secretary, he delivered a public lecture under the title of *Anthroposophy*.

The purpose of this paper is to introduce you to this very thing, anthroposophy. That is the name which Steiner gave to the movement which he himself founded, to his method of knowledge, and to the accumulating fruits of that method. He revived the ancient term *anthroposophia*, because the essence of it is that it is developed out of man himself by his own powers and of his own free choice. Anthroposophy is the rights of man carried into the sphere of knowledge. It leads in every department of life to a fuller and richer conception of the human being, of the 'rein menschlich' as the Germans are so fond of saying. But since it is founded on principles of knowledge, of which the essence is that they resolve the duality between subjective and objective, it leads at the same time and in the same degree to a fuller and richer conception of the world. We have already seen how the imagination knows instinctively what the Greek sages once taught — that all knowledge is self-knowledge — a proposition which may be said to conceal the root of all human wisdom. It is clearly a concept to be gradually approached, to be approached over and over again from totally different sides —— to be meditated on rather than glibly discussed. I should like nevertheless to try and characterise it a little further from one special point of view —— that of the difference between the typical Eastern and the typical Western attitude of mind.

We have approached these in the first place by showing that imagination, as the Romantics dimly divined it, as Goethe understood it, and as Steiner has shown us how to develop it, is not content with merely *looking-on at* the world. It seeks to sink itself entirely in the thing perceived —— "to resolve itself (you remember Lamb's phrase) into the element which it contemplates". It tries, we said, "to overcome the duality between subjective and objective". But now, if we take the bare expression, 'I am that', we shall probably note a certain difference between the tone in which it must have been uttered long ago by the Eastern Yogi and the tone in which it is uttered today by the Western devotee of imagination. There would be a difference of emphasis. For the Yogi, desirous of advancing further along the path of wisdom, the important thing is, or was, to feel, 'I am that' —— there is indeed such an entity as *I* myself and I can find it by looking at the outer world. That is his discovery. For the Westerner, on the other hand, as he develops his imagination, the novel experience is to feel 'I am *that*'. There was never any doubt about there being an entity called 'I', he feels, but the great discovery, the advance in wisdom, is the realisation that this 'I' is not shut up inside this physical body as if in a kind of box, as he had naturally supposed. No, it is out there in the flower and the stone. 'I' am not merely the seer but the seen. I am *that*.

Each of the two, the Eastern yogi and the Western poet-philosopher, can be seen trying to transcend the *normal* consciousness of his hemisphere. For the normal consciousness of East and West differs in just this way, that each has by a kind of native right what the other lacks, what the other can only acquire by its own efforts —— by becoming yogi or poet, as the case may be. It lies deep in the nature of the East, said Steiner, that its peoples are not fully *self-conscious* to the same extent as the Western peoples. There is there no such cult of the individual 'personality'. The idea, for instance, that this individual personality should survive death appears somewhat childish and unnatural to the deeper and better sort of Eastern mind. Eastern society bears about it still the marks of having grown uninterruptedly out of deep, unconscious, instinctive levels of human experience. Thus, we can still see standing behind it the old theocratic organisation, when the priest or the initiate directed all that should be done, not by theory and hypothesis and debate but by direct intuitions drawn from a spiritual world. Whatever Western ideas may for the time being take hold of his fancy and capture his brain, the Eastern man is still in the depths of his being fundamentally *religious*. So said Rudolf Steiner.

In the West, on the other hand, the typical kind of consciousness which everyone acquires without any effort — can hardly help acquiring nowadays out of the whole nature of his environment and education — is precisely the converse of this. Each man is a *personality*, alert, wide-awake, thinking in hard clear concepts and disposed to bring everything to the test of his intelligence and his senses. "I'm from Missouri," as the Americanism has it —— "You've got to *show* me!"

On one occasion Steiner summed up this contrast in the two words, *Maya* and *Ideology*. To the Buddhist (and Buddhism, he affirms, is still deep in the blood of the East, however much it may have been expelled from the brain) the outside sense-perceptible world is 'Maya' —— unreality. He hardly believes in it. What is real is that inner world of consciousness, into which his sages could sink themselves in meditation. Spirit is reality, matter non-existent.

In the West the opposite is the case. The doctrines of Marx spread wider and wider on the broad back of Lenin and there are millions of men who take it for granted today that matter is the only reality and spirit is —— an illusion, a nothing. Everything included under the term Religion, Art, Culture and the like, is no more than an 'ideology' —— a pale flickering reflection of purely physical and economic processes.

Yet the true human consciousness —— the consciousness for which man is, so to say, fitted and for which he longs, transcends these opposite distinctions of East and West. And for this reason we find in the East a kind of yearning towards the West and again in the West a longing and reaching out to the East. Thus educated Eastern people often have, or had until recently, a way of perceiving even more clearly than the Westerner himself the splendour of all that is most typically Western —— its debating societies and parliamentary systems and psychology and elaborately organised mechanical civilisation. They do not feel as acutely as the cultivated Westerner does the absence of the spirit from it all. For, in a certain sense, they *have* the spirit as a gift.

On the other hand the Westerner who is most keenly conscious of Westernism tends to reach out his hands towards the profound, silent, unconscious (or un-*self*-conscious) spiritual life which he at any rate thinks he perceives in the East. We have mentioned the Theosophical Movement, but in my opinion such phenomena as the popularity of Sigmund Freud, and in this country, of Mr. D. H. Lawrence are symptoms of the same unsatisfied desire — a desire for depths, dark, unconscious quiet depths — with less talk of this fussy little intellect, and this fiddling little 'personality' that we hear so much about.

This mutual need makes it very alarming to observe the rapidly increasing cloud of misunderstanding between East and West. It is not merely that misunderstanding is unnecessary; we must go further and say that, for both, a true understanding is exactly what is necessary. Neither can know itself without knowing the other. And yet there is in fact nothing but misunderstanding! The kind of misunderstanding that occurs is perhaps best typified in Gandhi's attitude to Christianity —— Christianity which, according to many Westerners themselves, has been justly discredited in the eyes of the East by the European War. Here one sees a personality that is clearly equipped to understand *one* aspect of Christianity so much better than anybody in the West that the West needs all he can tell it. It is that aspect which does not differ essentially from Buddhism, that call to a *passive*, self-surrendering love, which the East has always known and which it has elevated to a method of knowledge. Thus, Gandhi, with his policy of passive resistance, and seeing only this side of Christianity, is found affirming, not without a note of patronage in his voice, that Christianity does not differ in any essential from Buddhism —— except that its followers do not take it so seriously.

What Gandhi does not understand at all is that element which I can only call the other pole of Christianity —— that aspect of it which the West above all has developed, though often enough out of all connection with the name of Christ. I mean the fact that, through the incarnation of Christ in a human body, there was born into the world, not for the West or for one section of humanity only, but for all men, what one can only call a legitimate *self-consciousness*. Steiner has described on many occasions and from many different points of view how in the Christ the human Ego, the true Self, of Man descended from the purely spiritual heights, where it had hitherto dwelt, to the earth. Had Christ not come to earth, individual human beings would never have been able to utter the word 'I' at all. Steiner incurred here a good deal of opposition from theorists who insisted that all religions must be of equal value, and so forth, but his reply was always the same, that it was not his business to estimate the relative values of religions but merely to state the facts of human spiritual evolution as he knew them from direct intuition.

Now it is because a full consciousness of self depends precisely on a sense of the subjective-objective distinction — the feeling "I am here and the table is out there in space" — it is for just this reason that the West has had to develop its strong sense of that distinction, with the inevitable accompanying sense of exclusion from the unity of the spirit. Earlier I spoke of the 'overcoming' of the duality between subjective and objective as the goal which the Western romantic imagination set itself. The East *has never wholly fallen into the duality*; and that is why the West longs for all that it has to give.

If civilisation is not to come crashing about our ears, said Steiner over and over again in the most earnest words, there must be men not merely in the East nor merely in the West — but all over the world — willing to make the individual effort that is necessary in order to retain both —— the instinctive, pre-Christian spirit-consciousness typical of the East and along with it the clear, post-Christian *self*-consciousness typical of the West. That the whole of humanity should eventually acquire such a consciousness is the entelechy of the earth-evolution as a whole.

In a course of lectures delivered in 1923 at Vienna Steiner pointed out that he himself, in books such as *A Road to Self-Knowledge* and *Knowledge of the Higher Worlds and its Attainment,* had shown the way to such a balanced East-West consciousness. He began by comparing the ancient yogi, who by a *physical* process, the control of his breathing, drew his consciousness more and more into his body and thus increased his self-consciousness, with the modern devotee of Spiritual Science who, beginning with strictly *intellectual* exercises of concentration and the like, lifts his consciousness *out* of the body, where it is all too firmly embedded, and thus increases his consciousness of a spiritual world not identified with his personal self. He described how the instinctive Maya-feeling of the Eastern mystic — that dim dreamy realisation that the physical world is no more than a pale after-copy or reflection of a spiritual world from which he himself came when he was incarnated into the body — how this becomes, for the man who acquires self-knowledge by modern Western methods, a fully conscious, detailed *perception* of the way in which his own physical body, and then the whole physical world with which it is bound up, is indeed just a symbolic physical residue of the spirit. He showed how the practice of Yoga, well adapted for its own time, is yet unhealthy if conducted today, in that it paralyses the soul for its life of ordinary social intercourse and activity. It demands a certain retirement from one's fellows, which the needs of the time do not justify. And he showed how the modern 'exact clairvoyant', in the pain and suffering which come to him inevitably as he increases his self-knowledge, learns to comprehend Buddha's teaching of the escape from Maya to the Nirvana that is beyond suffering, while at the same time he transmutes this passive Nirvana of the Buddhist into that state of tireless spiritual activity about an inner core of peace, which we at any rate *ought* to mean when we use the Christian word Resurrection. *Maya* and *Ideology*; *Nirvana* and *Resurrection*; they are the key-words to an understanding of the true relation between East and West.

I have tried to show that romance is essentially something which lights up with the passage of Eastern wisdom towards the West. To anyone who has really come under the spell of that great Movement — to whom romance and imagination are not merely a pleasant means of whiling away an hour after dinner, but are — as they were to Coleridge and Shelley and have been to many others since —— a passion, a religion, a veritable key to the promised land, I have this to say. A man has recently died whose life-work has proved that that great enthusiasm of the Romantic Movement was no delusion, though voices on every side of us today will have us believe that it was. On the contrary, imagination is the most precious of all our possessions —— the chosen one of all our faculties to be our saviour. Only we must take it seriously. And then we can learn to receive as it were into our own consciousness the spiritual antithesis between East and West. And in this way an active and truly scientific mood of romance is born in us, a mood which does not merely sustain and please us, but makes us better able to serve our fellow-men and our age. Above all, we help to prevent, by our own 'esemplastic' power, that terrible material conflict between East and West which must surely be played out before long on the outer stage of history —— unless enough men are found with the ability and the will, not merely to say sentimentally 'we are all brothers', but to explain just *how* we are brothers and exactly what it is in our history, in our nature, and in our destinies that makes us so.

THINKING AND THOUGHT
first published 1927

THERE IS A difference between 'thinking' and 'thought'. One way of grasping this difference (which is of the utmost importance) is to consider the *history* of thinking and see how it differs from a history of thought. The following is intended to be a kind of digest of notes for a possible history of thinking — not of thought, but thinking — as it has developed in the Western world from the beginning of Greek civilisation down to our own day.

If we examine reflectively the manner in which we Europeans think today of the world about us, one of the first things we notice is that the concept of 'Law', explicit or implicit, as the case may be, plays an absolutely fundamental part in it. We might say that our thoughts take their whole shape and colour from this concept. The whole of what we respect as 'science', for example, is nothing but the investigation and revelation of 'laws', whether they be laws of nature in the stricter physical sense or the 'laws' which are assumed, albeit with somewhat less universal consent, to govern such regions as human behaviour, economic intercourse, etc. The familiar 'law of supply and demand' will do for an example of the latter kind. Nor is the idea merely one of those abstruse hypotheses which are deliberately adopted for the convenience of an accurate scientific method. It is fixed, as a reality, quite as firmly — perhaps more firmly — in the head of the proverbial man in the street than it is in the specialised mind of the professor expounding logic or the expert pursuing scientific research.

When we have realised the ubiquity of this idea in modern European thought, we may for that reason be inclined to stop and ask ourselves more precisely what is meant by it. What do we all mean? Do we, for example, think of a law of nature as corresponding at all to a Hebraic 'Law', that is to say, as being a definite *command* of the Almighty? I believe that very few modern Europeans and Americans conceive of the laws of nature in that light. Do we think of it, then, as a kind of custom or tradition, which Nature keeps tactfully agreeing to follow, as though, when she was bringing to birth a litter of puppies, she would say to herself: Well, I suppose I had better make them as like the parent dogs as possible —— after all, I always *have* done so? It would be absurd. No, it is only when we think of nature, life, reality, or whatever we call it, as being *obliged* to behave as it does, or — to translate the same idea from Latin into English — as being 'bound' to do so, that we begin to speak of 'laws of nature'. A law of nature is to us a something, an *x*, which binds or connects together otherwise discrete phenomena.

Now a history of thinking differs from a history of thought in that, not content with observing *that* men began to think thus and thus at a certain time, it goes on to ask *how* they became able to think so. Enquiring on these lines, it is quite easy to discover that the concept 'law' arose out of human practices and institutions and was only afterwards transferred, by analogy, to nature, or to processes in general over which the human will is conceived to have no control. But human laws have been created and conceived of very differently at different times and places; so that we have still to enquire what particular kind of human law it was, which was adapted by analogy and became such an indispensable instrument of modern thought. Now, just as the Hebraic 'Law' was much more of a command than a law, as we understand it, so the Greek law, as the word νόμος ('nomos') suggests, was rather in the nature of what we understand by 'custom' or 'tradition'. It is only in the Roman *lex*, with its etymological derivation from 'binding' (ob-*lig*-ation, etc.), that the modern meaning really begins to appear in human consciousness at all. Here at last, distilled as it were from the formidably practical activity of generations of Roman soldiers and statesmen, we have the true legal conception of a relation between human beings, not based on blood or affection or religion, but upon a purely abstract something which is 'binding' on them. This could be illustrated in an interesting manner from the meanings of all sorts of Latin words and English words derived from Latin. It could also be demonstrated, from such records as the writings of Augustine and Aquinas, old pictures of the Last Judgment, etc., that, as Steiner has pointed out, the peculiarly Roman conception of, and feeling for, law crept into all kinds of thought during the Dark and Middle Ages. But at the moment all this must be passed over. The question is, when did men first begin to think, in something like the modern manner, of 'laws of nature'?

As far as I am aware, the first writer to draw the analogy in England (though it was not in the English language) was the lawyer-philosopher, Francis Bacon.[1] Moreover, Bacon's place in the history of European thought makes it pretty certain that he was at least *among* the first to draw it at all. So that, in the history of thought, we have here a fairly definite point — round about the beginning of the seventeenth century — at which the concept 'laws of nature' first begins to reveal itself as working in human minds. But now, if we wish to go on from a history of thought to a history of thinking, we shall have to ask ourselves: then, how did men think nature before they had acquired this concept? I purposely avoid saying, how did they think *of* nature, because (as I hope to show) to think *of* nature, as we do today, the concept of 'law' must to some extent have been already absorbed by the thinker at first or second hand. History of thought is illusory just because we tend to *think back* in this way *in our own terms,* to project into the minds of our ancestors a kind of thinking which was only made possible by the subsequent events of that very history. For history of thinking we have to be much more conscientious; and, once having perceived that such a concept as 'law' in its application to nature only entered into human consciousness at a certain period, we must try for all previous periods, as it were, to *unthink* that

---

[1] For the *lex naturæ*, or *naturalis*, of the Schoolmen meant always the law of God implanted in the human reason for the guidance of human conduct.

concept together with all its intellectual and psychological implications and consequences. This requires a very real effort of the imagination, besides a fairly intimate acquaintance with the customary processes of our own intellects.

Now one of the most significant passages in which Bacon makes this strikingly novel use of the word *lex* (for he was writing in Latin) runs as follows:[2]

> It may be that nothing really exists except individual bodies, which produce real motion according to law; in science it is just that law, and the enquiry, discovery, and explanation of it, which are the fundamental requisite both for the knowledge and for the control of Nature. And it is that law, and its 'clauses', which *I* mean when I use (chiefly because of its current prevalence and familiarity) the word 'forms'.

The writer has just been vigorously condemning the scholastic science of his day, which consisted almost entirely of efforts to discuss and expound these 'forms' of which he speaks. It will thus be seen that he actually substitutes the meaning of the word 'law' for the meaning then commonly attached, in philosophical circles, to the word 'form' *(forma)* and only refrains from substituting the word itself because of its unfamiliarity. But subsequently — from about the time of the Restoration — this was actually done, with the ultimate results which we have just observed; and the word 'form' was dropped altogether in that connection. Thus, there is some reason to suppose

---

[2] *Novum Organum*, II, 2. Author's translation.

that, if we wish to grasp imaginatively the way in which men thought, before they had this transferred concept of 'law' both to help and to hinder them in their mental processes, it may be worth while to investigate the old meaning of the term for which, in effect, it was substituted —— I mean the word 'form'. As soon, however, as we attempt to do this, we find ourselves plunged into the world of Greek thought, for the meaning attached to the word 'form' in the Middle Ages was a definite relic of Greek philosophy. And in the kind of history which I am attempting to sketch Greek thought takes its place as the *result*, or product, of Greek thinking. We must consider the latter, therefore, first.

The pervasive quality of Greek thinking, and of Greek consciousness as a whole — the characteristic which distinguishes it most from our own and most delights us — is that it was in a certain sense *alive*. As a thinker or knower, the Greek tended to be at home, as it were, in the coming-into-being, or becoming; whereas our own thought, built as it is on the secure but rigid framework of *logic*[3] (which the Greeks did not succeed in evolving for us until Aristotle's day), can only deal with the 'become', the finished product —— except, of course, where it is willing to bring in the aid of poesy and metaphor. Ontologically —

---

[3] This is true of the average modern European, whether or no he is really capable of thinking with logical accuracy. There is all the difference in the world between the illogical and the pre-logical. The point is that he thinks *in the logical mode*.

and dismissing all moral and aesthetic values — it is quite legitimate to correlate 'alive' with 'becoming' and 'dead' with 'become'; and it is in this sense, as will appear more clearly, that I characterise Greek thinking as *alive*, when compared with our own. One casts about for a way in which one could try to convey this living quality of Greek thinking to those who had not had the opportunity of discovering it for themselves; and it must be confessed that it is not altogether easy. To take, however, a very homely example: the man of today knows quite well, of course, whether his hair is long or short; but if he examines this knowledge more closely, he will find that it is only knowledge of a *result*. Thus, he may look in the glass, he may see the snippets lying on the kind of surplice in which barbers envelop us, he may find that his new hat is now large enough to include his ears, or he may feel cold round the back of his neck as he goes out into the street. On the other hand, he may feel the heat or weight of long hair. But if we try to imagine that, instead of this way of knowledge, we could actually be conscious *in* the growing of our hair, could feel it as *movement* in something the same way that we still feel our breathing as movement, we should be making an approach towards the difference between Greek consciousness and Greek thinking, and our own. Consciousness and thinking are practically interchangeable here; for thinking, in this living sense, differs from thought in that it is not merely an intellectual operation connected with the brain, but involves the whole consciousness. Thought is only the *result* of this consciousness.

For this reason, history of thinking is often better revealed by the meaning of individual words (the study of which has been called *Semantics*) than by the parallel history of literature or philosophy. For the individual word is, in a sense, the point at which thinking becomes thought. Like thought, it is the product or *result* of thinking, and literature (apart from its redemption by poetry) and our thought, too, in so far as we have to think in words, is a kind of synthesis of these products. "It is only by recording our thoughts in language," says a recent writer on Logic,[4]

> that it becomes possible to distinguish between the process and the result of thought. Without language the act, and product of thinking would be identical and equally evanescent. But by carrying on the process in language and remembering or otherwise recording it, we obtain a result which may be examined according to the principles of Logic.

Thus, if we try to enter imaginatively into the meaning of many Greek words, comparing them with apparently similar words in our own language, we get all sorts of interesting results. In the case of long hair, for instance, we find that, besides the static, analytic method of statement, which arises from a knowledge of results only —— 'to *have* long hair', the Greek language in its early stages actually had a single *verb* to express this physical condition, a verb which is *ex hypothesi* untranslatable in modern English, and to which the nearest approach

---

[4] Carveth Read: *Logic Deductive and Inductive*.

would perhaps be 'to become long as to the hair', 'to bristle', etc.

The important thing is to realise imaginatively *the kind of underlying consciousness* which would have expressed itself in such terms. I mention these few words less as evidence than as *examples* of the fact that the Greek manner of thinking was determined by direct experience of *natura naturans*, whereas *our* direct experience is always of *natura naturata*. The proposition that Greeks did in fact think in this manner is no more capable of experimental proof than the proposition that a manuscript of *Hamlet* contains something else beside a certain weight of paper plus a certain weight of ink. Those who combine, let us say, a dram of imagination with some knowledge of Greek art and literature must take the responsibility of deciding for themselves whether or no they can venture to agree.

The Greek youth of Homer's day, as he approached manhood, did not 'have a beard', he did not even 'grow a beard'; he did not require a substantive at all to express what was happening —— he 'foamed'! And again, in order to attribute youth, the Greek language did not require, as we do, the static, logical mode of copula and predicate —— "So and so — is — young"; it could say "So and so 'blossoms' or 'blooms'," using the same word as it used for the flowers of the field. It cannot be too often insisted that this was not a poetical metaphor, but a bedrock element in the Greek language; it is *we*, when we use such expressions today, who are trying to get back, *via* poetic metaphor, into the kind of consciousness which the Greek had and could express quite naturally and straightforwardly.⁵

Nor is it merely a poetic fancy to connect in one's mind the whole flavour and freshness of Greek thinking with a blossoming flower —— a flower that is still moist, alive, in movement, becoming; and our own thought (again, in so far as it is not redeemed by the poetic) with the withered leaf and stalk of Autumn, the hard rind of the seed, the motionless, the dead, the 'become'. We can even take the connection in its most literal sense, when we find that the *popular* names of so many English wild flowers — *anemone, daffodil, bryony, celandine, cherry,* etc. — the names by which we instinctively call them when we see them blowing in the field, are traceable to a Greek origin, while the same flowers only acquire Latin labels, when they begin to appear, as dead, dried up specimens, in the botanist's scrapbook. In the same way one could consider all the medical terms that have come to us from Greek, or again the unsurpassed vitality and perfection of living form which breathes to us from the Elgin marbles, as revealing the manner in which Greek consciousness as a whole tended to be at home in the physically living, in the process of becoming.

It is only as a natural growth from this pre-existing soil, this instinctive *kind* of thinking, that the world of Greek

---

⁵ For an interesting discussion of the true meaning of the words ἄνθος and ἀνθεῖν and its distortion by the lexicographers' insistence on 'metaphor', see *Greek Metaphor* by W. Bedell Stanford (Oxford, 1936).

thought proper can really be understood. Philosophy may be defined as the most *wakeful* part of a people's consciousness. We find, accordingly, early Greek philosophy concerned precisely with this problem of 'coming into being' or generation. The kind of question which the first philosophers set themselves to solve would be expressed by us somewhat as follows: where, they would ask, is the flower's 'form', the shape and beauty which our eyes will see clearly enough when it blossoms, now that they can see nothing but the bare earth or the dry seed? It is not too much to say that all the famous puzzles of Greek philosophy, the puzzles about the One and the Many, about Being and Not-Being, and whether Not-Being *is*, and so forth, begin to be intelligible in the light of this underlying 'becoming' quality of Greek thinking. Now it is one of our four fundamental 'Laws of Thought' that a thing cannot both be and not be, and so obvious does this appear to us that when we find Heraclitus maintaining the opposite, we are inclined to stigmatise him as a verbal quibbler. This is because we can only think 'is'; we cannot really think 'becomes', except as a kind of cinematographic succession of states or 'is's'. Consequently Dr. Karl Unger, in an interesting article, has recently urged us to regard these so-called 'laws' of thought rather as subjective limitations to be overcome, and not as laws of Nature, in which sense they are sometimes accepted. We may thus compare them if we will with St. Paul's conception of the *Torah*, whose strict observance at one time was not more necessary than its supersession at another by a new impulse of Life.

With the Greeks themselves there could be no question of having to overcome such laws of thought; for no such laws had been formulated. Even by the end of Plato's career Greek consciousness had not yet succeeded in distinguishing either of the two opposed concepts of 'being' and 'becoming' from a third concept of mere logical 'predication', as we do. The struggle to achieve this can actually be overheard, at an acute stage, in the dialogue called the *Sophist*. And if we go a little further back, we come to a period when the Greek mind had not even succeeded in distinguishing 'being' from 'becoming'. For up to this point Greek consciousness had actually *lived* in this experience of 'becoming'. And because of this the Greek mind could not at first be conscious of it as such. Thus, although the early Greek philosophers were indeed occupied with a problem which we are now able to *name* as that of 'coming into being' or 'becoming', they themselves could have no such name for it, for being conscious *in* it, they could not get outside it and be conscious *of* it. So that, in a sense, this too was the problem of early Greek philosophy —— to acquire, as far as possible, the *idea* of such a world of becoming. And it began to do so, when Anaxagoras set over against the for-ever-changing world of growing and decaying substance (the 'universal flux' of Heraclitus) the other principle of *Nous* or Mind. This was the beginning of the antithesis (hitherto unapprehended) between Spirit and Matter,[6] and if enforced brevity may

---

[6] The idea of 'matter', however, was not really crystallised out into anything like its modern form before Aristotle's day.

excuse a somewhat amateurish expression, it may be said that by Plato's time the central problem of philosophy was how spirit, or *nous* 'becomes' matter, or how matter, at certain times and seasons imitates or takes the 'form' of spirit. It is no wonder that the Greeks were a nation of artists!

Note that our own problem tends to be the reverse of this: for we ask how (if at all) matter becomes spirit, and enquire into the 'origin of reason' which we often conceive of as having arisen at a certain point of time, in a world which previously consisted entirely of material substance.

We are therefore in a position to ask ourselves once more the question which was asked a few pages back: what were the 'forms' of which Bacon speaks, and which, by altering the meaning of the word, he wishes to eradicate from men's minds, putting in their place his own abstract 'laws'? They were nothing else than the memory, so far as it had been retained by European thought since Plato's and Aristotle's day, of those elements, as it were, of νούς ('nous') — of the mind — or spiritual world, which the best Greek thinking could still apprehend in its time as living Beings. They were a faint, shadowy recollection of those Thought Beings, neither objective nor subjective, which Greek thinking could actually enshrine within itself —— Beings, by whom the part of Nature which is perceptible to our senses is continually brought into being and again withdrawn, in the rhythm of the seasons and of life and death.

But by Bacon's time most, if not all, men had already lost the power to think these Forms. They could only think *of* them, filling their minds with the abstract, subjective 'ideas' of modern thought, which are at best no more than their shadows. Bacon transformed these ideas, already abstract in men's minds, to the still more abstract idea of 'laws'; and modern science has grown up since his day entirely as a system which deduces from sense-observation these laws, or rules for the changes which occur in the sense-perceptible part of nature.

Now to the most typical Greek thought this part of nature, as we saw, was itself but the sum of the accomplished deeds of another invisible part —— that of the 'Forms' as we will call them. Indeed the Greek tended to lose interest in the Nature which had *become*, dwelling only on the Nature which was still in process of becoming. We may even characterise this as its weakness. The 'law' type of thought, on the contrary, if strictly observed, can only deal with a nature that has already, in the physical sense, become. To it, the seed is a congeries of minute particles, which are disposed in a certain relation by the 'laws' of their being, and which, as the year proceeds, draw other particles towards them, building up, again according to certain 'laws', the leaf, the blossom, and so forth. And the flower is nothing else than these particles —— apart from the mysterious 'laws' which determine their changes of position.

But now if we ask again, as it was asked at the beginning of this chapter, what these 'laws' are, no scientist with a sense of his responsibilities can admit them to be more than the fact *that* certain changes *have been* constantly observed. He may, of course, add other ideas out of his religious or aesthetic convictions as a private individual, but that is the definition of 'law' which he has to observe in his work. He must deal with *facts*, and facts, alike in their real and their etymological significance, are simply — *facta* — 'things which have been done'. Natural law is observable in its effects only.

The result is, of course, a purely static type of thought which can deal adequately only with the most static part of nature —— the mineral, the inorganic, the dead. With that part it can deal in a marvellously skillful manner. The most elaborate machine which the Greeks ever even attempted would look like a drawing by Mr. Heath Robinson if it were placed beside the electrical installation that hums today in the power-house of a tiny Alpine village. That is the first result.

The second result is the modern civilisation which has arisen along with this static thought and the machinery which it has produced. But for those who see clearly how the *institutions* which make civilisation possible are but the bodies or husks of concrete creative thinking in the past, there is also a third result, as inevitable as the other two. It is the imminent disruption of this same civilisation. For this static, abstract thought has death in it. As far as being is concerned, it can *give* nothing; it can only classify what is there already and re-arrange somewhat its component parts.

For a long time our systems and institutions, grown up out of the ancient world in which this real thinking was still operative, have gone on working, as it were, by their own momentum. But the period which culminated in the

Industrial Revolution and the Great War has altered the world out of all recognition. Is it not painfully obvious on all sides that, if the continuity of Western civilisation is to be preserved, we need fresh creative thinking, the power to create fresh forms out of life itself, that is to say, out of the part of Nature which is still coming into being, the Spiritual World?

Not that this power to think life into the world has ever been wholly lost from Europe. As religious inspiration, as art, as poetry, it has continued to manifest itself sporadically right down to our own day. But it is a very long time since it appeared anywhere with strength enough to be *operative* in the practical, scientific sense. And it is the development of scientific thought with which I am here particularly concerned; when we want to cure a man of tuberculosis, we go today, not to religion or art, but to science.

By the end of the eighteenth century, then, apart from these isolated exceptions, the power to think in a living way may be considered as having died right out. The man of the eighteenth century lived in a clockwork cosmos. And because this static, clockwork cosmos which he had spun out of his abstract, scientific fantasy was remote from the truth, and because he was honestly seeking for the truth, he had at last to dislodge it from its repose with the idea of 'evolution' —— an attempt to get back again, in a new form, to the old notion of 'gradually coming into being'. But it was as yet no more than a notion —— even in its Lamarck-Bergson-Shaw evening-dress of 'creative' evolution it is not much more than an abstract shadow of the real life force, the true creative Logos, which was once not an idea for men but an experience and a Being. If 'evolution' today were not merely a *theory* for men, but an actual experience, it would be impossible for them, when speaking of it, to omit all reference to its meaning —— which is the evolution of *consciousness.* The spellbound teachers and parents, who must go on inculcating this lifeless, repressive dogma, do not introduce Shakespeare to their children by repeating what psychologists have said about the causes of the impulse to clap hands. This is because the genius of Shakespeare is, not somebody else's theory, invented to explain the repeated phenomenon of hand-clapping, but a concrete *experience* of the individual soul. There is no such experience of evolution.

How are we to get back this experience, this which will alone enable us to impart fresh life to our decaying civilisation? There is no question of going backwards and trying to be little Greeks. The Greeks are not to be our models; they are merely interesting examples, historically close to us, of a people who possessed something which we need desperately ourselves, though in a different form. Indeed, our problem is essentially different from theirs. The task which their philosophers instinctively set themselves was, as we saw, to get outside a plane of consciousness in which they normally lived, so as to be able to conceive of it: to turn thinking into thought. Our problem is the converse of this. We *are* outside it already. Our task is twofold, first to realise that it is still there, and then to learn how to get back into it, how to rise once more from thought into thinking, taking with us, however, that fuller self-consciousness which the Greeks never knew, and which could never have been ours if they had not laboured to turn thinking into thought. Thus, being normally outside it, it follows that we shall also be conscious *of* it as a different world, a world into which we can plunge at will. In this case, the Greeks did *not* have a word for it. We shall.

The first part of the problem has already been solved. Rudolf Steiner's comprehensive work is enough and more than enough many times over to enable any really unprejudiced, unobsessed mind to realise that this great world of formative thinking is still there, awaiting us, if we have but the will to reach it. His book, *The Philosophy of Freedom*, for example, is a bridge, itself compacted of ordinary, logical thoughts, which leads beyond and away from such thoughts right up to this other world of creative thinking. And the name which, in other books, Steiner has given to this world is 'etheric'.

But the second part of the problem is not solved, and it depends on ourselves, the men of this generation and the next. This is the problem of actually *reaching* the etheric in fully conscious experience of thinking. The preservation of continuity in Western Civilisation depends on how many and how active may be the spirits which shall succeeed in doing this. For the futile inadequacy of our method of knowledge to the rapidly changing realities by which its dignified Roman nose is being tweaked on all sides at present simply shouts at us. We understand what is at rest and what has become, and we can deal with it as never before; but when we try to grasp what is in motion or alive, we merely gibber fantasies in a vacuum hermetically sealed from the truth. Thus, in Medicine, the whole of the *surgical* branch has reached a point little short of perfection; but when it is a question of treating malignant growths and, in general, diseases of the living organism, where are we? In this country, no one who has been brought into contact with even the outer fringe of medical controversy on these matters (I mean, of course, outside the wide area over which the British Medical Association extends its virtual censorship) will need to wait for an answer. Indeed, the healthiest sign of all, probably, is the increasing number of doctors and others who are beginning to realise, and in some cases to admit, their helplessness. Not to admit it is to be led blindfold into a grotesque world of superstition in which our posterity will hardly be brought to believe, a world from which the sense of humour eloped long ago with the sense of proportion.

In 1924, when cancer research on orthodox bacteriological lines had been going on for more than twenty years and had already absorbed thousands and thousands of pounds, the Medical Correspondent of *The Times* (September 13th), in an article on a lecture, enumerated the following results, as "an important addition to knowledge":

(i) The first time a carcinoma has ever been produced in a guinea-pig.
(ii) The first demonstration that a mechanical irritant *can* produce cancer.

THINKING AND THOUGHT

(iii) The first time a cancer of the glandular type has ever been produced experimentally.

(iv) The first demonstration that a pathological substance developed wholly within the living body (i.e. a gall-stone) can produce cancer by prolonged irritation or injury.

But, as though his readers might feel almost too triumphant at these startling results, he prefaced them with the remark that:

> Rash conclusions cannot and must not be drawn. While mechanical irritation does cause cancer in the gall-bladder of the guinea-pig, there is no assurance that it will do this in other sites or in other animals. In all disease we have to consider the pathogenic agent on the one hand and the susceptible or refractory tissue on the other. Thus, if tar is applied to a mouse's skin, a skin-cancer will eventually develop, but no amount of tar-application will cause cancer on a rat's or a guinea-pig's skin....

We must also, he said, face the fact that tar applied to the inside of the bowel in a mouse does not produce cancer. It is as though he held up a warning finger: Steady! Do not be too optimistic, my friend. We can produce cancer in some of the animals some of the time, but, remember, we cannot yet produce cancer in all the animals all the time! Not a word, be it observed, of any *remedy*! But this is the sole method of investigation open to a mode of thought which can only perceive the formative forces in their effects: first produce similar effects, and then hope you will somehow chance on a remedy; ignore throughout as irrelevant all specifically human impulses of decency and compassion.

Or one could take Economics. The economic life is today the real bond of the civilised world. The world is held together not by political or religious harmony, but by economic interdependence; and here again there is the same antithesis. Economic theory is bound hand and foot by the static, abstract character of modern thought. On the one hand, everything to do with *industry* and the possibility of substituting human labour by machinery has reached an unexampled pitch of perfection. But when it is a question of *distributing* this potential wealth, when it is demanded of us, therefore, that we think in terms of flow and rate of flow, we cannot even begin to rise to it. The result is that our 'labour-saving' machinery produces, not leisure, but its ghastly caricature, unemployment,[7] while nearly every civilised and half-civilised nation of the world sits helplessly watching the steady growth within itself of a malignant tumour of social discontent. And this increasingly rancorous discontent is felt above all things by a cramping penury, a shortage of the means of livelihood, which arises, not out of the realities of nature, but out of abstract, inelastic thoughts about money!

---

[7] So, in the '30s, when this article was written. Since then the problem of over-production has been temporarily masked by the vast expenditure on industrial expansion that accompanied World War II and the vastly increased wage-distribution which that entailed—*plus* uneconomic 'consumption' of a large part of the product in the form of armaments. It has also (it is good to record) been partly remedied by 'giving away' programmes such as Marshall Aid and its successors.

It is a startling thing to go back to poetic writers such as Ruskin or Shelley and to find them forestalling already, out of the living thinking that was in them as artists, the most advanced and intelligent criticism that is being directed today upon the financial mechanism of distribution in our industrial civilisation. It is startling, but it is not very consoling. For what effect did their intuitive foreknowledge have on the problems upon which it was directed? About as much as Cassandra's. It is no longer enough that an occasional artist here and there should see his parcel of truth and speak it out, while the actual direction taken by civilisation continues to be wholly determined by a *soi-disant* scientific method of knowledge. Science must itself *become* an art, and art a science; either they must mingle, or Western civilisation, as we know it, must perish, to make room for one that may have spirit enough to learn how to know God's earth as He actually made it.

It is intoxicating to go on repeating the word 'must', besides giving one a very pleasant sense of superiority. But this time it was not the result of ignorance. Flirtations, it is true, are common enough, but it would be difficult to exaggerate the repugnance with which artist and scientist alike are generally inclined at present to contemplate any such spiritual marriage as anthroposophy desiderates for them. Indeed, for those few who have as yet been brought by the circumstances of their lives to comprehend how desperately Europe needs what anthroposophy can give her, it is an experience more moving and at the same time very much more bitter than the spectacle of high tragedy to see the indifference, misunderstanding, antipathy, and cold suspicion, with which Rudolf Steiner's work meets on every side. A kind of bigotry and arrogance is sometimes imputed to anthroposophists for their exclusive emphasis upon his work and their movement in so many different departments of life. The answer is in the facts themselves. Those who have accepted Steiner's priceless gift are not the choice and picked ones of the earth: they are simply those who have felt out of the depths of their being the fearful need of this living, creative thinking. They are only too glad to take and use such thinking wherever they find it. But where do they find it? Does the traveller, dying of thirst, stop to complain because the torrent gushes from a single spring instead of oozing up out of every stone beneath his feet?

SPEECH, REASON AND IMAGINATION
first published 1927

WE CAN QUICKLY learn from etymology that the meaning of practically every word we use has what may be called a sensual substratum. That is to say, the word can be traced back to a time when it, or some older word from which it is derived, had reference to either a material object or a bodily action. All sorts of deductions have been drawn from this. Anatole France, for example, in his *Jardin d'Epicure*, has an amusing dialogue between a young metaphysician and an elderly etymologist, in which the latter makes hay of the former by reducing all the words he uses (such as *God, spirit, Absolute*) to what he affirms to have been their original meanings (*fire, breath, untied*). With M. France it is, of course, merely a good opportunity for a little polite irony at the expense of bombastic philosophy. But in the last century, when men were taking etymology, and other things, more seriously, there was something like a real controversy on the matter. Such a conclusion, if true, appeared to many people to carry with it grave metaphysical implications; it would be debated, for example, whether such words as 'I' and 'God' could be excepted from the general rule. Finally, when at any rate the general principle seemed to be definitely established, a new question arose out of it: if speech is dependent on sense-perceptions, then what is the relation between Speech and Reason? Is the latter wholly dependent on the former or not? And on the whole, I think it can be said the tendency here too was to admit complete dependence. "No reason without speech," said Max Müller, "and no speech without reason."

It is easy, in looking through the books of that time, to see what was at the back of people's minds. 'Reason' had been regarded throughout the eighteenth century as the divine element in man, or at least, as the principal thing which distinguished him from the brutes. But if Reason depended on words for its existence, and words upon sense-perceptions, that important distinction began to look less important; the question affected one's whole conception of the relation between body and soul, and therefore, necessarily, of immortality. And these problems — the relation of man to the brutes and of the soul to the body — were just those which, for other reasons too, were uppermost in people's thoughts and feelings.

Today the word 'Reason' *is* somewhat ambiguous. Sometimes it is used to mean 'discourse' in the technical sense, that is to say, the *logical* or deductive process, and sometimes it is intended to include all possible intellectual activity. This very ambiguity suggests that yet a third question may arise out of the other two: is there any intellectual activity other than the logistic one of deductive, *abstract* thought? Thus, we get a kind of connected series of questions: (i) are words dependent on sense-perception for their meaning? (ii) if so, is Reason dependent on Speech? (iii) if so, is there any intellectual activity which is *not* dependent on 'Reason'? I do not suggest that it is impossible for these questions to occur to people in any other order. Kant, for instance, tackled the last question without reference to words at all, and ended by answering it in the negative. But whatever their proper order, it is these three questions which I wish to consider here.

Let us begin by approaching the matter historically. If we ask, have men always felt convinced of the interdependence of these three things — thinking, words and sense (waiving for a moment the previous question of the exact nature of thinking), then the answer is emphatically no! To Plato, dialogue was a τόκος ('tokos') —— a begetting; the words of one speaker were conceived of as merely the instruments by which true thinking, itself beyond words, was 'begotten' or generated in another. It is only in the Middle Ages that the words and the thought begin to be identified, and intellect therefore conceived of as waiting upon the senses. The human being, wrote Dante, who was so deeply read in Scholastic philosophy: "solo da sensato apprende Cio che fa poscia d'intelletto digno" —— only takes up through the senses what he afterwards makes fit for the intellect.[1] Hence the medieval period was above all the age of Logic —— it worshipped Logic, in which — through the concept of the 'term' — the word and the thought are kept as close together as possible.

But if we scrutinise the men of the Middle Ages more closely, contrasting them with ourselves, we shall find something yet more significant. And it is this, that they identified *themselves* with their thoughts. This is of the utmost importance. It is this that is at the bottom of all

---

[1] One may compare with this the later pronouncement of John Locke, derived from Aristotle: "*Nihil in intellectu, quod non prius fuerit in sensu.*"

that strikes a modern observer as most incomprehensible and alien about the men of that time —— for example, their intolerance. Identifying the thought with the words, they felt that truth could be wholly embodied in creed and dogma and identifying the self with the thought, they were — quite rightly — intolerant. A wrong thought could strike them as far more immoral than a wrong action.

Now, when we are confronted with a phenomenon like this universal intolerance of the Middle Ages, we can only explain it in one of two ways. Either common sense, kindliness, and self-control have miraculously increased among us, and the great men of that time were therefore a kind of foolish children compared with ourselves; *or* we may feel a little uncomfortable about this explanation and ask ourselves accordingly whether the cause may not be otherwise, whether it may not be that thinking was actually something different then from what it is now —— not only *believed* to be different, but *actually* different. And those who find a certain difficulty about the picture of, say, St. Thomas Aquinas grovelling in intellectual chains, while, say, Mr. H. G. Wells basks without effort in the sunshine of intellectual freedom, will no doubt consider what there is to be said for the latter view. They will be led, in fact, to consider whether there is not such a thing as the evolution of consciousness.

Today, they will notice, everybody is tolerant. We are really extraordinarily polite to each other nowadays, even on such subjects as religion. "Oh, I see, my dear Sir," one theologian is reported to have said to another, whose meaning he had at length succeeded in grasping, *"your*

God is *my* Devil!" —— whereupon they took each other's wives in to dinner. And so these suspicious people may ask themselves: does this universal tolerance arise from the fact that we have at last succeeded in subduing the evil passions that formerly drove men to quarter and burn one another for their opinions, or is it — can it possibly be — that we no longer *care* very much whether people agree with us or not?

Really, there is no doubt at all about the answer. The fact is, we have *ceased to identify ourselves with our thoughts* —— at any rate, with such thoughts as can be expressed in words. We are for 'the spirit and not the letter' today. We distinguish between thinking and believing. And not only is this so, but it is one of the most typical modern experiences. I quote from *More Trivia*, the second of those two remarkable little books, in which so many typical modern experiences are summed up with an odd mixture of suppressed pathos and cynical humour, and in such musical prose:

WELTANSCHAUUNG

When, now and then, on a calm night I look up at the Stars, I reflect on the wonders of Creation, the unimportance of this Planet, and the possible existence of other worlds like ours. Sometimes it is the self-poised and passionless shining of those serene orbs which I think of; sometimes Kant's phrase comes into my mind about the majesty of the Starry Heavens and the Moral Law; or I remember Xenophanes gazing at the broad firmament, and crying, "All is One!" and thus, in that sublime exclamation, enunciating for the first time the great doctrine of the Unity of Being.

> But these Thoughts are not my thoughts; they eddy through my mind like scraps of old paper, or withered leaves in the wind. What I really feel is the survival of a much more primitive mood — a view of the world which dates indeed from before the invention of language. It has never been put into literature; no poet has sung of it, no historian of human thought has so much as alluded to it; astronomers in their glazed observatories, with their eyes glued to the ends of telescopes, seem to have had no notion of it.
>
> But sometimes, far off at night, I have heard a dog howling it at the Moon.

"These thoughts are not my thoughts." That is the feeling. And it is an experience which really distinguishes our own from all previous civilisations. It is the reason why irony — not irony over some particular matter but just irony in general — is expected of the poet or artist who claims to be 'contemporary'. Other peoples, of course, have known what it is to weigh one hypothesis against another, but never before has it been such a vital personal experience —— this sense of thoughts which are 'not my thoughts'. Never before has it existed on such a vast scale, so that a man may run through three or four entirely different and contradictory explanations of the Universe before breakfast. Even the Sceptic had his intellectual conviction — concerning the impossibility of knowing — and he at least felt *this* conviction to be a part of himself. The true Agnostic —— the man who says, not 'men can't know', but '*I don't* know', is a much later arrival; for he is speaking out of immediate personal experience. And today the world is simply full of him. There he goes, in the street, on the bus, in the factory, the office, the bank-parlour, the consulting-room — his mind full of a queer mixture of odds and ends of scientific and religious theories — but personally convinced (if he really examines himself) of none of them. These thoughts are all very interesting —— but they are not *his* thoughts.

That human consciousness is perpetually evolving was, of course, Steiner's perpetual theme; and he often described this particular stage of it, which I have tried to depict, as the Ego developing in the 'Consciousness Soul'. The Consciousness Soul indicates the maximum point of *self*-consciousness, the point at which the individual feels himself to be entirely cut off from the surrounding cosmos and is *for that reason* fully conscious of himself as an individual. He has attained complete self-consciousness —— at the cost of practically everything else. It is easily distinguishable from the Intellectual Soul, an earlier stage of development, in which, though clearly discerning itself from perceptible objects over against it in space, the Ego still feels its words and thoughts to be a part of itself. In the Middle Ages the Ego was still working in the Intellectual Soul.

Starting, then, from this pronounced difference between ourselves and the men of the Middle Ages, we can gradually begin to see more and more clearly what it means, this evolution of consciousness, which, at any rate up to the present, is also the evolution of *self*-consciousness. We can see the successive stages following and overlapping each other in the history of man as a whole, and in our own day we can see them succeeding each other all over again — on the principle of what Mr. Bernard Shaw has called "condensed recapitulation" — in the life-history of the individual. The very small child has, properly speaking, no self-consciousness at all. He cannot say 'I'. But then, through the operation of his physical senses, he gradually comes to realise: On the one hand there is something that is 'I', and on the other, there is something out there in space which is 'Not-I'. At this stage he still feels the *words* which he speaks as emanating wholly from himself, the 'I' division. But, sooner or later, because words, too, have this sensual substratum, he begins to feel detached even from them. They are instruments which he picks up and uses and drops again. He begins to discover that, even when used in quite ordinary prosaic, logical forms, they can be made to prove the most contradictory things —— can be made to prove almost anything. If he is a philosopher or a logician, he may develop his elaborate system of 'antinomies'; but if he is a 'plain man', he will only become vaguely confused by the variety and disharmony of all the different systems of ideas (each apparently quite convincing, when taken by itself), with which he is deluged from press, pulpit and platform. "Well, I dunno!" he will say; and, with more or less awareness of what he is doing, he will transfer words from the 'I' to the 'Not-I' division of his consciousness —— just as Hamlet did, at the moment when he cried out "Words, words, words!" in that mood of loneliness and despair. And at last comes the experience — possibly a deep and painful one — that not merely words but thought itself —— abstract thought — 'Reason' (and by many, as we have seen, no other kind of thinking is admitted) — must be transferred in the same way; for in its inmost nature it is wholly dependent on words.

Thus, from the standpoint of the Consciousness Soul, we can see how the Ego at first, as it were, hovers over the physical body, and then gradually, through the medium of language and abstract thought, uses that body as a 'tool' (in the words of the American psychologist, J. M. Baldwin)

> for turning all the series of external things into copy for his mental manipulation. He thus achieves the wonderful step whereby all objects alike become *his* objects, *his* content of meaning, *his* experience.[2]

And now, when this has occurred, the Ego has reached rock bottom. It feels itself to be alone, on an island, cut off from all sense and objective meaning. This is the full price of self-consciousness. This is the experience which the English poet, Matthew Arnold, tried to express — in its social bearings — in the fine poem that begins:

> Yes, in the sea of life enisled,
> We mortal millions live alone!

And we are the more justified in regarding it as an experience of special present significance, and in agreeing with Steiner that it represents a definite stage which we have reached in the evolution of consciousness, when we find that it can *either* come as an intellectual discovery in such diverse departments of study as

---

[2] *Thought and Things*, I, v. 7.

etymology and philosophy, or much more indirectly, out of the very conditions of life as we know it today. This conviction is strengthened further, when we find the same experience expressed in various forms by the poets. It is still more strengthened by the following consideration.

A little reflection must persuade anybody that personal experience of just this nature — the living in the Consciousness Soul — is the foundation, and the only possible foundation, for something which only began about four hundred years ago, and which has very special historical associations with England. I mean the Scientific Spirit. Men had investigated natural phenomena before, but the scientific *spirit* means very much more than this. It means absolute, unqualified *open-mindedness*. It means the deletion of the word *belief* from one's vocabulary, and the readiness to unite one's sympathies temporarily with any conceivable hypothesis, for which the barest *prima facie* case can be made out, in order to give that hypothesis a completely unbiased consideration. The rarity of this attitude at present among what are popularly called 'men of science' is of course a sign of the times; but it need not be unduly emphasised at the moment. For, if it is true that the pundits of the scientific world are now respected as 'authorities' in much the same way as the Church Fathers once were, it is also true that allegiance is only given to them because they are at any rate in some vague way *believed* to be really open-minded. And that is equally a sign of the times. We are determined to believe something, so we believe this. We go on living in the Intellectual Soul, because we want something to lean on, but all the time we know in our hearts that the Consciousness Soul is something beyond and above it; for, whether we like it or not, we are born into the age of the Consciousness Soul. Why is it that, today, while everybody praises the scientific spirit, practically nobody takes the trouble to acquire it? It is because (let me whisper it very softly), today, the scientific spirit really is a *virtue*!

To those, however, who really are living with all their might in the Consciousness Soul, who are really open-minded, really imbued with the scientific spirit —— to such persons, whether they find themselves inside or outside of laboratories, the third question asked at the beginning of this article must sooner or later occur: Is there any kind of thinking not dependent on the reason and therefore not dependent on the senses? Is there a kind of wordless thinking, with which the self can actually unite, as in the Middle Ages it united with ordinary logical thinking? In other words, what is Truth, not for Aristotle, or Thomas Aquinas, or my great-great-grandson, but for myself here and now?

I am going to cut right across the main thread of the argument with another question. What is anthroposophy? Believing (some would answer), without a shred of evidence, everything that Steiner chose to say. And this is exactly what it is not. Anthroposophy is knowledge, as it is expressed and grasped by the Consciousness Soul; and the Consciousness Soul (if it really is the Consciousness Soul and not the Intellectual Soul dressed up to look like it) knows first and foremost that *anybody's* thought, once it is conceived in ideas and expressed in words, must be alloyed with error. It is easy to understand Steiner's extreme reluctance to have his lectures recorded; and it is easier still to realise why, in his lectures and books, he kept on repeating, almost to exasperation, such phrases as "what is contained in", "what is reflected by", and so forth —— if we only recollect that, of all men, he spoke from the Consciousness Soul to the Consciousness Soul. "Think these thoughts without believing them," he once said; and in nearly all his utterances he employed the mode, not of discursive argument, but of pure assertion —— though he could syllogise as well as anyone if he chose to, as he showed in *The Philosophy of Freedom*. And this reluctance, and these phrases and habits of his, and the essential nature of anthroposophy, place — so it seems to me — rather a heavy responsibility upon its adherents. I cannot think it is unduly paradoxical to say that it is really a kind of betrayal of the founder of anthroposophy to believe what he said. He poured out his assertions because he trusted his hearers *not* to believe. Belief is something which can only be applied to systems of abstract ideas. To become an anthroposophist is not to believe, it is to decide to use the words of Rudolf Steiner (and any others which may become available) for the purpose of raising oneself, if possible, to a kind of thinking which is itself beyond words, which *precedes* them, in the sense that ideas, words, sentences, propositions, are only subsequently *drawn out of it*. This is that concrete[3] thinking which is the *source* of

---

[3] The word 'concrete' may here be taken as meaning 'neither objective nor subjective'.

all such ideas and propositions, the source of all meaning whatsoever. And it can only take the form of logical ideas and propositions and grammatical sentences, at the expense of much of its original truth. For to be logical is to make one little part of your meaning precise by excluding all the other parts. To be an anthroposophist, then, is to seek to unite oneself, not with any groups of words, but with this concrete thinking, whose existence can only be finally *proved* by experience. It is to refrain from uniting oneself with words, in the humble endeavour to unite oneself with the Word.

For this concrete, wordless thinking is not something which has only just been discovered. Men were united with it long ago —— though not men who had developed the Consciousness Soul. Very small children — lacking full self-consciousness — are still united with it, as we may see in their faces. A sense of its living presence pervades alike the Platonic dialogues and the opening of the Fourth Gospel. And this may bring us to reconsider something of what has been said already. I have been expressly distinguishing this kind of living thinking from words, suggesting that it could not by any means be expressed in words, was 'wordless'. But in doing so I intended 'words' and 'language' to be taken in the sense in which a logician would understand those terms. There is another sense besides this, and a very different one. I mean the sense in which a poet would understand them. As users of language, the poet and the logician stand at opposite poles. To the logician the *sound* of a word means nothing at all, while to the poet it is of the utmost importance. To the logician those words are of most value which change their meaning as little as possible when they are used in different contexts; the poet likes the meanings which change most, and is always trying to change them further himself. The logician tries for statement, the poet for suggestion. And so we could go on. But the object of this digression was to point out that, while this other kind of thinking is certainly not expressible in words taken in the first sense (though certain *results* of it may be, and for definite practical purposes *must* be, so expressed), yet it has a very close connection indeed with words taken in the second sense. In their sound and rhythm, and in all that is metaphorical and figurative about their meanings, there we should listen for its voice. The presence or absence of that voice is the difference between poetry and prose.

Consequently it is often those who are much concerned with the beauty of words who most easily catch an echo of it. Throughout the ages it has been the poets who have talked most of 'inspiration'; while the Romantic poets of the last century (I allude especially to Coleridge's conception of the Imagination —— a word whose meaning his thought perceptibly altered) actually had a glimmering of the special relation of this concrete, or inspired, thinking to the Consciousness Soul. And what is this special relation? There is a concrete thinking (experience alone can prove it), which is independent of the senses, and there is an abstract, logistic thinking, which is entirely dependent on them. But between these two there is an intermediate stage, at which consciousness takes the form of pictures or images. In the history of mankind that intermediate stage contains the mystery of the Myth. It still contains today the mystery of Poetry, and with that the whole great mystery of Meaning. It is Imagination. Imagination is the marriage of spirit and sense. Therefore the Consciousness Soul, which is the Ego cut right off from sense by its abstract thoughts, will have, in its passage back to its home in the spirit, to pass through this intermediate stage of Imaginative Consciousness. That is the peculiar relation of the Consciousness Soul to concrete thinking, or to the Word. The Consciousness Soul is cut off from knowledge. Does it wish to know again? Then it must become the Imaginative Soul.

We may very well compare the self of man to a seed. Formerly, what is now the seed was a member of the old plant, and, as such, was wholly informed with a life not wholly its own. But now the pod or capsule has split open, and the dry seed has been ejected. It has attained to a separate existence. Henceforth one of two things may happen to it: either it may abide alone, isolated from the rest of the earth, growing dryer and dryer, until it withers up altogether; or, by uniting with the earth, it may blossom into a fresh life of its own. Thus it is with the Consciousness Soul. Either it may lose itself in the arid subtleties of a logistic intellectualism, which no longer has any life, though it once had — preoccupying itself with a nice balancing and pruning of dogma, theory, and memory — *or*, by uniting itself with the Spirit of the Earth, with the Word, it may blossom into the Imaginative Soul, and live. It differs from the seed only in this, that the choice lies with itself.

Thus it is, if we describe it from outside. But from within, it would have to be put quite differently. Having abandoned all beliefs, the man slowly begins to gain — whence he hardly knows — a certainty of a different kind. The experience is a difficult one to express. It has already come to many people, and must come to many more. It had come to Keats, when he wrote in a private letter to a friend: "I am certain of nothing but the holiness of the heart's affections and the truth of imagination."

Steiner was never content with general statements. Consequently, besides the delicate revelation which he gave of the stages of evolution of man's consciousness as a whole, he frequendy pointed out the way in which the nations and races, and certain historical individuals born into them, have their special, several relation to each stage. Thus, he often said that the English nation is the nation of the Consciousness Soul. England is the island nation; it is England whose greatest writer creates a matchless gallery of individual 'characters', each standing on his own feet and valuable for his own sake —— every conceivable type of man, as someone has pointed out, *except* the mystic; it is England, out of which the scientific spirit arises; it is England, who, alike in her notions of sport and her economic and biological theories, sees the world as an aggregate of free competing units; and it is the English-speaking peoples who, for good or ill, are taking the lead externally in the present age, which is the age of the Consciousness Soul.

When Steiner said such things, he always used to assume that he was speaking to people who were capable of viewing them quite objectively and apart from the accident of their own birth. To say this of the English nation, then, is not to suggest that it is ultimately more important in the scheme of things than any other nation; it is only to suggest that in the present age it bears a specially heavy responsibility. To be born an Englishman, a German, a Russian, or a member of *any* nation whatsoever, is to have certain things (different, of course, in each case) given to you, which other nationals can only acquire by their own efforts as individual men. And, for the reasons given above, the things which are — generally speaking — born into Englishmen have their peculiar relation to the present age.

And now, what signs are there that England may live up to her responsibility and perform her mission? She can only do this by a right development of her *consciousness*, for out of the consciousness all free actions spring. It is not easy to be very optimistic on the subject. If there are any signs at all, they are at present to be found — so it seems to me — not in the centre, but at the periphery —— not in the public man, but in a few private men, and not so much in the town as in the country. Perhaps the growing popularity of Blake's *Jerusalem* heralds a dim awakening of purpose. I should have liked to say more of William Blake. The problem of the right action of England must clearly be connected with that of the right development of the Consciousness Soul; and Blake seems in a remarkable way to have felt himself as the spokesman of this development, besides connecting it obscurely with the Spirit of England. Mr. Foster Damon, in the introduction to his book on Blake, points out that the man is really complementary to Shakespeare; for if Shakespeare (the spokesman of the Consciousness Soul undeveloped) represented every type *except* the mystic, Blake could apparently conceive of no other type! To Blake logic is always something that has to be, not ignored, but conquered —— overcome. Imagination and the Redeemer are almost synonymous, and Albion — the old name for Britain — is a symbol for universal Man. Logic, and with it the whole experience of Nature as matter, and, with that, the unfree morality that is based on the law —— all these emanate from the Daughters of Memory. But the Daughters of Memory are to be overcome by the Daughters of Inspiration, who are also Jerusalem. 'Nature' is to be redeemed by Imagination, is to become Imagination.

These are only broad outlines of his elaborate symbolical system, the details of which are, for the most part, perhaps beyond my comprehension. It is conceivable, however, that the fault is not entirely Blake's, and that, as time goes on, the Prophetic Books may begin to take an increasingly important place in the English consciousness. Careful and sympathetic studies have now been made of them —— in at least one case by those who came to scoff and remained to pray. In the meantime no very deep study is necessary to see the bearing of Blake's work on what I have been trying to say here. Let anyone read enough of it to get at the essential notions I have selected above. Albion is Humanity. Jerusalem is the Daughters of Inspiration. And then let him ask himself: What does it mean, "I will not cease from *mental* fight!"? And let him turn to one of the hundreds of passages in which Blake explains exactly what it means. Suppose it to be the first Chapter of *Jerusalem:*

> I rest not from my great task!
> To open the Eternal Worlds, to open the immortal Eyes
> Of Man inwards, into the Worlds of Thought, into Eternity
> Ever expanding in the Bosom of God, the Human Imagination.

Or his description of the enemy:

> A dark and unknown night, indefinite, immeasurable, without end,
> Abstract Philosophy warring in enmity against Imagination
> (Which is the Divine Body of the Lord Jesus, blessed for ever).

And at last let him ask himself: What does it mean, then, to "build Jerusalem in England's green and pleasant land"? And what *can* it mean except this, which is not the concern of England alone, but of all humanity, to rise from the Consciousness Soul to the Imaginative Soul? —— The other Jerusalem — the visible one — can only arise as the outward form of this invisible City of the mind. The 'Satanic Mills' which have arisen over England since Blake's time, will never be thrust down from their hideous tyranny, until those of which he actually sang — the dead thinking of Newton, Locke, and Hobbes — have been burst asunder from within.

OF THE CONSCIOUSNESS SOUL
first published 1928

ANYONE WHO WISHES to reflect on the human being in greater detail than usual may decide to take help from the classification and analysis which Rudolf Steiner spent his life in developing. This classification, which upon a first introduction has a cold and forbidding sound, is no end in itself. It is no more than a means to a more intimate and loving understanding of the human being. A map, with its pink and blue patches and its rigid lines of latitude and longitude, would look cold and forbidding if we mistook it for the world. We do not do this. We use it to enable us to travel through the world.

One may say that man has on the one hand a body and on the other a soul or a mind. But if we stop at this, we immediately find ourselves involved in all kinds of confusion and complication and arguments as to which, in any particular case, is which. Sterner did not stop at this. Man, he said, has a *physical body*, in this resembling the mineral world, an *etheric body*, which the plants can also claim, an *astral body*, which he shares with the animal kingdom and which is the vehicle of his sensations and passions, and lastly an *Ego*. In virtue of the last principle alone is he entirely differentiated from all other earthly creatures. He alone can say 'I'.

Among the many and varied trains of thought and investigations for which such a classification and all that follows from it has been found fruitful is that metaphysical conception of the human being which sees him as a 'microcosm' evolving from a 'macrocosm' and finally returning, in a sense, to the great whole from which he took his birth; which sees him reposing at first unconscious in the bosom of the Father, then, like a shed seed, separating himself from this unity and finally regaining in some remote future his 'at-one-ment' with the Father principle, only now in full self-consciousness, as a self-poised, self-contained 'Ego'. It is from this point of view that the following article is written.

The addition of an Ego to the other three principles does not leave them unchanged. Just as it raises the physical body from the horizontal to the vertical position, so it works in other ways into the astral and etheric bodies. Man does not merely experience appetites and passions. Because there is an Ego working in his astral body he is also capable of a new experience —— he is now capable of *mere* sense-perception, without desire or aversion. With this is closely connected his life of sensuous, artistic pleasure. Out of the astral body, in other words, he develops the *Sentient Soul*, and one is not far wrong if one thinks of this principle as being the vehicle of his whole *aesthetic* experience, taking 'aesthetic' in the wider sense. In a similar way, working in the etheric body, the Ego leads to the development of the *Intellectual Soul*; and here we are at once at a crucial point of its evolution. Man has now reached the stage at which he can *think*, and about thinking there is something essentially paradoxical. When I think the truth (let us say that $2 + 2 = 4$) my thought is not individual to myself: one cannot say that there is *my* 2 + 2 = 4 and also someone else's. It is the same thought —— the same thing. To the extent, therefore, that I think truth, I am one with all other Egos and with the macrocosm. Yet it is only because I have my *separate* existence as an Ego that 'I' can think at all! What does this suggest? That here in the intellectual soul is the crucial point of this great mysterious process of separation, that is to say, of the separation of the Ego from the objective world, of the microcosm from the macrocosm. Inasmuch as man is experiencing in the intellectual soul, this separation is actually taking place.

And where there is a process of separation, or severance, going on, one will be able to detect a certain point at which the severance is finally accomplished —— a birth-point, a cutting of the navel-string. In the evolution of human consciousness, Steiner named this stage the *Consciousness Soul* or *Spiritual Soul*. What, then, do we mean when we say the Ego is working in the consciousness soul? We mean that this severance, or birth, of the human microcosm from the macrocosm has just been completed. The consciousness soul, we might say, *is* 'the having been cut off'.

Thus, expressing human consciousness and its evolution diagrammatically, we obtain, to begin with, a scheme such as the following.[1]

---

[1] The reader is referred to Steiner's book *Theosophy* for a full statement, as well as a justification, of the material in this grossly inadequate preliminary sketch.

Consciousness Soul
Intellectual Soul
Sentient Soul
Astral Body
Etheric Body
Physical Body

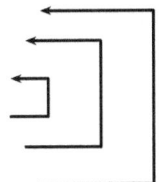

In all the other principles but the two extremes the human being maintains a certain primeval connection with the universe, the source of his creation. But his physical body is complete in itself, enclosed within its own skin, like a little island. And when the Ego works right down into this principle, then on a higher level of consciousness is developed the consciousness soul with its corresponding spiritual isolation.

Now let us suppose an impossibility. Let us suppose that a man develops up to this point of unfolding the consciousness soul and then stops dead. What would he be? Considered as a self-conscious individual, what would he actually be? He would be precisely nothing. We could never say what he is, only what he is not. We could only define him as 'that which is cut off', as 'what is left'. His actual content would be zero. Of course it is impossible that this should happen. What has been described is a *pure* consciousness soul condition; whereas, in fact, the stages of development must continually overlap and interweave. But for the purpose of clear thinking it is also well to be able to abstract them and consider them apart; and then we can say that, in so far as a man is experiencing in the consciousness soul, he tends towards this condition, this paradoxical zero-point, where self-consciousness and nonentity coincide.

Now one can go a step farther. The evolution of human consciousness, as Steiner saw it, must not be thought of as a kind of flat race where the competitors run parallel courses between strings. Much more is it presented as an orchestral symphony, or dance, in which each individual has his own figure to perform in harmony with all the rest. And here we have to consider, not merely the Egos of individual human beings, but the souls of groups of men such as families or nations; and indeed this orchestral development of human consciousness was, as he depicted it, the rationale of that manifold division of humanity into races and nations, which has brought about all that we read of as history. Over and over again Steiner traced out some particular theme in the universal symphony into a loving wealth of detail; here we have to do with one only among these intuitions —— when he pointed to the English nation as the special vehicle for the unfolding of the consciousness soul.

Few things are more startling than the sheer *effectiveness* of this occult key to the quiddity of the Anglo-Saxon genius. The indications are innumerable, and I can only select two or three. In the first place there is the geographical one —— the island form, the 'piece of land surrounded by water' as we learnt at school, with all its reverberations into character and history. "Every Englishman," wrote Novalis, "is an island." And so we find the Englishman developing out of an instinctive feeling the rule that 'his house is his castle'. Nothing will do but he must have another little island inside the big one! And this raises the whole question of that social and political freedom of the individual which Europe has so long connected with the name of England. For, curiously enough, if we examine the Law of the Constitution to see what documents and principles this is based on, we do not find any. Nothing is said of what the citizen may do, but much of what policemen and the King and civil servants may *not* do. In other words, his much-vaunted liberty is nothing in itself: it is 'what is left'. We do not know what it is; we only know what it is not. But it is none the less real for that.

It is important to understand the real relation of the Englishman to liberty. Liberty is not something which he understands better than other nationals; it is not something that he puts enthusiastically before him as an ideal. It is not something which he is especially competent to talk about. It is something that he *takes for granted*. That is the point. And it shows us immediately something of what is meant by saying that a certain nation 'is the vehicle for the unfolding' of a certain human principle. It means that the people of that nation have this principle, as it were, 'given' them, whereas other nationals have to work their way to it by individual effort.

Where else can we trace the working out of this instinctive consciousness-soul experience of the English people? In the sixteenth and seventeenth centuries there gradually spread over Europe that outlook on life which is commonly called the 'scientific spirit'. England can by no means claim a monopoly of great scientists, but when we are talking of the scientic *spirit*, it is English history and literature that we must study in order to understand its origin. And now if we come on to consider the system, the cosmogony, at which the scientific spirit, as such, at last arrives (this is quite different from saying that all scientists have this outlook), what is it? It is a system in which Nature is seen as a structure of unalterable laws. And what is Man? Nothing can be said of Man except what concerns his least distinctive principle —— the physical body. Sweep this aside, and ask: What is Man *as Man!* And the answer is: 'What is left.' This is perfectly true of everything that can be said out of the real scientific spirit, when it is applied only to data at present regarded as admissible, and is not affected by the fact that the British Association now recognises all sorts of *demi-mondaine* 'ologies'.

To understand the scientific spirit in its essence and to realise the enormous gulf that yawns between it and the medieval way of thinking, one must read Bacon. And then one realises how the scientific spirit is really identical with the spirit of English philosophy. And the spirit of English philosophy is —— materialism. Only this word, materialism, is not necessarily a term of abuse, as we shall see. It is impossible to go deeply into this; but one has only to consider the extraordinary detachment of our philosophy from that great and distinctive modern European movement of thought — pure mathematics — in order to perceive something of what is meant. England can show no Descartes, no Leibnitz: she has mathematicians, but they are not philosophers. Newton employed his mathematics in practical scientific investigation, while the philosopher Hume built up his system on the work of his predecessor Locke, ignoring the Cartesian and Newtonian mathematics. If we are looking for a Newtonian philosophy, we must go to Germany, to Kant.

Now what is meant by the label 'materialism'? As a term of abuse, as a missile weapon slung by anthroposophists at the rest of the world, it commonly signifies a refusal to admit the reality of anything but matter. Whereupon we come upon another paradox; for it is a peculiarity of materialism in philosophy that it actually renders this other, naughty kind of materialism impossible; it does this, by carrying it to its logical conclusion and showing it up for the nonsense it is. If, for example, we consider Hume's scepticism over the concept 'causation', we see at once that its effect is to emphasise and bring into the light the loose thinking on which this naughty 'materialism' depends. For if we are consistently materialistic, we are obliged to maintain that the world consists of an arbitrary collection of objects and events entirely unconnected with one another, and that in every instant of time it holds itself together and creates itself anew. This, in effect, is what Hume brings home to us. And so from English philosophy we learn the important lesson that pure *honest* materialism cannot be materialistic!

What then does English philosophy do? Instinctively it seeks the material everywhere; it deals with the material, with the physical, in which it feels itself at home. That is one side of the picture. On the other side we have —— *what is left!* If you laid your finger on everything material, wherever it is to be found, it follows that whatever is left is non-material. You have detached the material from the immaterial, and the immaterial that is left rejoices, as it were, in its freedom. And such is indeed the gift of English philosophy to Europe —— the license for free speculation in the realms of pure thought, unhampered by disguised forms of materialism. One cannot of course say that the English philosophers had any such purpose in view; but there are other purposes besides conscious ones. In the light of the whole history of Western consciousness it is very clear that English philosophy proper, that the English folk-soul as philosopher, so to speak, was engaged on a definite task. It sought for matter everywhere —— *in order not to confuse it with Spirit.*

And by doing so it detached 'what is left' from the cosmos and made it free. Man as a physical being is not free; he is inseparably bound to the rest of the physical world, though the insulation of his body does indeed give a sort of picture of detachment. But this immaterial remnant — once it has been detached from matter — is free from the whole world; for the other kind of attachment (through the soul) is already left behind with the earlier (sentient soul, intellectual soul) stages of development. At last the microcosm is fully and finally severed from the macrocosm. Only the uneasy question arises: has this microcosm any content? Does it really exist? *Am* I? Such is the typical consciousness-soul experience.

The answer may come in many different ways. And we will consider at first the way in which, given a certain honesty, it arises out of the consciousness soul itself. The paradox that honest materialism cannot be wholly materialistic is nowhere better illustrated than in English literature and particularly in the English manner of dealing with its favourite subject of death. It would be possible to write at considerable length of this; but at the present I will only take two passages, the first from Landor's *Imaginary Conversations*:

> Laodomeia died; Helen died; Leda, the beloved of Jupiter, went before. It is better to repose in the earth betimes than to sit up late; better than to cling pertinaciously to what we feel crumbling under us, and to protract an inevitable fall. We may enjoy the present while we are insensible of infirmity and decay; but the present, like a note in music, is nothing but as it appertains to what is past and what is to come. There are no fields of amaranth on this side of the grave: there are no voices, O Rhodope! that are not soon mute, however tuneful: there is no name, with whatever emphasis of passionate love repeated, of which the echo is not faint at last.

The second from *Love's Labour's Lost* is more extraordinary. We are in the middle of a practical joke; the 'fantastical Spaniard', Armado, playing Hector, is being bated by all the courtiers; everywhere laughter. And then suddenly the following pathetic protest is made by Armado, not on his own behalf but actually on behalf of the character he is representing. He stops in the middle of his part and protests to his chaffing audience:

> The sweet war-man is dead and rotten; sweet chucks, beat not the bones of the buried! When he breathed, he was a man!

This sudden, half-whimsical drop into pathos on the subject of mortality is very typical of the English genius.

It is the poetic aspect of that honest materialism which we have already traced in philosophy. The consciousness soul can only see the physical; and the most certain thing about the physical body is that it dies! Yet here too we find abundant evidence of the truth that has already been indicated —— that honest materialism cannot be wholly materialistic. Why is this? It is because, if we examine the sonorous word-music to which English literature tends to rise, when it speaks, as it so often does, of death, we shall find that the nameless, unknown *content* of the isolated human soul sounds mysteriously through it. It is not mentioned. But it is *suggested* —— often quite without design on the writer's part.

It is surprising how far genuine honesty and clear-headedness will carry one. The truth does not consist of a collection of isolated facts; it is all woven together into a single fabric. Consequently, even if you are so constituted that you can only see one small part of reality, yet if you make it your whole endeavour to state that part with absolute accuracy *and without saying anything you do not mean*, you will not be able to help suggesting the whole truth. This is a very important fact. Its application to English Literature is as follows: that you cannot write well and truly of death without suggesting the resurrection. Let us say that you are absolutely incapable of 'seeing' the spirit that rises as the body falls, and that you are rigidly determined to say no more than you know. You may put it in the simplest terms that you can find, stating the bald fact that such and such a being was and is not. And all the time there will ring through your words something of which you had no idea, the overtone, the music, the glory of the spirit that rises as the body falls. The art of Literature is not much more after all than an exceptional faculty for utterance that is honest, absolutely honest with one's whole self. And so, if there exists in you somewhere a real capacity for *seeing* the spirit, and you ignore it and try to write of death in the manner of your forefathers, you will not achieve this mysterious overtone. Many modern writers are unaware of this.

To understand English Literature, to acquire any sort of taste for it, one must really be able to appreciate this gentle art of *suggestion*. One must learn to read the thing that is *not* said and to see how important it is that it should not be said. Then one will appreciate that hovering lightness of touch which is the essence alike of English lyric and of English humour. One will appreciate, for example, that remarkable old English carol of the *Seven Virgins*:

> All under the leaves and the leaves of Life
> I met with virgins seven,
> And one of them was Mary mild,
> Our Lord's mother of Heaven.
>
> "O what are you seeking, you seven fair maids,
> All under the leaves of life?
> Come tell, come tell, what seek you
> All under the leaves of life?"

I will only pick out a verse here and there:

> Go down, go down, to yonder town,
> And sit in the gallery,
> And there you'll see Sweet Jesus Christ
> Nail'd to a big yew-tree.

and so on, up to the last verse but two, the climax of the poem:

> Then He laid his head on His right shoulder,
>   Seeing death it struck Him nigh —
> "The Holy Ghost be with your soul,
>   I die, Mother dear, I die."

We have reached the climax. And now how does the poem go on? These are the two last verses:

> O the rose, the gentle rose,
>   And the fennel that grows so green!
> God give us grace in every place
>   To pray for our king and queen.
>
> Furthermore for our enemies all
>   Our prayers they shall be strong:
> Amen, good Lord; your charity
>   Is the ending of my song.

You see how it is. Nothing is said of the resurrection —— and yet... Perhaps in this context, where the ultimate object is an earnest attempt to come nearer in all love and humility to the Spirit of a nation, it would not be unduly flippant to say: 'the poet was too much of a *gentleman* actually to *mention* the resurrection!'

One could equally well take a poem by a living English poet — one of the most beautiful which the language contains — I mean Mr. Walter de la Mare's *Nod*.

> Softly along the road of evening
>   In a twilight dim with rose,
> Wrinkled with age and drenched with dew,
>   Old Nod the shepherd goes.

> His drowsy flock streams on before him,
>   Their fleeces charged with gold,
> To where the sun's last beam leans low
>   On Nod the shepherd's fold.
>
> The hedge is quick and green with briar;
>   From their sand the conies creep;
> And all the birds that fly in heaven
>   Flock singing home to sleep.
>
> His lambs outnumber a noon's roses,
>   Yet when night's shadows fall,
> His blind old sheepdog Slumber-soon
>   Misses not one of all.
>
> His are the quiet steeps of dreamland,
>   The waters of no-more-pain,
> His ram's bell rings 'neath an arch of stars:
>   Rest, rest, and rest again!

In this case there is no outward sign that the writer is thinking of death at all. All is symbolism — suggestion — a kind of slyness. One need not labour the point further. The thing is in the very blood of English Literature. I am personally acquainted with a student who, after graduating with first class honours in English Literature, had the greatest difficulty in understanding the French 'Symbolist' movement in poetry, for the simple reason that he could not conceive of any other kind of poetry. It might just as well have been an Ink or Paper movement, for all it meant to him.

From what was said at the beginning it will be fairly clear that the interest of all this extends far beyond the limits of England. If Steiner was right, what we have been describing is not merely the English Genius but, in a deeper sense, Man —— Man seeking to express himself as he unfolds the consciousness soul. And we will ask again: What is the typical experience of the consciousness soul? It is the experience of nothingness —— of having no content. 'Perhaps I am not'; it says uneasily: 'for one thing is certain. I do not *know* what I am. I only know what I am not!' To this we may add what is not yet perhaps a typical experience, but an occasional one, a possible one. Out of the nothingness and uncertainty overtones begin to sound forth, bringing with them an extraordinarily sweet certainty of their own. At first this may be a certainty of pure *feeling*, and then perhaps a conviction, an absolute knowledge, of the truth that resides in beauty and imagination. This is the stuff of which the English Romantic Movement was made. "I am certain of nothing," wrote Keats in a letter (and he meant every word literally), "but the holiness of the heart's affections and the truth of imagination."

But human consciousness can never, in its forms of expression, come to a state of rest. The moment it seeks to do so, it begins to degenerate. How common an experience it is for the individual to discover something new in his inner life, some fresh experience such as may come from a piece of music or a mountain, and to say to himself: 'Ah, now I have got this! I shall always be able to return to this for fresh inspiration, or to restore the equilibrium when things are awry.' And then he finds that this is not the case at all; the more he seeks to draw from the treasured memory, the more flaccid and lifeless it becomes. No. He is obliged to metamorphose it, to give it new life by incorporating it in other experiences, if it is to remain a real inspiration.

It is the same thing with the march of human consciousness as a whole. And in this way we can understand the tragedy of the Romantic Movement. For this movement first arose out of the fact that human forces which could no longer find any expression for themselves in the increasingly abstract forms that European thought took on in the seventeenth and eighteenth centuries, that these forces broke through these forms, smashed them up, and made of the pieces a vessel of a different kind that was better able to hold them. This new vessel was imagination —— symbolism. For Literature it meant the finding in words of other meanings than the superficial reference. All over Europe there was a flaming up of enthusiasm, and one may perhaps see in Blake's picture *Glad Day* a sort of prophetic vision of these flames. But now in our own times we are living out the tragedy. For on the one side is an intense desire to retain this romantic-imaginative consciousness, and the will to keep it sacred, as something quite apart from the scientific-logical element in experience. And yet on the other side it is being steadily undermined. A wealth of ideas which have sprung up since Keats's day (for example, ideas connected with the *demi-mondaine* sciences of psychology and anthropology) are all tending to do to Romance that most dangerous of all things, to *explain* it! At the same time we find a tropical growth in the practice of introspection, which leads to the same end. One could mention Mr. Aldous Huxley as a striking example of this gnawing desire for romance living in perpetual strife with a psychological necessity for introspection. Now one way of approaching anthroposophy is to see in it the solution, or, since that has a somewhat facile sound, let us say the λύσις ('lusis'; in Aristotle, the resolution or denouement of the plot of a drama) of this tragedy of Romance.

It will be easiest to plunge *in medias res* and to enquire precisely what Steiner said of the further development of the human Ego beyond this stage of the consciousness soul. We have arrived, then, at the point of development at which the macrocosm is so to speak focused to an invisible point in the isolated Ego. What next? The answer of anthroposophy is that there are two alternatives open to it: ultimate death or nonentity on the one hand, and on the other the first step towards an expansion outward again to the macrocosm —— an expansion of such a nature that the centre and source of life is henceforward within instead of without.

Steiner spoke of future as well as past stages of evolution, and we may now add to the six principles of the 'scheme' given at the beginning, the three which are concerned with future development. Thus we have:

Remoter future	Spirit Man
Seventh civilisation	Life Spirit
Sixth civilisation	Spirit Self
A.D. 1450 → now →	Consciousness Soul
B.C. 750 → A.D. 1450[2]	Intellectual Soul
Egypto-Chaldean period	Sentient Soul
Ancient Persian period	Astral Body
Ancient Indian period	Etheric Body
Remoter past	Physical Body

[2] Græco-Roman period. These dates are of course fixed for convenience only and should be taken as approximate centre-points of a period of transition.

To the unfolding of each of these principles a whole period of civilisation, lasting over 2,000 years, has been or will be, dedicated. All these periods themselves are for the most part recapitulations of infinitely longer periods of development, which took place in the remote past. Such was the account of the Earth's history which Steiner gave, claiming to speak not from theory, but from direct knowledge. There is no verifying it, except by experience of the same kind. Failing that experience, everyone must decide for himself whether or no it appears reasonable; and these essays will have succeeded in as much as they are attempting, if they show how reasonable it can appear, when worked out, in at least one direction, into detail.

From this completer point of view, which directs our gaze to the remote future, we can see how the three soul-principles, sentient soul, intellectual soul and consciousness soul, are really regarded more as stages on the way to the ultimate transformations than as ends in themselves. And it will be noticed that with the consciousness soul we have (for the first time in the long period specially under review —— more than 8,000 years) a working back into the lowest, or rather the *earliest* — for in a sense the physical body is the most perfect of all — of all the human principles. With this fact there are two important matters connected.

It is with the working of the Ego right down into the physical body that the impulse to *self-knowledge* first really becomes a serious matter. Now it is, to take one example, that man demands to know, that he *must* know, more of the way in which the reproductive part of his organism pulsates through the whole of his soul-life. Psychoanalysis is a symptom of this necessity. Anthroposophy differs from it in realising that genuine self-knowledge is another name for the knowledge of higher worlds; for the microcosm is the germ of all worlds. It is good to bring to the surface of consciousness the hidden workings of the body, but only if one is prepared to go further and unmask in that body itself the hidden workings of the spiritual hierarchies. Secondly, if we realise that the Consciousness-Soul age only began in the fifteenth century, and that we are still only in its first quarter, we can see the importance of an understanding of English History since this date. The history of England from the fifteenth century, when it first began to play a leading part in Europe, down to today, is the history of the consciousness soul in its *nascent* condition. It is therefore an important study, not for English people alone, but for all. For we are all in the *age* of the consciousness soul, whether we like it or not, and by studying an element in its nascent condition we can often learn things about it which can be learnt in no other way.

In the present day this nascent or 'unconscious' development of the consciousness soul is drawing to a close. The instinct for self-knowledge, one might say for the body, is growing at a rapid pace and undermining not only 'Romantic' experience, but all experience of an emotional nature.[3] People can no longer say, with Keats,

---

[3] See C. S. Lewis's Riddell Lectures (*The Abolition of Man*, Oxford University Press, 1944; republished Zondervan/HarperSanFrancisco, 2001) for a wonderfully firm and powerful expression of this fact and its inevitable results.

"I am certain of the truth of imagination." No. They must know *in what way* imagination is true! Otherwise they cannot feel its truth. And here it is that the enormous difference between the consciousness soul and the intellectual soul begins to appear. If we ask for the *meaning* of something, it is to the intellectual soul that we must go for an answer. The consciousness soul can suggest and depict —— but it cannot utter. It is to the intellectual soul that we must look for our answer to questions concerning the *meaning* of Romance and Imagination or (which is the same thing) to the question "in what *way* is Imagination true?"

For consider: anyone who objects to this statement that imagination is true will probably do so on the ground that imagination is entirely an inner, 'subjective' activity. That is indeed the popular meaning of the word —— especially of the adjective 'imaginary'. In seeking to answer the above question, therefore, we are brought up against the whole question of the relation between 'inner' and 'outer' in human experience, between the 'objective' and the 'subjective'. The consciousness soul cannot tackle this question. It is already cut off. Subjectivity is its essence, as I have tried to explain. But in the Intellectual Soul, as was said near the beginning of this essay, we have the human Ego still actually in process of being 'cut off' from the macrocosm. It is to the intellectual soul, therefore, that we must look for an understanding of these questions and an answer to them.

Anthroposophy is, in one sense, the intellectual soul speaking to the consciousness soul. It is the science of meaning. "In genuine creative imagination" it says to the consciousness soul, "you are already taking the first step towards reunion with the macrocosm; for it is not man alone who creates in Imagination, but Nature herself!" Let us, for the moment, express the whole course of human evolution in the following diagram:

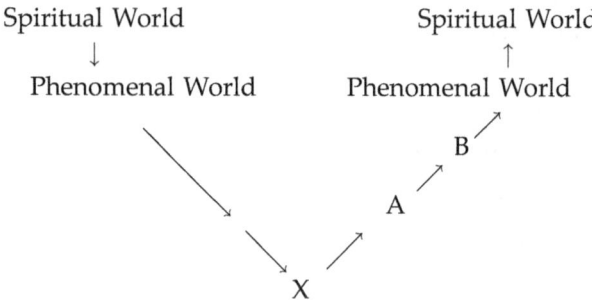

Then, if the point A is the consciousness soul, B represents the developed consciousness soul, the consciousness soul on its way to becoming what Dr. Steiner once called the 'Imaginative soul'. And at X, which marks the intellectual soul, we have, says anthroposophy, the human nadir, the true mystery of the resurrection, the mystery of the New Man from the Old. Let us look at it historically:

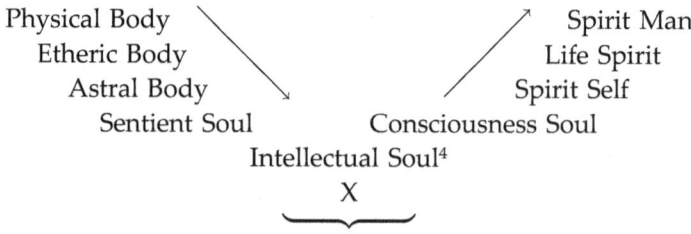

---

[4] 750 B.C.—1450 A.D. These dates are of course fixed for convenience only and should be taken as approximate centre-points of a period of transition.

Then we see how it is that the intellectual soul has an understanding of this great problem of the relation between a 'subjective' and an 'objective' world. It has this understanding, because just at the time when it blossomed on Earth, that question arose, and arose not as a matter of knowledge but as a matter of action. It arose and was answered, not by words, but by a deed. This deed, the incarnation of Christ in a human body, and subsequently in the 'aura' of the Earth, was the solution in fact of that divorce between a subjective and an objective world which had only recently arisen in human experience. We may put it another way. In the last great period of civilisation a question stood before the whole Earth —— the question whether it should henceforth have any *meaning*. And the question was answered by the deed of God, who brought meaning to the Earth from the Sun. In our own period the *same* question stands before, not the Earth, but individual souls, and must be answered, not by God, but by themselves. Yet it is the God Who gave the Earth its meaning in the age of the Intellectual Soul, the Græco-Roman age, who also makes it possible for them to give the positive answer now. That is the teaching of anthroposophy, as I understand it; and its whole object is to give what assistance it may to humanity, to the humanity of the Consciousness-Soul age, in answering that question.

THE FORM OF *HAMLET*
first published 1931

SOME YEARS AGO Mr. Clive Bell, who is sometimes regarded as an expert in the subject of Aesthetics, wrote a book called *Art*, which attracted a good deal of attention. The burden of it, if I remember rightly, was that a work of art is to be distinguished from all other things (including cheap imitations of itself) by the possession of something which he called 'significant form'. My impression is that if the reader went on to ask the question: significant of *what?* —— he got his knuckles smartly rapped for having already left the sphere of pure art and departed away into philosophy, which is, of course, a miserable abstract science that has nothing to do with Art. I think the book consisted largely of reasons why it was better *not* to say anything else about works of art except that they had 'significant form'.

The impression which Mr. Bell succeeded in making with his phrase proves that 'form' is a very suggestive word. Most modern writers on art try to conjure with it in one way or another; I have done so myself; and I only pick out Mr. Clive Bell's book because it happens to be a particularly good example of the sort of disability under which people labour who write authoritatively and at length on something, in the existence of which they do not believe.

What is form, the form of a work of art, the form of anything? I think it is fairly safe, to begin with, to say that it involves some kind of unity in variety. Neither mere unity nor mere haphazard 'multeity' (to borrow Coleridge's word) have form, but something between the two. The one theme, with many variations, this is not only the basis of all musical form but the basis of all form. So far, if it can be called far, all are agreed. It is when the critic seeks to go beyond, or to apply, this elementary maxim that he commonly gets into difficulties. This is especially so in the case of literature. For what is it that makes the form of a play or a poem into a real solid *thing*, something to be reckoned with, something that is able, so to say, to send a little shiver down the back? What is it that gives life to a work of art? It is, that the unity which is at the base of its form is itself a real being. At the lowest it must be a part of the author's own finite being, informed with his own life, so that if you prick it it will bleed. At the highest it will be something altogether beyond any one personality. But it will be a being, not an idea.

Whereas the only unity which your modern critic can conceive of as underlying a literary work is —— an idea. Hence his difficulty. Supposing, for example, that we were to have had a really deep experience, a specifically artistic experience, of the unity which underlies all the rich variety and seeming inconsequence of the play *Hamlet* and that we were then to approach this experience, armed with the above conception of form as 'unity in variety', in the hope of throwing some light on it. Well, our efforts to name the mysterious unity which we had experienced would end, inevitably, in our turning it into an idea, a theory. We might, for instance, try to demonstrate that some such notion as 'uncertainty' or 'mutual distrust' was the theme of the play and seek to show how this same theme is variously expressed in the characters of Hamlet, Laertes, Ophelia, Polonius and so on. All this is very interesting while we are working it out, but we have only to forget it for a moment and go and see (or read) the play itself again, the whole play and nothing but the play, and the theory suddenly crumbles through our fingers. It looks hopelessly thin, dry and mouldy. It explains nothing, has left everything that matters out. It is simply talk. We feel all the discomfort of the eminent zoologist who, on opening his study door one day, found awaiting him not the MS. of his new book on the Lion, but a lion.

As a reaction against this somewhat doctrinaire interpretation of form (it is the type of criticism which tends to conceive of writers as having a 'purpose' or 'message') there is another way of approaching the problem of the nature of art, which has come to the fore more recently. This second sort of criticism approaches 'form' more from the genetic point of view. It asks, not so much what form is, as how it came into being, and the reply it gives is that the artistic activity is a function of 'the Unconscious' and that artistic form is the product of the impact of this dreaming, unconscious part of the self upon its ordered and conscious, waking world. It is the unconscious caught in the act of becoming conscious.

Here again, however, as in Mr. Clive Bell's case, a certain amount of tact or awe seems to be demanded of the student. He is not to inquire too persistently what is meant by 'the unconscious'. At any rate, the more he does inquire, the more he finds himself fobbed off with all sorts of 'impulses', 'tendencies', 'complexes', 'states of the organism', 'hypnoses', 'reintegration of the personality at a higher level', and so forth, which are really not a whit more concrete than 'uncertainty' or 'mistrust'. There is indeed a curiously close resemblance between the writings of the modern whole-hogging psychological critic and the stiffer sort of medieval allegory, in which such abstractions as 'Courage' and 'Fear' are brought on to the scene to fight a full-dress battle for the vacillating soul of the hero.

This is a good example of the way in which ordinary present-day ideas, striving as they do to limit themselves to the sense-world even when considering things which are *ex-hypothesi* supersensuous, are brought over and over again into an *impasse*. From such tight places the transition, as into another dimension, into the anthroposophical world of ideas appears to those who are familiar with it to be not only natural but inevitable. Thus, whereas from one point of view the works of Steiner seem full of the strangest stuff, from another he seems merely to utter what is trembling on everyone's lips.

What is 'the unconscious'? Anthroposophy *answers* this question. It answers it with a library. The unconscious is the whole world of spiritual beings, of the Folk-Spirits, the Time-Spirits and the Hierarchies above and below them. It tries by all the means in its power to make exactly clear the ways in which these beings are related to each other and to man, and the part they have played in his evolution. We learn from it that they interpenetrate with the human Ego in a way so foreign to the physical world that, although they are *other* than self, it is correct (speaking from the point of view of everyday consciousness within the body) to say that they are experienced *within* the self.

The same spiritual world is there as the unconscious part of every human being. But among human beings there are some whom we call geniuses. In such beings the world of spiritual beings has already begun to break through into the conscious self. They are therefore able to create form.

So, too, there are among geniuses certain great representative ones — it may be, nationally representative — such are Dante, Shakespeare, Goethe. And again, among the productions of these representative geniuses there are certain specially typical or representative ones —— as the *Divine Comedy, Hamlet, Faust.*

In the case of such world-famous productions of the human imagination as these latter are, we should expect to find, and we do find, that that which constitutes, if I may put it in rather an ugly way, their representativeness, is also that which constitutes their unity —— the unity underlying their artistic form. And so, making use of anthroposophical ideas and the anthroposophical vocabulary, we are able to say that the one spiritual essence which gives life to the play of *Hamlet* and which at the same time makes it so typical, so representative, can be properly named the Spiritual Soul or the

Consciousness Soul.¹ We ask: what is the consciousness soul? Anthroposophy replies neither with silence nor with the pat scientific substitution of another name. It does not say 'there is no answer', but it does say that the answer cannot be given in a formula, in one chapter, or even in one book. Just because the consciousness soul is not a subjective idea but a real being, Steiner did not attempt to reveal its nature by a definition but by approaching it from continually new directions, under new aspects, in new environments, new departments of its activity. Thus, the answer is in the library. There, if you are interested enough to seek for it, you will find it. From such a course of lectures as the *Karma of Materialism* and again from the book *Mysticism and Modern Thought* the fact will become apparent that the consciousness soul is that part of the whole human entelechy which comes to expression in the history of the world during a period beginning in the fifteenth century and extending far into the future beyond our own time. Again, from the course entitled *On the Altered Conditions of the Times*, the consciousness soul gradually takes form as the principle in the human being which expresses itself more particularly in the nature of England and of the English Genius; while from reading such fundamental works of Steiner as *Theosophy* and *Occult Science: an Outline* (from these but also from scattered references in many other books and courses —— the selections I am making are

---

¹ According to which translation we adopt for the German *Bewusstseinseele*. I have taken "Consciousness Soul", which seems to me to be a more appropriate term when it is the *past* that is in question.

fairly arbitrary), it is made clear how the consciousness soul is the part or principle of man by virtue of which he acquires a separate and independent consciousness, a separate mental existence. Now for the first time a completely self-conscious Ego *detaches* itself from the rest of the spiritual world which rules in his unconscious. Fully responsible at last for his own actions, he is deprived of the instinctive guidance of spirits, even including his National or Folk Spirit, on whom, up to now, he has leaned. This is described in an illuminating way by Steiner (in this case actually with especial reference to Hamlet) in the first lecture of the course on *St. Mark's Gospel*. Living in the consciousness soul man experiences isolation, loneliness, materialism, loss of faith in a spiritual world, above all —— uncertainty. The soul has to make up its mind and to act in a positive way on its own unsupported initiative. And it finds great difficulty in doing so. For it is too much in the dark to be able to see any clear reason why it should, and it no longer feels the old (instinctive) promptings of the spirit within.

We must conceive of this being, this living mansion, so to speak, of the spirit of man, as present in the fullness of its power just below the crust of Shakespeare's waking consciousness, and we must conceive of it as the spiritual unity which, in the act of breaking through to the surface of that consciousness and stamping itself upon the sensuous manifold that constitutes our daytime world, gives rise to *form* —— to the form of the play *Hamlet*. Diagrammatically the representative nature of *Hamlet* may perhaps be expressed as follows:

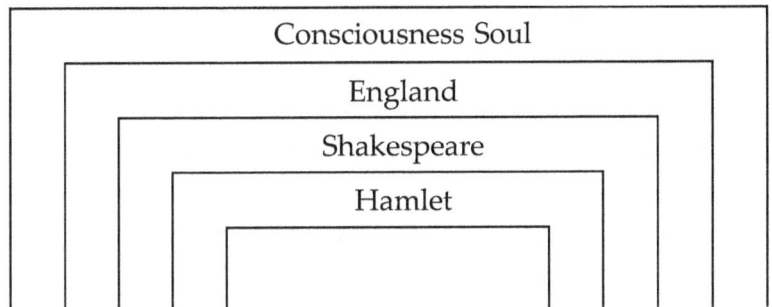

If it seems perverse to speak of the soul-principle by which man becomes self-conscious, as being itself present *in the unconscious*, it must be remembered that Shakespeare lived in the very dawn of the Consciousness Soul age when it was still, so to speak, within the womb. That his imagination was secretly pregnant with the whole nature and history of the age that was to follow him, this is at the base of that modernity and vast forward reach which has surprised so many critics. That he was *unconsciously* the bearer of —— consciousness! this is at the bottom of what is often baffling and even unsatisfactory about him. This, I believe, is why sometimes, after reading or seeing a play, we have the uneasy feeling that Shakespeare does not *mean* anything. He has nothing to say. His characters know what they mean and can utter it in the most beautiful language. They know also what they want, have individuality. Not so the author. He is indeed 'not one but all mankind's epitome'. He has no existence apart from the characters. He will be as *you* like it, undertake what *you* will; but he has no like or will of his own. Such at any

rate is the impression left by his work as a whole ——
with the possible exception of the Sonnets. If we can imagine
a state of *mere* consciousness without any individuality,
without any will, then there we have Shakespeare.[2]

It is particularly interesting to observe how this mood
of isolation in excessive consciousness, of individual
uncertainty, of 'will-lessness', is what gives the play of
Hamlet its characteristic 'form'. So much so, that critics
who are insensitive to this mood are often heard
complaining that the play has *no* form, that as a work of
art it is a failure. For example, the farewell scene between
Ophelia and Laertes and between Polonius and Laertes is
often criticised as a mere excrescence and the same has
been said of the scene between Polonius and Reynaldo, in
which the former directs Reynaldo to spy upon Laertes'
doings in Paris by employing all sorts of exceedingly
cunning pretences and devices. Such critics do not see
how the reciprocal relations between Ophelia, Laertes,
Polonius and Hamlet are carefuly modulated variations
of the central consciousness soul theme of isolation,
uncertainty and distrust of all outside the self, including
other selves.

From the mild but nevertheless slightly stinging retort
made by Ophelia to Laertes:

---

[2] I realise, after having written it (and gladly acknowledge the forgotten debt), that this is almost exactly the point of view taken by Mr. Middleton Murry in his admirable book, *Keats and Shakespeare*. Mr. Murry, however, would not have agreed that there is anything unsatisfactory about such a state, which indeed he identified with poetic inspiration, and with much more.

> ... But, good my brother,
> Do not, as some ungracious pastors do,
> Show me the steep and thorny way to heaven;
> Whilst, like a puff'd and reckless libertine,
> Himself the primrose path of dalliance treads,
> And recks not his own rede.

to Laertes' stilted and even priggish sowing in his sister of distrust for Hamlet's motives —— thus revealing at the same time his own lack of confidence in *her*:

> ... Perhaps he loves you now;
> And now no soil nor cautel doth besmirch
> The virtue of his will: but you must fear,
> His greatness weighed, his will is not his own;
> ...
> Fear it, Ophelia, fear it, my dear sister,
> And keep you in the rear of your affection,
> Out of the shot and danger of desire.
> ...
> Be wary, then; best safety lies in fear ...

it is really remarkable how the whole speech is directed towards inculcating *fear*. Laertes is a 'Safety First' man. From the careful watering of these seeds of misprision by old Polonius ("Aye, springes to catch woodcocks!") to Ophelia's perhaps weak abandonment of her faith in Hamlet and too ready obedience to her father, the whole scale is played, until the diapason closes in the pathetic scene, not actually played on the stage but described so graphically by Ophelia herself, in which, after she has suddenly returned him all his letters and gifts, Hamlet comes to her in his wild and dishevelled state, seizes her hand and simply stares questioningly into her eyes:

> He took me by the wrist, and held me hard;
> Then goes he to the length of all his arm;
> And, with his other hand thus o'er my brow,
> He falls to such perusal of my face,
> As he would draw it. Long stay'd he so;
> At last — a little shaking of mine arm,
> And thrice his head thus waving up and down —
> He rais'd a sigh so piteous and profound,
> That it did seem to shatter all his bulk,
> And end his being: that done, he lets me go:
> And, with his head over his shoulder turn'd,
> He seem'd to find his way without his eyes;
> For out o' doors he went without their help,
> And, to the last, bended their light on me.

Superficially we know that Hamlet is asking himself — and Ophelia's face — the question: Are you honest? Have you simply been acting in obedience to Polonius's commands? Or are you after all only a heartless coquette? But actually —— and this comes out both in the quality of the poetry and in the whole structure of the play (the *place*, for instance, at which this speech occurs) he is asking much more than this. He is asking the question: Is there such a being as Ophelia at all? A body no doubt; I have hold of it; but is that island inhabited? He is being forced back into an unwelcome solipsism. He looks into her eyes and he asks the question that is asked, in this age, many thousands of times a day all over the Western world by people who cannot see the other being —— the telephone question: "Are you there?" And so we are led by this play through the whole gamut of uncertainty and mistrust, not excluding the central uncertainty of all —— Hamlet's mistrust of the revelation he receives from the other, the spirit-world from which, as from his fellow creatures, he is severed by his excessively insulating self-consciousness.

In the same way it has often been complained that the episode of the Players' entrance and their long practice speeches made at Hamlet's request is tacked on for no artistic reason and spoils the shapeliness of the play. Critics who make such a complaint have not noticed what the First Player's speech is about. Let us consider it for a moment. Hamlet himself selects the particular passage to be spoken, from which we see that a dim recollection of the scene it conjures up is already running in his mind. But with what else has his mind been preoccupied? With the practical result of uncertainty —— indecision. He is come to the moment in his life at which his destiny calls on him to act, to act positively without excessive hesitation, without being held up and paralysed by an excess of that kind of sympathy which is based on blood-relationship and the divinity that hedges kingship. The world of Denmark is out of joint and *his* action is needed to put it right. He does not want to. He wants to do nothing, to retire, to have, or say he is having, a nervous breakdown. Moreover, he himself is alive to this danger; he knows well that alleged moral scruples may mask a mere supine inactivity —— that "conscience" may "make cowards of us all". He knows that he is in need of a little 'ruthlessness'. Instinctively, therefore, he draws on the Player to put before him an imagination of the opposite state of mind to this of his own; and the Player at his request recites that scene from the fall of Troy, in which Pyrrhus has to kill the aged and venerable Priam ——

as Hamlet knows *he* ought to kill his uncle. The verse describes in ranting terms how Pyrrhus seeks out Priam amid the smoking ruins and strikes at him, and how, though he strikes wild, the old man falls "with the whiff and wind of his fell sword". And now comes the crux of the speech. Pyrrhus pauses. He is, so to speak, becalmed.

> ... for lo! his sword,
> Which was declining on the milky head
> Of reverend Priam, seem'd i' the air to stick:
> So, as a painted tyrant, Pyrrhus stood;
> And like a neutral to his will and matter,
> Did nothing.

This is the picture with which it is so important that Hamlet should be confronted. For it is an imagination of his own condition. It is surely no accident that the last two words are given a line to themselves.

What does this mean for the *form* of the play? We are nearing the centre of the drama. And now there is put before Hamlet's soul the very picture of the crucial moment of the consciousness soul. It is his chance. Lost in uncertainty, no longer moved by divine promptings or commandments from within, the dramatic question that stands before him is the question whether he will now choose to act and to act out of his own initiative; not for any abstract reason or logical compulsion but freely imitating a picture set before him and *known* ("What's Hecuba to him or he to Hecuba?") to be no more than a picture.

For myself at any rate this has long been one of the most dramatic moments in the whole play. In this moment, Hamlet *is* the Consciousness Soul. He is every soul that has lost all its bearings, all its motives and springs of action, its very *raison d'être* and which now has indeed to decide for itself the stark question "To be or not to be". The soul has to assert its own existence as a separate, self-moved, spiritual entity. Nobody else will do that for it. But it can find no *reason* for asserting itself and its own existence —— no balance of pleasure over pain and so forth. —— If it could, it would not be consciousness soul, and (what matters) it would not be free. Reason compels. Instead of reasons, therefore, it has pictures set before it —— imaginations or examples, which it may imitate in freedom if it chooses. Such imaginations, mirroring its own true nature, are —— other souls, the events of history, inspired works of art. In fact the play of *Hamlet*, properly understood, may itself function as such a picture. It may bring to the consciousness of its spectators in the age of the consciousness soul the drama of their own souls, just as the play in the play was used to "catch the conscience of the King".

In order to make perfectly clear what is meant, a further distinction must be drawn here. Hamlet has been called 'representative' of mankind as a whole at this particular stage of their development. He is so in the sense that not only he, but every soul, in order to become a free, self-moved moral agent, must first go through this purely negative experience —— must be 'becalmed'. Every soul is faced at some time with this problem of transition from obedience (whether the obedience was to instinct, to the Law, or to a categorical imperative) to free imitation.

And the imitation will always be of some picture or example. But inasmuch as he is the *representative*, Hamlet is also more than a mere random *sample* of consciousness soul humanity. As the type and symbol of this experience, his crisis must represent the experience in its intensest possible form. And this is achieved by Shakespeare's selecting as the particular picture which is set before Hamlet at the psychological moment, not the soul of another human being, not the Christ, not any symbolical glimpse of the glorious future open to his soul, but simply a stark imagination of *the bare consciousness soul experience itself.* Hamlet is shown, in the picture of Pyrrhus, the bare sequence: Action — paralysis or becalming — renewed initiative and action. And that is all. That is the only imagination that is put before him —— his own experience. For there is certainly nothing very admirable or inspiring *per se* in the deed which Pyrrhus performs.

Involution, a sort of Chinese box structure, is thus characteristic of the whole form of this play. What is its central point, the crisis in the middle of the third or middle act? It is the play within the Play; and the plot of this play within the Play recapitulates in brief the story on which the Play itself turns. And as if this were not enough, this play within the Play is itself preceded by a Dumb Show (the play within the play within the Play) which recapitulates the same plot more briefly still. I am not concerned to suggest that Shakespeare was fully aware of all he was doing, but there is no question that the form of *Hamlet*, taking the word 'form' here in quite an obvious, external sense, is able to cast an almost magical spell —— especially on the young. It induces a sort of 'ecstasis' —— a sense of looking on at ourselves in the same moment.

What does Hamlet himself do at this crisis of his life? He fails. He does not imitate the imagination. The Player's speech goes on:

> But, as we often see, against some storm,
> A silence in the heavens, the rack stand still,
> The bold winds speechless, and the orb below
> As hush as death, anon the dreadful thunder
> Doth rend the region; so, after Pyrrhus' pause,
> Aroused vengeance sets him new a-work;
> And never did the Cyclops' hammers fall
> On Mars's armour, forg'd for proof eterne,
> With less remorse, than Pyrrhus' bleeding sword
> Now falls on Priam.

The words "with less remorse" should be especially noted. But, unlike Pyrrhus, Hamlet does not take any action. He only curses himself for not doing so. He needs something to *drive* him to action. He needs a violent force of external circumstances, such as was provided by the King's treacherous plot through Rosenkrantz and Guildenstern, the pirates' attack on his ship, and again at the very end of the play.

Hear his own account of some of the things that happened on the voyage to England:

> Up from my cabin,
> My sea-gown scarf'd about me, in the dark
> Grop'd I to find out them; had my desire;
> Finger'd their packet; and in fine withdrew
> To mine own room again; making so bold,

> My fears forgetting manners, to unseal
> Their grand commission; where I found, Horatio,
> O royal knavery! an exact command, —
> Larded with many several sorts of reasons,
> Importing Denmark's health and England's too.
> With, ho, such bugs and goblins in my life,
> That, in the supervise, no leisure bated,
> No, not to stay the grinding of the axe,
> My head should be struck off.
>
> Being thus be-netted round with villainies, —
> Ere I could make a prologue to my brains,
> They had begun the play — I sat me down,
> Devis'd a new commission, wrote it fair. ...
>
> I had my father's signet in my purse,
> Which was the model of that Danish seal;
> Folded the writ up in form of the other;
> Subscrib'd it; gave't the impression, plac'd it safely,
> The changeling never known. Now the next day
> Was our sea-fight; and what to this was sequent
> Thou know'st already.

The sea-fight he had already described in a letter:

> Ere we were two days old at sea, a pirate of very warlike appointment gave us chase. Finding ourselves too slow of sail, we put on a compelled valour; in the grapple I boarded them; on the instant they got clear of our ship, so I alone became their prisoner ...

Promptitude, courage, startling initiative, and after it is all over a curt, pungent report of the naval incident —— a masterpiece, as Coleridge has pointed out, of coherent brevity! Here is the amateur introvert of the Elsinore soliloquies in rather a different light! Certainly he is not the man to set right a disjointed world by obeying the summons of a purely spiritual intuition; but let someone else 'begin the play'; demand of him a *compell'd* valour; put him to sea with the toughest definite job to do and in the tightest possible corner you can think of —— and you get 'the Nelson touch'.

Perhaps enough has now been said to explain the difference between saying, on the one hand, that 'uncertainty' or 'mistrust' is the theme of *Hamlet* and, on the other, that it is a representation of the consciousness soul. But it is by no means all that could be said. There are many important aspects and qualities of the play which have not been touched.

A recent reviewer in *Punch* concluded his criticism by recounting, apparently with some self-approval, that he could not say how the final scenes of the performance under notice had been played, since he had followed his usual practice of leaving before the gravediggers' scene, thus escaping the vulgar ranting about death and the melodramatic claptrap which mar the conclusion of this otherwise fine play. This critic was, I think, an exceptionally insensitive one. Others do at least accept the gravediggers and the pile of corpses at the end as an integral part of the play, even if without quite knowing why. The truth is, of course, that *Hamlet* without the gravediggers, without the whole atmosphere of death and corruption which permeates the play even into the very metaphors the poet selects, and of which the scene in the graveyard is not more than a fitting climax —— *Hamlet* without all this is only a little less inconceivable than *Hamlet* without the Prince of Denmark.

Our immediate and quite unsophisticated perception is enough to tell us that this is so. But it is quite another matter when we attempt to explain why. And vagaries such as those of the *Punch* critic suggest that we are reaching a stage when attempts will have to be made to explain why. For, crude as such criticism may be, we must at least accept this about it, that it is there. It is written, and it is read. The time may come therefore when it will have to be answered.

The objection that the gravediggers' conversation, Hamlet's soliloquy over Yorick's skull, and the fight in the grave are mere sensations, introduced without reference either to the plot or to the inner psychological development of the play, is at first sight plausible. Certainly they cannot be derived from the 'uncertainty' theme and, as long as we see no further than that, they will also be felt to mar the unity of the play. But, as has already been pointed out, to say that *Hamlet* is a representation of the consciousness soul is to say very much more than that it is built up on the theme of 'uncertainty' or 'diffidence'. That is only one aspect of the consciousness soul.

From other of Steiner's numerous writings (and this time I find myself at a loss for specific quotation) it can be seen how intimately related is the consciousness soul to the experience, *and especially the imaginative experience,* of death. Of the many startlingly obvious truths to which Steiner was nevertheless alone in drawing attention, there is none more paramount to the whole of human experience than the truth that consciousness, based as it is on a perpetual wastage of the nervous and sensory tissues, is a direct concomitant of —— death. Other Central European psychologists have spent their lives indicating out of a muddled sort of empiricism that there is *some* vague connection between the unconscious life of the soul and the metabolism of the body. Steiner, beginning his investigations before psychoanalysis was heard of, had set in a beautifully clear light before he died the truth that — reflected physically in the cerebro-spinal system and the metabolism — Consciousness and Life stand at opposite poles. There is not space to go further into this here, but to grasp the nature of this conscious principle of the human being is to perceive at the same time, and now not merely aesthetically but with the intellect too, how perfectly appropriate all the gruesomeness in *Hamlet* is, how even the flavour of rant and exaggeration (which was obviously imparted deliberately by Shakespeare)[3] is appropriate, as delicately stressing the fact that it is the *imaginative* experience which is pointed to. Regarded as an event, the fight in the grave is, of course, preposterous. It is neither actually possible nor (what is twice as important) artistically convincing. As an imagination, however, it is colossal. The very stage direction, the laconic *"leaps into the grave"*, has an electrifying effect on a reader, coming precisely where it does in the play.

It is interesting in this last respect to contrast *Faust* with *Hamlet*. Nothing more opposite could well be conceived.

---

[3] Hamlet actually cries to Laertes:
  Nay, an thou'lt mouth
  I'll rant as well as thou.

Where *Hamlet* has death in every line, *Faust* has life in every line. From the wonderful moment of the outburst of the Easter hymn near the beginning of Part I to the very end of the Second Part, we are constantly being overwhelmed, positively submerged in deep floods of life. And the two characters are a no less perfect contrast than the plays. They are not so much opposed to one another as complementary. They are like Jack Sprat and his wife; each lacks all the qualities which the other possesses, and possesses all the qualities which the other lacks. Both together would make a whole man.

It is, for instance, nowhere indicated that Faust found any difficulty in asserting himself. This seems to have come to him as naturally as breathing. He soars freely above it. His problem, which he only succeeds in mastering near the end of the Second Part (when he gives way to the old couple), is to become able to do something which Hamlet simply cannot help doing with every other word he speaks —— that is, to display a piece of ordinary generosity. We again see how much wider a thing these characters are than any theory of them. How is this open, generous quality in Hamlet's nature related to the main thread of his character? The very acuteness of Hamlet's consciousness of his surroundings has this effect too, that he *lives* much in them. He is interested in the people he meets, critical and penetrative of their absurdities and dishonesties, but generally speaking in a kindly way. Thus, the nothingness of his own soul has its good side. Above all, he is interested in people *for their own sakes* and not with any conscious eye to their possible part in his own destiny. When they come in, we feel he is glad to see them.

Whereas the mood and manner in which Faust's character is drawn leave the impression of its being doubtful whether — when not under the influence of infatuation — he is ever really glad to see anyone, except possibly his own face in a mirror. Of course it is in a way absurd to react to Faust personally in this way. But, as far as it goes, the comparison stands and is, I think, 'significant'.

Again — and this takes us still further away from the 'uncertainty' motif — Hamlet seems to possess in a marked degree the virtue of constancy. It is the Saturn virtue. Somehow through all Hamlet's weakness we feel the bracing, astringent power of that death-nature which permeates the consciousness soul. This is really a deep meditation. Life as such, whether it be the life of an organism or the biography of a human being — or even perhaps the life of a Society — always has the metamorphic tendency. It is fissiparous. Its nature is to keep passing into ever new forms, to divide and again to subdivide. It is a good thing to be "lebendig", but a living creature is held together, kept from mere riotous multiplication, only by its death force. It is the skeleton that binds the body together and keeps it on the earth. It is the force we acquire from having, or having had, a skeleton which makes constancy and stability possible even in the spirit.

It would be possible to continue making cursory observations of this kind, but they lack force unless each can be traced separately from the roots of the play in the same way as has been attempted in the case of that aspect of the consciousness soul's manifestation which can be called 'uncertainty'. For it is not that it is incorrect to say that the theme of uncertainty is there, but only that it is incomplete. If it were said that this is *the* theme of *Hamlet*, it would be both incorrect and cramping to the imagination. For there are all these other themes as well. That is the difference between a work of literature which has form and one which merely has doctrine. It is the difference between myth and allegory. A doctrine or a 'message' in a work of art only says one thing; and when the thing is said, it is said. So too, a being who is the allegorical personification of, say, 'Courage', has only one quality —— courage; only one function —— to be brave. Whereas the 'Nemean Lion' or the mythical figure of Hercules, though they mean that, mean very many other things too. Thus, with a play such as *Hamlet*, which rises to the imaginative level of a Greek myth, criticism that treats it as mere allegory or mere doctrine will maim the play and cramp the reader's appreciation. Whereas criticism which treats it *as* myth, criticism which sees underlying its form not a theoretical but a spiritual unity, will be in a position to illuminate *all* the meanings it contains, instead of only one, and will enable us to trace them out more distinctly, if we want to.

Such criticism may itself rise to the level of an art. For it will each time come back from its journeys out into the particular aspects of the myth to the centre again, returning as in a dance to the underlying spiritual unity and bringing light from without to assist in raising the hidden centre to consciousness. And, in looking at a work of art, it is precisely when we are aware of having enjoyed such an interior dance that we know we are in the presence of 'form'. Only the unity to which we return must be, however dimly apprehended, not an idea but a spiritual being.

A spiritual being? Let me add in conclusion that the understanding of the nature of the three 'souls' is immeasurably deepened when they are related to the three mysterious female figures, *Philia, Astrid* and *Luna*, who appear in Steiner's Mystery Plays. In particular the figure of *Luna*, together with the fourth figure, *'the other Philia'*,[4] is important for an understanding of the consciousness soul. He is especially careful to affirm of these three characters that they are *not* mere symbolic or allegorical figures but actual individual beings. How can a principle of the human being, a stage, so to speak, in the development of his consciousness be at the same time a Being? This is an exceedingly difficult thought and I do not profess to be able to think it through, though I believe there must be a sense in which it is true. I come nearest, however, to being able to understand it along such lines of thought as I have attempted to put forward here.

---

[4] See also "The Inspiration of the *Divine Comedy*", p. 167 *et seq.*

OF THE INTELLECTUAL SOUL
first published 1929

I HAVE PREVIOUSLY pointed out that the great outburst of feeling and enthusiasm which marked the turn of the eighteenth century, and which we may loosely describe as the Romantic Movement, is for us today a tragic spectacle; and further that the increasing impulse towards self-knowledge is tending to undermine by 'explaining' Romance. I have suggested that anthroposophy is a genuine solution of this tragedy, describing it as the 'science of meaning' and again as 'the intellectual soul speaking to the consciousness soul'.

It will now be necessary to try and give some clearer idea of what the last phrase means. I say 'try' because there is really, by the very nature of the subject, an almost insuperable difficulty about describing or 'explaining' the intellectual soul, as seen from within, that is to say, from the Ego itself. It is much more a question of living with certain kinds of thought for a long time, turning them over and over, concentrating on them, relating them to ever fresh phenomena of inner life and outer observation, and so on. And then this understanding of the Ego-intellectual-soul nature grows up of its own accord.

One can, for instance, reflect, not once, but many times, on a curious fact that penetrates nearly all our experience. I mean the fact that what one *is* one cannot at the same time contemplate, or experience in full consciousness. We must be in some sense outside an experience — it must have become a memory — before we can realise its objective nature and significance. Those who are interested in problems of artistic creation and criticism will have a ready approach to thoughts of this kind, but they can also be understood out of the feeling life as a whole. From this one can go on to dwell on the opening chapters of St. John's Gospel and feel how, according to the author, this same fact is at the heart of all creation. The light, the divine creative principle, was in the world —— in a sense, it *was* the world, for through it all things came into being —— but the world *knew it not* —— was not conscious of it.

Again (to take an example), one can, if possible, immerse oneself in the whole nature of Greek thought, experiencing how the more self-conscious, Socratic intellection emerges gradually from the more universally conscious, but more dreaming, Platonic mind. One can feel the significance of such an historical fact as the following: On the one hand the philosophic problem of an opposition between 'subjective' and 'objective' was not heard of until the time of the Stoics, and on the other hand it is in this same sect that we first meet with a theory of the divine Logos. Men begin to be *conscious* of an indwelling creative principle, precisely as they *begin* to feel themselves detached from it.

Now, if one throws upon all that one knows of history the light that comes from an intimate acquaintance with such thoughts as these, then one can see the inward meaning of the scheme which was given in the essay on the Consciousness Soul (I will remind the reader of the three crucial periods —— see diagram next page).

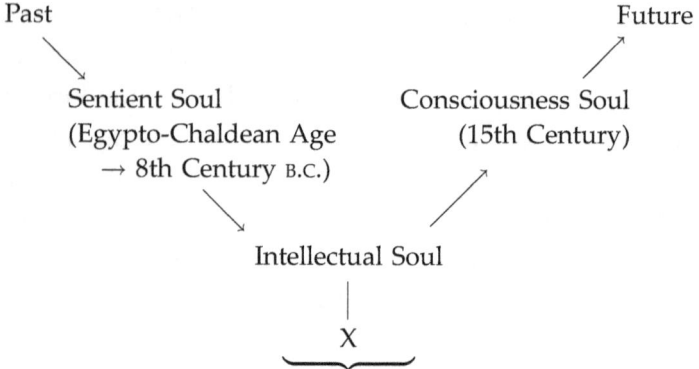

The result is that one begins to assert with confidence, and out of one's own experience, that *some* remarkable event must have taken place at 'X', some gift of power to arise from the depths, some passing over of life and meaning from the macrocosm to the microcosm, some mystery, let us say, of resurrection. And then the question arises, not so much, do I believe in the Gospels? but rather "How far do the Gospels present a consistent and illuminating account of just such an event?"

In this way questions of faith, belief, and knowledge take on rather a different complexion; and we begin to grasp the true nature of *certainty*. Certainty of knowledge must be a very different thing in the consciousness soul age from what it was in the age of the intellectual soul. And this, I think, is felt instinctively by all minds which are in any sense abreast of their time, whether their bent be scientific or romantic. The consciousness soul will only say "I know", when it can add: "because I have experienced".

Thus, the ability to say 'I know what happened on Golgotha' really depends, for the consciousness soul, on having experienced it. Experienced, not suffered (though there must of course have been some suffering with it). It is painfully easy today to write glibly about Christ. Every quill-driver, who has just discovered that life is not all beer and skittles, rushes into the market-place to explain that he has been 'crucified'. For that reason I want to emphasise that what I mean here is rather a thought experience than an emotional one. To do so is neither to be emotionally casual nor to overlook the supremacy over both thought and emotion of the moral issue; only it is impossible to say everything at once. Indeed, the decision to *imitate*, taken irrespective of belief or knowledge, is for the consciousness soul the typical moment of *metanoia* —— repentance, or change of mind.[1] But once that moment is past, the most inflexible and lasting choices of the will are those which originate in response to neither emotion, exhortation nor command, but because of knowledge. Before such decisions can be taken the eyes must be opened, the mind, as the idiom has it, 'made-up'. After they have been taken, the heart will be warmed and strengthened in ever increasing measure by circumstances themselves, alike by success and failure, happiness and dismay. It will be found that all creation is in the conspiracy to satisfy and uphold them.

Certainty, then, about the central event of the Intellectual Soul age is only possible, when we have, so to say, recapitulated the event in consciousness. It is only possible, when we have re-experienced as a problem of

---

[1] See "The Form of Hamlet".

consciousness what was once a problem of history. The historical problem was the problem of the resurrection —— the problem of establishing a living umbilical connection between macrocosm and microcosm, in order that life might pass from one to the other. It is easy to see how this problem, when we recapitulate it in consciousness, must be the problem of 'subjective' and 'objective'. In what way does the macrocosm, the world which presents itself as 'outside' me, live in me, so that it is indeed I, so that its tremendous forces are some day to become forces of my will? *In what way* is imagination 'true'?

And the first step towards the solution of this problem is the grasping of a right theory of knowledge. The mind which has grasped a right theory of knowledge, and has *experienced* it, that mind is on the road to certainty — the only kind of certainty that is open to the consciousness soul — because it has begun to cross the threshold between the objective and the subjective worlds.

Now the Romantic Movement never properly crystallised into a theory of knowledge. In this country — apart from Coleridge — there was hardly even the desire for such a theory. But in Central Europe it was somewhat different. Apart from the group of Romantic philosophers, Goethe, with such conceptions as that of the 'exact percipient fancy' and with all his scientific work, brought an initial confidence in the truth of imagination at any rate to the verge of a theory of knowledge. And Steiner, in his *Philosophy of Freedom*, carried it over that verge and established it firmly in the promised land of philosophy. Almost from birth Steiner had felt it as his task to break down the theoretic barriers between the objective and the subjective worlds and he had hardly reached the age of thirty before he succeeded. His subsequent work — the fruit of his own method of knowledge — enables one to perceive, among other things, how infinitely much is hidden behind this apparently trifling phenomenon, the divergence in the paths of development taken by the Romantic impulse in this country and in Central Europe. Bernard Shaw has used the phrase 'condensed recapitulation' to describe the course which evolution takes. And this is the principle which we always find at the heart of that larger, all-embracing evolution of the world and of humanity, the *evolution of consciousness*, which Steiner depicted. Thus the achievements of the two great periods which preceded our own — the Egypto-Chaldean and the Graeco-Roman — are in a sense picked up in the present age by different parts of Europe. And we may, I think, conceive, in general, of the sunny Mediterranean lands south of the Alps as the home of a Sentient Soul development, while the continent north of the Alps and West of Russia is peculiarly the vehicle for the Intellectual Soul. The British Isles develop the Consciousness Soul in the age of the Consciousness Soul.[2]

[2] The only definite pronouncement of Steiner's with which I am acquainted on this subject is a lecture in which he identified Italy as especially the Sentient Soul and *France* as the Intellectual Soul nation. The peoples of Central Europe were the carriers of the Ego itself. From the present point of view, however—the resurrection point of view, if I may so call it—the relation between Intellectual Soul and Ego is peculiarly close. The Intellectual Soul, as Steiner himself characterises it in *Occult Science: an Outline*, "since it partakes of the nature of the I—since in a certain respect it *is* the I, though not yet conscious of its spiritual being—may be designated simply as the I or Ego." Compare "The Inspiration of the *Divine Comedy*" at page 185.

Thus it is in Central Europe that we find this instinctive impulse to grasp the *meaning* of life. And this comes out, not only in vast highbrow philosophical 'Strömungen', but in all sorts of delightful little ways. Notice, for instance, how fond its inhabitants are of such words as 'significant' and 'deep' (*tief*). We have only to cast our minds back to the scheme of evolution depicted earlier in these articles, with the Intellectual Soul at its inverted apex, and we can see how natural it is that they should all have this vague instinctive sense of living over a dark, unplumbed abyss. This is the abyss in which all those 'deep' meanings to which our attention is constantly directed will somehow, they believe, be found; this is the abyss into which Faust descended to find the Mothers, and in which Goethe discovered the Primal Plant. This is the abyss from which the fashionable theory of the Unconscious was muckraked up by the Freudians.

> O Mensch! Gib Acht:
> Was spricht die tiefe Mitternacht?
> Ich schlief — ich schlief!
> Aus tiefem Traum bin ich erwacht!
> Die Welt ist tief,
> Und tiefer als der Tag gedacht:
> Tief ist ihr Weh —
> Lust — tiefer nach als Herzeleid!
> Weh spricht: Vergeh!
> Doch alle Lust will Ewigkeit —
> Will tiefe, tiefe Ewigkeit.

One might almost say that the Ego in Central Europe lives always at the point of incarnation, and the Intellectual Soul is that point. It is as if constantly surging up and down between life and death. It is naturally adapted therefore to understand the Johannine mystery of the light shining into the darkness, the mystery of resurrection, the mystery of meaning. And it is to the culture of Central Europe that we in the West must look if we would find the actual concrete *meaning* of life — the living heart of nature — the Eternal Feminine.

We in the West are so placed that, as our self-consciousness increases, we feel: over there is the material world, all that I experience as sense-perception and ordinary thought, and over here is the 'I', a mysterious entity (perhaps non-entity) about which I can never know anything, and between the two there is no connection. Sentient Soul: Consciousness Soul. At best we can jump restlessly to and fro from one to the other. It is only as we get nearer to the true heart of Central European culture, it is only as we begin to penetrate the loving darkness of the intellectual soul, that the connection between the two, which is indeed *Ourselves*, begins to glimmer into conscious experience.

$$\begin{array}{ccc} \text{Sentient Soul} & :: & \text{Consciousness Soul} \\ \downarrow & & \uparrow \\ & \text{Intellectual Soul} & \end{array}$$

Then we begin to understand that another relation between the senses and the too acutely self-conscious Ego is possible, besides that unhappy jumping to and fro which characterises the life of the modern intelligentsia. For we begin to understand how we can resolve the two once more into one. We go back now to all the richness and colour of the sentient soul, but in such a way that it is redeemed. Sense-perception has become spiritual perception. And this is precisely the dramatic choice which lies before Imagination, as the Romantics understood it. Either it must go boldly forward and turn itself into clairvoyance (for clairvoyance *is* a partial reunion with the macrocosm) —— or it must fall back and become —— at best idle fancy, at worst sensuality.

The last act of this tragedy is performed over and over again —— every time an ego which has begun to live intensely in the consciousness soul tries to turn back, to turn back, as it were, *directly* to the sentient soul, without deepening itself in the intellectual soul first. The Western Ego repudiates the earnest search for the meaning of life, repudiates all that Central Europe stands for in the history of modern European culture, and seeks instead a place in the sun —— in the old easy-going *instinctive* imaginative experience of the sentient soul. If one wished to sum all this up in a kind of occult formula, one might say: "The Englishman should travel to Italy —— but he should go by way of Central Europe." The other route is a tragic one. And we can trace the tragedy of it far back into the earlier days of consciousness soul development, back even to the time when it was the only route possible.

To understand the cultural relations between England and Italy one must, I think, realise that for the spiritual life of the ordinary Englishman Italy is a kind of *temptation*. Just as in our own day the English critic gives up Coleridge for Croce, just as we have Mr. Chesterton and his school of beer and tobacco Catholics, with their intense dislike of Teutonic culture, succumbing to the same sensuous Roman temptation, so a little while back there came the Oxford Movement in religion and the pre-Raphaelite movement in art, both tending to a simple, but affected and essentially rootless Romanticism. The *struggle* against temptation comes to light with peculiar force in a soul such as Cardinal Newman's.

But the extraordinary thing is that we find this same tragedy further back still. We find it, for instance, in John Milton, whose relations with the culture of Italy were so close that he wrote poems in that language which won praise from Italians themselves. In Milton the struggle between sentient soul and consciousness soul never ceased, and indeed gave rise to his finest poetry. Over and over again, while the Puritan in him wished to reject as unlawful the beauties of the senses, there was something else, a deeper voice, which told him that these beauties must have a spiritual reality of their own. Alike in his life and in his poems the discord is always there, sounding through the rest. It comes out in the rhetoric of *Comus* and hovers behind the magnificent dialogues of Adam and Eve in *Paradise Lost*. And it is peculiarly noticeable how Milton often brings forward his glorious wealth of pagan imagery with a half disapproving air. He never fully resolved that discord —— and it was out of his perception of this failure in the great poet's life and experience that Blake subsequently wrote his poem, *Milton*. It is especially significant (especially 'tief') that both poets should have been 'modern', inasmuch as they remained throughout unable to shake off a certain preoccupation with the matter of sexual indulgence. One cannot help wondering what it might have meant to both of them, but especially to Milton —— if time had been kinder and allowed them to encounter the spiritual voluptuousness of, for instance, Novalis.

In this way we gradually begin to behold the interplay between the three soul-principles more as a moving historical spectacle. Can we not almost see with our eyes the warm, brilliantly-coloured Italian painting of the Madonna working its way underground up through Provence, through the medieval French courtly tradition, to blossom at last in the pure inward experience of Goethe's 'Eternal Feminine', or in that profound imagination of Isis which runs so curiously through Novalis's work?

At the same time we can begin to understand the real significance of a phenomenon which punctuated the transition in another part of the world —— Puritanism. It really is more useful to try and understand what Puritanism means than to sneer at it. Puritanism went furthest in scouring the last echoes of the senses from the religious self, as English philosophy went furthest in scouring them from the speculative self. We may perhaps grasp its true meaning best in an imagination —— if we think of a vast empty whitewashed cathedral, with every carven image removed, with not a single object to catch the eye, and, whispering and welling out through the living space beneath the dome, re-filling it, so to speak, out of the depths of the Ego itself, the grandeur of a Bach Fugue or the rich feminine tenderness of one of his Cantatas. Milton loved playing the organ. And again the picture dissolves into an image of the *human* temple. Body and soul are swept and garnished; vanished are the last echoes of the unredeemed senses of the old Adam. The temple is empty —— ready at last to be re-filled with the voluptuous yet pure imagery of the soul's own conscious making.

And so once again we are brought back to the mystery of the resurrection, of the passage through the little wicket gate from the old man to the new. And we see the relationship between consciousness soul and intellectual soul in yet another light; for the consciousness soul is the little wicket gate, and the intellectual soul is the passing.

What has been spoken of here as the resurrection might also be called the resurrection of the body; for that is the full re-union with the macrocosm. It seems as if minds which pass beyond a certain level of sublimity acquire as of right a presentiment of this final goal of creation, and it is interesting to compare the way in which this presentiment echoes in the language of two representative poets. First Novalis's *Hymn*, of which I have attempted to give a very free English rendering, though it is unfortunately hard to imagine a more untranslatable poem, and I am only too well aware that nearly everything is lost:

HYMN

Very few listen
To the secret of love,
Feel the unquenchable
Undying thirst!
The Supper
Hath a heavenly meaning
Passing the understanding of the senses.

Yet whosoever
From hot and dearest lips
Hath drunken breath of life:
Whose heart the holy glow
Hath ever melted into tremulous floods —
Whose gaze hath risen
Even to heaven,
Plumbing its fathomlessness,
Will eat of his body
And drink of his blood
Everlastingly.
How few have guessed
The holy meaning of the earthly body!
Who dares
To say he understands blood?
One day — all body —
One body...
A blissful pair
Swimming in heavenly blood —
Oh! that earth's pale seas
Were flushing *now*
And into odour-dropping flesh
These rocks were passing!
Fair never-ending meal!
For love can never take enough.
Nearer! More in me! More mine own,
Beloved!
By softer, ever tenderer lips
The elements are changed
Inwarder — nearer —
Fiercer and fiercer longing
Thrills through the soul:
Thirstier and hungrier
Grows the heart.
So must love's banquet last
From eternity to eternity!
Had the abstemious
Only tasted,

> All would they leave
> And would sit down with us
> To the table of love-longing
> That never is bare.
> They would hail love's magic bounty
> And praise their commons
> Of body and of blood.

Is there not, in this poem, a certainty, a grounded *knowledge*? It is not content to stop in imagination and hint and suggestion. One feels that its meaning, its *openly expressed* meaning, reaches right down into the solid earth and again right up into the empyrean. It is the resurrection of the body —— in terms of the body.

Over against it let us set the song from Shakespeare's last play, *The Tempest*, which is so full of invisible meanings.

> Full fathom five thy father lies;
> Of his bones are coral made;
> Those are pearls that were his eyes.
> Nothing of him that doth fade,
> But doth suffer a sea-change
> Into something rich and strange.
> Sea-nymphs hourly ring his knell:
>
> *Burden:*   Ding-dong.
> Hark! now I hear them — Ding-dong bell.

Now this song is not of the earth at all. It never touches earth. Everything in it is imagination, hint, suggestion. The deeper meanings are not expressed but rather fly off like the invisible vapour from the surface of volatilising spirits. This is the resurrection of the body in terms of pure imagination.

'Puritanism' — 'pure' — the words themselves give us a further clue to the manner in which intellectual soul and consciousness soul dovetail into and complement one another. It is the function of the intellectual soul to inspire —— of the consciousness soul to correct. Only the intellectual soul knows what is the meaning of life —— but the consciousness soul knows what is *not* the meaning of life —— and therefore either is helpless without the other. Earlier I said that we in the West must go to the culture of Central Europe to find the meaning of life. Yes, but we shall find it in solution with all sorts of waste matter —— nonsense, sentimentalism, credulity, ruthless egotism. We ought to be able to purge it of this dross. In this connection we might consider one of those little peculiarities of expression which often tell us so much. There is a word which springs very naturally to the lips of English people endeavouring to characterise their general impression of German literature, and that word is 'earthy' —— not 'earthly', which is something quite different. I cannot go into it further, but one can see at once that this is a quality in which the good and evil elements are likely to be hard to disentangle. Even in the *Hymn* of Novalis, which has just been quoted —— one can feel how open it would be to a false, or too easy reading. In a sense one has the feeling that only dead people ought to be allowed to read this *Hymn*. This is where the consciousness soul, like a spiritual policeman, steps in. It never forgets death. It is not going to allow us to forget that, before there can be a resurrection, there must be a death. It knows at any rate what is *not* the meaning of life; and so it keeps a humorous, suspicious, weather-eye open, and if it finds the intellectual soul groping secretly backward to the sentient soul —— if, for instance, it finds Romanticism slipping back into Pantheism or catches the Eternal Feminine crystallising too easily into the pretty lady, it picks up a death's head, strikes an attitude, and with a certain grim satisfaction, declaims: "Now get you to my lady's chamber and tell her, let her paint an inch thick, to this favour she must come!"

In a word, the Consciousness Soul strives to purify by baptising in the waters of Jordan. We might say that the Central European 'should not travel to Italy until he has crossed the Channel'. It is perhaps no more than an accident that Shakespeare's poem is as watery as Novalis's is 'earthy'. But we may remark in passing that the unsatisfactory interpretations to which the former is open are of quite a different order. The danger here is that the poem may seem to have *no* substance —— so that, for example, I might be accused of fancifulness for connecting its meaning with the resurrection of the body at all. And yet every day we find more and more that we cannot do without substantial certainty upon these great subjects. We must have the substance of knowledge, the substance of meaning, not only its beautiful overtones and shadows.

Anthroposophy, arising out of Central Europe, contains in it precisely this substance of knowledge; and the soul which makes 'anthroposophia' a part of itself gradually begins to *know* this mystery of the emergence of the old man from the new as a fact of concrete experience. For it begins to grasp meaning, not merely in those abstract shadows of thoughts from which the intelligentsia are already beginning to shy, but in that concrete thinking which reveals itself as being functionally related to (for instance) the breathing. Thus, it does not merely read about the light shining into the darkness, interpenetrating the darkness, but experiences the process —— experiences it, for example, as the counterpart of its bodily breathing. Gradually it begins to feel the in-breath as a light experience, as a red experience, as the old man, and the outbreath as a dark experience, a blue experience, as the new, resurrected man. Upon such a soul the meaning of the old prophetic exhortation "Know thyself!" suddenly dawns in its full reality, as it perceives that all genuine wisdom involves the overcoming of precisely that dilemma which was referred to at the beginning of this essay, where it was said: 'What I *am* I cannot at the same time experience or contemplate.' The human heart *can* overcome this dilemma. It is a contradiction which would only be really true of a creature without a heart, without any rhythmic experience of heart or lung. Man need not be such a creature. Nor need our civilisation. If anthroposophy remains true to itself, over in the centre of Europe the Goetheanum should stand as the heart of an otherwise ever more heartless civilisation. The consciousness soul, critical without being negative, can see that it does remain true to itself.

Of course it will make nonsense of all this if it is taken in such a way, as to think: Yes, all English people have the consciousness soul strongly developed, and all Central Europeans the ego and intellectual soul. It is meant much rather that the nature and function of the consciousness soul can be *better understood*, if the English culture is sympathetically grasped, the intellectual soul, if French and German culture are so grasped. 'We' means, not so much 'we English' or 'we Westerners' as 'we anywhere in the world who are Western in spirit or Westernised by tradition'. It would be equally false to read into what has been said any sort of political meaning. In this connection a final word remains to be added.

I have been treading to a certain extent on dangerous ground. When we turn our minds to the description of national characteristics, passion and prejudice die hard. The elimination of bias is a much harder matter than those imagine who, having achieved a superficial smear of the anti-nationalism that is given away nowadays with a pound of socialism, smile complacently at anyone who demurs to their facile manifestos. Even if we feel pretty confident that the super-national conceptions of Spiritual Science have already given us complete 'objectivity' in these matters, we shall do well to be especially on our guard. Perhaps then more than ever. National pride works underground and penetrates to surprising depths, nor is it in absolutely every case love of our *own* nation which blinds our critical faculties.

At the end of the essay on the *Consciousness Soul* I ventured to describe anthroposophy as 'the intellectual soul speaking to the consciousness soul'. In front, so to speak, of this idea I should now like to place something in the nature of an imagination. Let us try to call up two divinely tall spiritual forms, and suppose them meeting each other for a moment in the intricate figure of a dance. And let us suppose that this dance is also a choral hymn, so that these two gracious, serenely moving spirits interchange not merely motions and positions, but words. As they meet, the Spirit of the German Nation calls across to the Spirit of the English: "Seek life! Know yourself! Go down with Faust to the Mothers, to the Eternal Feminine, go down into the teeming earth and rise again in full certainty, having found both yourself and the world. Take the confidence that is based on this knowledge. Know yourself! Seek life!" And the English Folk-Soul calls back: "Seek death! Yes, *know* yourself and the world! Do not merely *believe* in the old way, substituting one creed for another. Rather live in the very breakdown of all belief. Even encourage your own opposition, as men do in games. Immerse in the destructive element! And so learn to tear your true self free from all thought and all feeling in which the senses still echo. Leap, with Hamlet, into the grave, in order to wrestle there. Seek death!"

In such a way, starting from what we know best, we might gradually learn to fill in the rest of the picture, until that greater imagination, of which Rudolf Steiner once spoke, of *all* the Nation-Spirits moving in solemn dance round the blinding brilliance of the Central Figure, should stand before us in all its majesty and terror and yet at the same time in all its little and intimate charm.

THE INSPIRATION OF THE
DIVINE COMEDY
first published 1934

IN THE LAST of Steiner's four Mystery Plays a figure appears on the stage, whom we have not hitherto seen, called the "Spirit of Johannes Thomasius' Youth". The spirit makes two or three very brief appearances and each time it is in conjunction with another character, "the other Philia".

It is noticeable that in the list of dramatic personae prefixed to the second and third plays "the other Philia" is described as "the spiritual being who hinders the union of the soul-forces with the Cosmos"; this is in clear contrast with her three companions, Philia, Astrid and Luna (recalling the sentient, intellectual and consciousness souls), who are described as the spiritual beings who mediate that union. In the dramatic personae to the fourth play *The Souls' Awakening*, on the other hand, the same being is described as "the bearer of the element of love in the world to which the spiritual personality belongs". No explanation is offered of this apparent discrepancy.

Those who have seen or read *The Souls' Awakening* will certainly recollect those musical words of the other Philia, which run throughout the play as a sort of refrain:

> Und wachendes Träumen
> Enthülle den Seelen
> Verzaubertes Weben
> Des eigenen Wesens.

of which a rather lame translation would be: "And may waking dream unwrap from souls the enchanted weaving of their own nature." Now it is in the second scene of this play, while Johannes is murmuring over to himself these lines, which he has just heard spoken by the "other Philia," that the spirit of his youth first appears. The spirit explains that he is kept alive by Johannes' *wishes* and nourished by the dreams of his youth (*Mein Atem schlürfet deiner Jugend Träume*). And he implores Johannes not to forsake him, leaving him to do service in the cruel shadows.

In a later scene Johannes, under the impression that he is listening to the other Philia, awakens to find that the voice is that of his own Doppelgänger or double, who then at once leads him before the Guardian of the Threshold. The Guardian explains that this shadowy double can only be freed from "enchanted worlds of soul" (Seelenzauberwelten), if Johannes will kill out of himself the wishes which still accompany him on his path of spiritual progress. Until that happens, Johannes will be led each time, not over the threshold, but past it. The Doppelgänger, too, is connected with Johannes' past. He says to Johannes: "Leave to its life in the realm of shadows that in yourself which is lost to you. But give it light from your Spirit light, for then it will not have to suffer pain."

So there are two beings connected with Johannes' youth —— parts of himself, it seems, which he has left behind as he grows older, but which he has left behind in a wrong way. They are forced to lead a shadowy and

THE INSPIRATION OF THE *DIVINE COMEDY* 169

painful existence from which they seek redemption. And they are nourished by the youthful wishes and hopes which are still not quite eradicated from Johannes' soul. What is to be done with these beings? The wishes and hopes themselves, says the Guardian sternly, must be killed before the threshold can be crossed. It seems to follow that the Doppelgänger and the Geist von Johannes' Jugend are to be simply starved to death. But this is a hard saying, in view of the dramatic symphony which they have been allowed to excite. We expect, and in the tenth scene we get, some further reference to the "redemption" which has already been spoken of.

It appears that the instrument of this redemption is to be the other Philia. She tells him that he himself has created the Doppelgänger out of himself and she goes on to say that she (the other Philia) must remain with him as long as shadows continue to surround him —— until he himself redeems the shadow into which his guilt has breathed an enchanted life. We begin to gain a little insight into the two different descriptions of her given in the dramatis personae. She tells him what to do: *Gib mir, was du dir denkend selber bist*, and then she explains who she is:

I am in thee, a member of thy soul. I am the power of love in thee, the heart's hope which stirs within thee, the fruits of long past lives on earth which are preserved in thy being; oh, behold them through me —— feel me in thee and behold thyself through my power in thee.

Gib mir was du dir denkend selber bist ... Give to *me* what thou thyself thinking art to thyself. The line is reminiscent of one of the thought-weighted lines from Dante's *Divine Comedy*, and is equally untranslatable. What does it mean? In the superficial sense this is clear enough; but its *content* will depend on the wealth of emotional and imaginative experience with which anyone can relate it. With this in mind, we may begin by asking: Do we know of anyone who has actually done what the other Philia bids Johannes do, when she speaks this line, who has redeemed the spirit of his youth, or who has at any rate done something very much like it, taking into account the different circumstances of the age in which he lived? And if we have really felt and understood some part of the great poem to which I have just referred, I think we shall be able to answer: Yes, we know of, at any rate, one such person; we know much of him; and his name is Dante Alighieri.

Many people know that the *Divine Comedy* is divided into three long books called the *Inferno*, the *Purgatorio* and the *Paradiso*. The details of the story which they tell are not so well known. At the opening of the *Inferno* the poet describes how in the midst of the path of this life he came into a situation, a "dark forest", in which his courage failed him. The scene changes to heaven, where the Virgin Mary, who has observed his trouble, sends a message to Beatrice, herself also in heaven, to enquire why she is doing nothing to help her former lover. Beatrice summons the Spirit of the Latin poet, Virgil, from the region on the outskirts of hell, where he dwells with the other virtuous pagans, and bids him encourage Dante. Virgil descends and does so. He tells Dante that he will show him the whole universe, both the sorrowing and the rejoicing. The poet is at first reluctant but on his hearing of Beatrice's intercession, all fear is dispelled.

The rest of the *Inferno* describes Dante's journey through hell under the guidance of the Latin poet and his encounter with the various types of sinner who inhabit the different circles of hell. Dante's hell is much more varied than the "everlasting bonfire" which is commonly imputed to the medieval imagination. It is located in the interior of the earth and only some parts of it are involved in flames, the inmost circle (where Judas and Satan are found) being a place of freezing cold. When Satan fell from heaven, he fell head-first, and, penetrating the earth's crust at a point in the southern hemisphere, which is the antipodes of Jerusalem, he finally came to rest with his head and shoulders in the hollow of hell which had been prepared for him in the interior of the northern hemisphere, while his nether extremities stretch upward into the south. When, therefore, Dante and his guide, who of course start their journey from Italy in the northern hemisphere, reach the centre of hell, they come upon the head of Satan. This happens in the last book of the *Inferno* and there follows a brief, grotesque, yet somehow awe-inspiring account of the continued journey of the two poets past the earth's centre of gravity, when Virgil, who is leading, astonishes Dante by turning round and apparently standing on his head (sotto sopra), and *up* Satan's hairy legs, flying in the dark from frozen shag of hair to frozen shag —— until they emerge beneath the stars of the southern hemisphere at the foot of the mount of Purgatory. The mount of Purgatory is comparatively small. It was thrown up, like a sort of molehill, when Satan's fallen bulk suddenly penetrated the mass of the earth. The ascent of the mount by the two poets and their encounters and conversations on the way is the story told in the *Purgatorio*.

Purgatory is the country of the soul, as the heaven of the *Paradiso* is the home of the spirit. The mountain is cut into a series of terraces (in the old prints it looked rather like a wedding cake) and on each terrace there are souls being purified by suffering from all traces of the different grades of sin. A soul which has been but slightly affected by any particular sin only stays a short time in that particular circle. It remains longest in the circle which corresponds to its besetting vice, but its time may be shortened even there by the prayers of the living. On the summit of the mountain is situated the Garden of Eden, for at the end of its path of purification the soul regains the pristine innocence from which it fell through Adam's transgression. This is the *earthly* paradise. It is in the earthly paradise that Dante's first meeting with Beatrice since her physical death takes place. She approaches in a cart drawn by a grifon (that is, griffin), the animal symbol of Christ Himself, amid crowds of blessed spirits flinging flowers. She comes from the spirit world of the *Paradiso*, to which Dante is about to ascend with her. Her cart is symbolical of the Church and the reader can already see her in the light in which she is to appear throughout the rest of the *Divine Comedy* —— as the embodiment of divine wisdom or revelation. But for Dante in the earthly paradise at this moment she is still a Beatrice of the soul-world. The language in which he describes the scene is closely reminiscent of the account which he had given in his earlier work, the *Vita Nuova*, of their first meeting upon earth. At first he does not see her face, for she is veiled. The revelation which she is to be is still scarfed in a cloud of the bewildering wishes, hopes and fears which once beset his awakening adolescence. But already, before she unveils, Dante feels her presence through some hidden virtue that goes out of her. "I felt the mighty power of ancient love," he says. *D'antico amor sentì la gran potenza.* He turns to Virgil like a frightened child, crying:

> Men che dramma
> Di sangue m'é rimaso che non tremi;
> Conosco i segni dell' antica fiamma.

Less than a drachma of blood is left in me that does not tremble. I recognize the tokens of the ancient flame.

He turns with these words to Virgil, only to find that Virgil has disappeared! It is a poignant moment; doubly so when the last words are recognised as a quotation from Virgil's own *Aeneid*.[1] The name "Virgilio" echoes like a dirge through the succeeding terza, in which Dante bemoans the loss of the "dolcissimo patre" who has been his help and stay so long. But Virgil has done

---

[1] *Agnosco veteris vestigia flammae.* The words are spoken by Dido to her sister Anna.

his task and can go no further. Henceforth Beatrice is to be the guide.

We are now in the 30th Canto of the *Purgatorio* and nearing its end. Beatrice begins by chiding Dante for his shortcomings since her death. He has plenty to weep for, she says, besides the loss of Virgil! Dante is overcome with shame and misery at the thought of all that he has become since that first meeting and since he lost her. He is bidden to look on her and, on raising his downcast head, sees how she now surpasses her earthly self in beauty as much as she formerly surpassed all other women. His remorse becomes so bitter that he loses consciousness. At last he is allowed to be plunged in the waters of Lethe, which wash away all memory of sins, except as occasions of divine mercy. And when he emerges, it is to see Beatrice gazing on the grifon and Christ reflected in her eyes.

"A thousand desires hotter than flame held my eyes fast bound to the shining eyes, which remained ever fixed upon the grifon."

There is nothing more about trembling blood. The poet is ready for his journey to the stars.

It is important to gain a clear picture of the scene in which the *Divine Comedy* is laid and through which Dante's journey proceeds. It is nothing less than the whole universe of Ptolemy, whereof the earth is at the centre surrounded by nine concentric spheres. The first six of these are the spheres of the planets, Moon, Mercury, Venus, Sun, Mars, Jupiter, Saturn, and the three outermost spheres are those of the Fixed Stars, the

Primum Mobile and the Empyrean. The centre of gravity of the earth, therefore, is the centre part of the whole universe and it is here that, at the end of the *Inferno*, Dante encountered and passed the source of all evil (Satan) congealed, as it were, in the maximum condensation of matter. Henceforward his path is outward from the centre towards the circumference, slowly at first, as he winds his way with Virgil up the comparatively diminutive cone of the mount of Purgatory until, caught up into the spheres with Beatrice from its summit, he traverses in a series of effortless leaps (salite), of which more hereafter, the enormous distances between the orbits of the planets, in each one of which he stays some while. At the beginning of the 11th Canto, having reached the sphere of the Sun (which is the fourth planet outward from the earth in the Ptolemaic astronomy) the poet takes a look backward and downward at the earth and apostrophises the insensate care of mortals hurrying to and fro on their mundane affairs.

> Quando da tutte queste cose sciolto
> Con Beatrice m'era suso in cielo
> Cotanto gloriosamente accolto.[2]

While freed from all these things I was high in heaven with Beatrice so gloriously received.

---

[2] I give the Italian in many of these quotations in the hope that their cumulative effect will convey to readers unacquainted with Italian some impression of the weight and resonance of that musical language in which, the vowels always predominating, every syllable is given its full and distinct value.

Each sphere is inhabited by different ranks and orders of the spirits of the dead and in each one Dante meets and converses — often at very great length — with some who on earth were either known to him personally or, like Justinian and St. Thomas Aquinas, famous among all men.

Beyond the sphere of Saturn Dante and Beatrice come into the circle of the Fixed Stars and next into the Primum Mobile, the First Mover which, itself unmoved, is the source of all spatial motion. Here, in the 28th Canto, Dante describes how, as he was gazing into Beatrice's eyes, he beheld something reflected in them which made him turn his head to see what it was. He saw a point of light so intense and concentrated that an ordinary star as seen from the earth would appear as large as the moon beside it. Round the point of light nine circles of fire were swiftly wheeling. These are the nine hierarchies as manifested in the Primum Mobile. Dante notices that the inmost circle is the swiftest. He is told that this is because it is the most divine and therefore nearest to the centre. It is the circle of the Seraphim. Now the speeds of the Ptolemaic spheres through which Dante is passing are arranged in the opposite order. The *outermost* of these spheres (the Empyrean) is the most divine and the swiftest. Beatrice explains that there is indeed a correspondence between the hierarchies and the spheres, but he has forgotten, she says, that since he reached the sphere of the Fixed Stars he has left the world of space behind. His only "where" now is in the divine mind.

> E questo cielo non ha altro dove
> Che la mente divina.

THE INSPIRATION OF THE *DIVINE COMEDY*

Light and love encompass the heaven of the Fixed Stars even as it encompasses the other spheres and only He Who "Himself girdles this girdle" can understand it. Thus the point of light, is God Himself. It is the non-spatial centre of the universe, just as Satan is located at the spatial centre. The innermost (in a non-spatial sense) of the fiery rings represents the Hierarchy of the Seraphim and corresponds with the outermost of the heavenly spheres; while the outermost ring (the Angels) corresponds to the innermost sphere of the Moon.

The conception, or rather the *experience*, of the Universe as composed of two interpenetrating contrasted worlds, one of them spatial and the other non-spatial, is one of the most striking characteristics of the *Paradiso*. The point is that *both* worlds are experienced objectively; both worlds are experienced in that perceptual way in which the modern soul can ordinarily only experience one of the two —— that of the senses. It is not simply that Dante expresses the *theory* that there are two such worlds (though, as we have seen, that is done — pictorially — in the 28th Canto) but rather that the whole style and quality of the poem, the choice of language and imagery, make us feel, as it proceeds, that we are actually living in two such worlds. To illustrate this in full, it would be necessary to pick out a line here and a phrase or word there throughout the poem and to write on them at some length. I will only give two or three examples.

When, today, we speak of "seeing" the truth, it is little more than a metaphor. Axioms and self-evident propositions are for us experiences of an inner subjective nature. But Dante makes us feel how, for the Spirits in his heaven, to say that they "see" the truth is a literal expression. Thus, in the 6th Canto the spirit of Justinian, describing how a contemporary had convinced him, while on earth, of the dual nature of Christ, adds: "I believed Him and now I see clearly what was contained in His faith ...

> *Si come tu vedi*
> *Ogni contradizion e falsa è vera*

"just as *you* see that contradictories cannot both be true!" Observe the argument. I *believed* then, but *now* I see ... I see as clearly as you on earth see ... we should expect "daylight" or some similar expression drawn from the perceptible world. Instead we get: "That every contradiction is both false and true." So in the Second Canto Dante, describing his entrance into the first heaven of the moon, uses the beautiful simile of a ray of light entering water: "The eternal pearl (*i.e.*, the sphere of the moon) received us, as water receives a ray of light and yet remains undivided." How was this possible, he asks, if I was in the body? And he adds: If we cannot conceive how two bodies can occupy the same space, that should fire us all the more with the longing to behold Christ, in Whom the divine and human natures are united. There what we hold by faith will be *seen*; not demonstrated but ... again we expect a metaphor drawn from the vision of the physical eyes. Instead we get: "But self-known like an axiom" (*a guisa del ver primo che l'uomo*

THE INSPIRATION OF THE *DIVINE COMEDY* 179

crede)! For the poet himself the thoughts which come to him are not only "seen," they are *tasted*. He receives them and takes them into himself almost as the body takes food and in one place those which are difficult to understand are called "acerbe" (bitter). Still more striking is the line with which in the 10th Canto Dante designates the whole of creation:

> Quanto per mente o per loco si gira (whatever revolves through mind or space).

Another quality which is characteristic of the *Divine Comedy* as a whole, but which finds its paramount expression in the *Paradiso*, is the perfect welding of lyrical emotion with intense, concentrated and (as we should say) *abstract* thought. Again the problem is to select examples which will tell, though taken out of their context. For an instance of the condensation of Dante's thought we may perhaps revert to the meeting, in the heaven of Mercury, with the spirit of Justinian, the imperial legislator.

> Caesare fui, e son Giustiniano.
> Che, per voler del primo amor ch' io sento,
> d'entro le leggi trassi il troppo e il vano.

Caesar I was, and am Justinian who, through the will of the primal love which now I feel, purged from the laws the excessive and the idle parts.

There is a long conversation between him and Dante. To begin with, Justinian briefly resumes the history of the

Roman eagle until the time when it came into his hands. His narrative reaches the reign of Tiberius, when the Roman power was allowed by *la viva giustizia che mi spira — gloria di far vendetta alla sua ira.*

> "By the living justice which inspires me — the glory of avenging His wrath."

From the intense concentration of thought embodied in such an allusion to the crucifixion as is contained in the line "Gloria di far vendetta alla sua ira," the poem passes without strain or bathos to a description of Dante's diffident desire to ask Beatrice to explain one of the difficulties that had arisen in his mind as a result of Justinian's speech and the boyish shyness which comes over him.

> Io dubitava e dicea: "Dille, dille"
> fra me, "dille" diceva, "alla mia donna."

> I hesitated and said to myself, "Speak up now, speak to her. Speak to my lady!"

She can't eat you! But his courage fails under that excess of reverence which overcomes him, even if he only hears detached syllables of her name such as "Be" or "ice" spoken.

> Quella riverenza, che s' indonna
> di tutto me, pur per "Be" e per "ice."

Until she herself comes to his help, reading his thoughts and, radiating upon him (*raggiandomi*) a smile that would make one blessed even in the flames, immediately proceeds to enunciate in a long speech full of intellectual vigour and apt imagery the majestic drama of the fall and redemption of man. I do not know if such transitions would be possible in any other language. In the *Paradiso* all is carried forward without effort or strain on the never-ending stream of light and colour with which the poet's choice of imagery fills the mind and the noble clangour of the sounds of which his language is composed. I wish there were also space to quote the beautiful simile of the two rainbows, one born from the other, which occurs at the opening of the 12th Canto. All the metaphors and tropes in the *Paradiso* seem to have to do with light, colour or music. The spirits are referred to as "torches," "lights," "flames," "stars," indifferently and their movements likened to dances. Thus, when in the sphere of the sun St. Thomas Aquinas and a group of learned doctors approach, Dante describes them as being "like ladies interrupted in the dance (*non da ballo sciolte*), listening silently until they can catch the notes of the music again." And when the spirits resume their wheeling dance and song, they are "like the clock that calls us to prayer, in which one part draws and impels the other chiming 'tin tin' so sweetly that the well-disposed spirit swells with love."

> tin tin sonando con si dolce nota
> che il ben disposto spirto d'amor turge.

The question may be asked of Dante, as of other poets, how much of the quality of his work is due to his own individuality and how much of it to the age in which he lived. Instead of posing the question in this rather barren form let us approach it in another way. Let us suppose that one were to gather together all the threads of experience of many different kinds that come from the study and enjoyment of the *Divine Comedy* and place them side by side in the mind without, for the time being, forming any opinion. Thus one may set side by side, firstly the actual picture of the Ptolemaic universe as it is portrayed in the *Divine Comedy*, the picture of the nine heavenly spheres by means of which the nine Hierarchies work out of the spaceless into a space which has the earth for its centre; secondly, the intense, abstract quality of the thought and above all the objective perceptual way in which precisely that kind of thought is experienced, and thirdly, the peculiar fusion of just this seemingly abstract kind of thinking with *feeling*, with that intense lyrical feeling which presents itself to the imagination as the essence of all feeling. And then one can picture Dante on his journey through Paradise taking into himself, absorbing into his mind almost as the body absorbs food, this whirling world of hierarchies or "intelligences" ("Quanto, per mente o per loco si gira"), which is at the same time the *substance*[3] of the phenomenal world.

And then, when this has been done, and the mind is resting, with full attention, but without undue theorising curiosity, in contemplation of these three

---

[3] In the true philosophical sense — that which "stands beneath," or sustains — that which *is the ground of*.

qualities, it may happen to a student of Steiner's writings that another experience will come, a distinctly "anthroposophical" experience. I had almost said *the* distinctively anthroposophical experience. The three qualities may unite themselves with all that the imagination and memory hold between them of what Steiner described from so many diverse points of view as the intellectual soul. And in so doing they will become, not three qualities, but one quality —— one single æsthetic experience. The concept drawn from spiritual science acts, in chemical parlance, as a "catalyst," fusing diverse substances into one, and it is in such experiences that I, for one, find the most convincing proof of spiritual science itself.

The age of the Intellectual Soul extended from the foundation of Rome to the 15th century. Dante lived and wrote at the end of the 13th century and at the beginning of the 14th. Steiner has, more than once, given an account of how in the latter part of the 4th Post-Atlantean era (that is, the age of the Intellectual Soul) a process was taking place which may be described as the incorporation of the cosmic intelligence into the human being. We can see from the *Philosophy of Spiritual Activity* — and also from the study of psychology — how this absorption, or individualising, this subjectivisation of thought is accomplished. It is accomplished through the union of thinking with feelings or sensations (for sensation is, after all, only a hardened kind of feeling). In this way are produced those "after-images" of which psychology speaks and which become, at a later stage, "ideas." The shadowy world of ideas in which the modern mind lives and moves and has its being is a world for the most part of passive experience, but it had its origin in the union of an *active* cosmic principle (that of concrete thinking) with the passive or sensational element in human experience. It need not then surprise us that in the *Divine Comedy*, and indeed in medieval literature as a whole, a type of thought which we must today classify as "abstract" should yet seem to have a living and even poetic quality. (It is along this line, too, that we shall best understand the medieval cult of allegory for which the present generation has lost all taste.) It is because the "abstract" thought which we meet in the literature of that time is *not yet* fully abstract; it is still in process of becoming so, still active in its own noumenal nature, not yet spellbound by sensation into the form of idea.

Gradually, then, the *Paradiso* reveals itself as the dramatised picture of an historical epoch in the evolution of human consciousness —— of that epoch which was itself a repetition or recapitulation in the *soul* of man of an event which had already taken place without his conscious participation at an earlier period, in Atlantis. Both the whole of the *Divine Comedy* and some of its smallest parts, as individual lines and even words, are alive with the urgency of this event. We feel it happening in the style; in the genius of the Italian language at that date. We feel the Ego of man in the act of uniting with the soul of man, the Ego which is alike that in him which thinks and one with the substance of the universe by which, as a physically embodied being, he perceives himself to be surrounded in space. No wonder that we are struck with the perceptual, *recipient* nature [*Ed.*, in the 1966 edition, this word is "quality"] of the poet's experience of the thoughts that come to him. No wonder that we are struck by that close welding of thought and emotion of which I have spoken. For the union of thought and feeling is the exoteric nature of the Intellectual Soul just as the union of the Ego with the soul is its inner nature or "mystery." The intellectual soul, writes Rudolf Steiner in chapter 2 of his *Outline of Occult Science* ... "partakes of the nature of the Ego and in a certain sense *is* the Ego, not yet conscious of its spiritual nature."

In the preciseness of the visual representation and in other qualities of the poem, but above all in its light-filled imagery (the whole of the *Paradiso* is as if bathed in gold) something else becomes apparent to us. The *Divine Comedy* was written by an Italian. It is the paramount expression in literature of the sentient soul, just as *Hamlet* is of the consciousness soul and *Faust* of the intellectual soul. But unlike the other two, it was written *in the age of the Intellectual Soul*. It is the characteristics deriving from this last fact which are for us the most distinctive and the most difficult to apprehend with sympathy, and it is these which I have especially tried to delineate. I can understand many readers of Dante shrinking from subtleties of this sort. I can only say that to ponder on the *Divine Comedy* as the sentient soul flowering in the age of the Intellectual Soul has never done any harm with me. I have only found it a richer mine than ever. And I must add that a distaste for subtlety of thought *as such* in any case is an absolute bar to anything like full appreciation of that poem.

It is a commonplace that the sequence of events in the *Divine Comedy* has, and was intended by Dante to have, more than one meaning. Thus, besides its literal interpretation as a description of the spiritual and material universes, it is throughout an allegorical representation of moral experience. For the modern reader the thought often remains profoundly true on this level, even in those parts whose literal interpretation is the most harsh or difficult.

The desperate situation of the souls in hell,[4] for example, as contrasted with those in Purgatory, is a very clear imagination of the difference between a soul which has not, and a soul which has, taken the step known to Christian experience as "repentance", when the soul accepts its own responsibility for its own sufferings and those of others. This experience may also be mediated by a conviction of the truth of reincarnation. In fact it may be deep in the heart, but it cannot today be taken seriously by a mind which will not take the fact of pre-natal existence equally seriously.

But besides these two meanings the poem has a third. It is an imaginative account of the experience known as initiation. There are many indications of this. For example, if we study the way in which the poet describes each 'rise' or 'salita' into a higher sphere, we

---

[4] It is, however, doubtful if Dante really confused eternity with infinite duration of time. At any rate it is clear from the *Paradiso* that the crudity often imputed to his theological notions by those who are not at the disadvantage of being acquainted with them exists mainly in the minds of the imputers.

find that in each case it takes the form of a *discovery that he is already there*. (The occasion of this discovery may be the increased beauty of Beatrice or the reflection of a new light in her eyes.) Again at the end of the whole poem, Dante says of the beatific vision of the Trinity with which it closes, not simply that he cannot describe it, but (as Steiner has said of the experience of clairvoyance) that he cannot even *remember* it. It is the feeling, the increase of joy that comes to him as he speaks, which makes him believe he saw it:

> Credo ch' io vidi, perchè piu di largo,
> dicendo questo, mi sento ch' io godo.

It is also clear from the course of the narrative as a whole. The descent into hell, followed by purification and enlightenment, are easily recognisable steps even to those with no more than a nodding acquaintance with the writings of the mystics. What is, however, perhaps peculiar to Steiner's descriptions and accounts of initiation is an intenser and more conscious form of that which every human soul is suffering or must at some time suffer. Thus, the *Divine Comedy,* and particularly the *Paradiso,* appears to represent, on the level of an initiation experience, that which the human soul in general was suffering at the time in which it was written. *Gib mir was du dir denkend selber bist.* It is the union of thought with feeling, but carried so far, so intense, so vividly and consciously experienced, as to amount to inspiration or enlightenment. Intense, youthful feeling — not extinguished but purified, but redeemed — becomes a grail into which the light of the world is poured. Intellectual Soul becomes transmuted into Life-Spirit:

> Luce intellettual piena d'amore,
> Amor di vero ben pien di letizia,
> Letizia che trascende ogni dolzore.

Light of thought full of love, love of the true good full of joy, joy which surpasses all sweetness.

How is this transmutation, this enlightenment accomplished? It is Beatrice who accompanies the poet on the whole of his journey through Paradise, from the first 'salita' into the Sphere of the Moon — that 'eternal pearl' which receives them into itself as water receives a ray of light — until the final 'salita' out of the Primum Mobile into the Empyrean

> fuore
> Del maggior corpo al ciel, ch' è pura luce

"Out of the greater body into the heaven which is pure light."

Nor does she merely become a pale allegorical figure, as is often objected, representing Theology in the abstract. Quite the contrary.[5] Thus, even in the 30th Canto of the *Paradiso*, near the end of the *Comedy*, when her beauty becomes so great as to make it impossible to describe it any longer in verse, Dante refers back quite naturally to

---

[5] See Charles Williams's delightful and spirited book, *The Figure of Beatrice* (London, 1943), which is (*inter alia*) one long refutation of this miserable error. It is also a splendid general invitation to the work of Dante.

the day when he first saw her face. Still more striking, and much harder to convey, is the quality of the *light* which shines through every canto of the *Paradiso*. It is in very truth the brilliant, warm, thrilling light in which the eyes of an unspoilt adolescence perceive the world to be bathed —— only purged of all those vaguely personal hopes and wishes and all that element of strangely projected egotism to which the term 'erotic' is properly applied. The spirit of Dante's youth, redeemed, no longer wanders in the shadows, but carries the poet with him into the light. And the result is a poem, in very truth, of light, made firm with the philosophy of Aristotle and filled with colour and music and with an inspiration as intense as it is sustained.

At the same time it is important not to try and read into the inspiration of the *Divine Comedy* things which are not there. Dante tells us that he was nine years of age when he first saw Beatrice and she eight. Between then and her death, at the age of twenty-five, he saw her once or twice, and it is probable that she knew very little of him and his feelings. From the point of view of Beatrice's own development, therefore, the whole connection with Dante appears to have been, at any rate for her life on earth, quite unimportant if not non-existent. The intellectual soul would appear to be very little concerned with personal relationship as such. This is matter for the consciousness soul (which does not find cultural expression until our own age); and accordingly it is our own age which is grappling in the modern novel and drama with the psychology of marriage, the woman's point of view, and so forth. For a woman to understand anything written about women before the fifteenth century it is first necessary to think herself masculine or make in some other way the required readjustment of imagination and sentiment. Spiritual science should help her to do this. It should help to remove out of the way of a sympathetic understanding of medieval 'romance' — and perhaps also of its nineteenth century after-echo — the typical feminist revulsion of feeling against the symbolical, lay-figure position occupied there by the woman. This revulsion of feeling is the critical reaction of the consciousness soul, rightly stressing the element of reciprocity and mutual equality, rightly insisting that love and affection can only be a relation between two equal units. But such an insistence, good in itself, is none the less bad if it is allowed to cramp appreciation of a monument of the human spirit such as the *Divine Comedy*. The event of our own age is the union of thought with *will* rather than with feeling, and accordingly the relationships of human beings, not only with the whole spiritual world but also *with each other as spiritual beings*, are increasing in spiritual significance. But that union cannot be achieved otherwise than *through* the grace of feeling and therefore that event cannot happen, unless the human soul continues to be sustained and deepened by the fruits of its evolution in former ages.

COLERIDGE'S "I AND THOU"
first published 1931

COLERIDGE AS PHILOSOPHER by Professor Muirhead is an extremely important book and I would, in a way, rather thank the author than write a review of it. For he is one of the few people in the world who are really well acquainted with the whole of Coleridge's published works, not simply with the *Poems*, the *Biographia Literaria*, and the *Lectures on Shakespeare*; and this acquaintance extends, fortunately, to the extracts recently printed by Miss Alice Snyder in her *Coleridge on Logic and Learning* from unpublished works such as the *Logic* and the *Semina Rerum*. Writing out of this abundance of material, Mr. Muirhead has, in effect, rebutted once and for all the two principal charges commonly brought against Coleridge's metaphysics, of incoherence and insincerity. The fact is, it has long been the custom for English men of letters to think traditionally rather than immediately, and honestly, on such matters; Coleridge was incoherent because he wrote on the margins of books, and thought upon many subjects (whereas it is now authoritatively known that one man can understand one subject only): he was insincere because he reported that his conclusions were compatible with those of theological orthodoxy. This is, or was, 'all ye know and all ye need to know!'

This essay is a review of John H. Muirhead's book *Coleridge as Philosopher* (George Allen/Macmillan, 1930).

An unprejudiced study of the lesser known prose-writings quickly reverses these facile judgments. As for his toadying to orthodoxy, Coleridge held that faith 'does not necessarily imply belief,' he described the doctrine of hereditary sin as a 'monstrous fiction', and his theology was sufficiently correct to win from Cardinal Newman the golden opinion that he had 'indulged a liberty of speculation which no Christian can tolerate, and advocated conclusions which were often heathen rather than Christian.' Again: Coleridge's system of thought is incoherent in its outer form alone. The more we study it, the more infallibly shall we recognize the same clear principles working their way to the surface from beneath whatever he wrote. For their precise formulation we have to go, as with all philosophers who beg none but the inevitable questions, to his exposition of the nature of thought. This he developed most fully in the *Logic*; but, once understood, the principles themselves can be discerned as clearly in the *Essay on Faith* as in the *Theory of Life*; they are there as unmistakably behind the lecture on *Romeo and Juliet* as behind the political lucubrations of the *Friend*.

What is wanted, therefore, is such an arrangement and exposition of Coleridge's voluminous and scattered philosophical writings as would serve to reveal these principles to those who have not yet penetrated to them for themselves. And this is what Professor Muirhead, with his systematic arrangement of chapters under the heads of Logic, Metaphysics, Philosophy of Nature, Philosophy of Religion, etc., and above all with his generous and skillfully linked chains of quotations, has attempted to do.

He has succeeded in a measure which far surpasses any work on Coleridge that has yet come to my knowledge. Professor Muirhead has, in fact, done some of the work which Coleridge's disciple, J. H. Green, ought to have done, but signally failed to do, in his *Spiritual Philosophy*, and I shall not pass on to my more critical consideration of his book without again expressing the thanks due to him from all those to whom, in Keats's phrase, 'the truth of imagination' is an experience and therefore the theory of imagination a matter of the first concern.

This confirmed, I pass on to the reviewer's more arrogant task of distinguishing the better from the worse. Coleridge's world of thought may, for the purpose, be divided into two hemispheres —— one of which turns on the relation of the self to other selves. The first he may be said to have very largely absorbed from the German philosophers other than Hegel, with whom he came in contact early in life; the second, which he himself regarded as the necessary complement of the first, was more definitely his own contribution to philosophy. It was his own, that is, as far as any thought other than palpable error can be termed a man's own. Scholars interested in 'influences' could, and no doubt will, some day, represent it as a mosaic of fragments culled from Greek philosophy, the Gnostic and Mystic writers, Giordano Bruno, the Church Fathers, Hegel, and so on, just as the *Ancient Mariner* (as Professor Lewes showed us in the *Road to Xanadu*) can be plausibly resolved into elements, all of which are in some sense 'borrowed'. This does not affect the point that both the

Ancient Mariner and this part of Coleridge's philosophy are his own in a sense which is not true in quite the same way of the first part.

German philosophy found the unity underlying that sensuous manifold which we call 'nature' to be necessarily and only grounded in the self of man. Coleridge found that self itself to be necessarily grounded in at least one other self. German philosophy proclaimed as the last word '*I am!*' Coleridge replied: '*I am, precisely because I can say "thou art"! — for it is just the power and will to say so which makes me an "I".*' I doubt if there is anything more sublime in the whole range of philosophical thought than the brief passage in the *Essay on Faith* in which Coleridge demonstrates the relation between consciousness and conscience:

> This is a deep meditation, though the position is capable of the strictest proof, namely, that there can be no I without a Thou, and that a Thou is only possible by an equation in which I is taken as equal to Thou, and yet not the same ... but the equation of Thou with I, by means of a free act, negativing the sameness in order to establish the equality, is the true definition of conscience. But as without a Thou there can be no You, so without a You no They, These or Those; and as all these conjointly form materials and subjects of consciousness and the conditions of experience, it is evident that conscience is the root of all consciousness — *a fortiori*, the pre-condition of all experience — and that the conscience cannot have been in its first revelation deduced from experience.

And this relation between the I and the Thou, between two conscious selves, so far from being, as is often assumed, specially evolved to square with theological dogma or with some private sense of sin, is itself only one aspect of that central intuition of 'polarity', which is (to employ something more than a metaphor) the immovable axis about which the whole cosmos of Coleridge's thought perpetually revolves.

With such first principles it is inevitable that Coleridge should dissociate himself from that semi-oriental tendency noticeable in German metaphysics to submerge the individual spirit completely in the Whole. Indeed, to judge from such little indications as the joke about Fichte which he retails with such gusto in the *Biographia Literaria*, one can well suppose that he was able even then to foresee its logical culmination in Schopenhauer's western variant of Nirvana. Nor was it less inevitable that he should find a fuller measure of truth in the Christian writers than elsewhere. For they alone had concerned themselves with the same problem. (I must mention at this point that I am, of course, fully aware of the impropriety and even absurdity of 'potting' philosophy in this way. But then either books of a philosophical nature must cease to be reviewed or else philosophy must continue to be potted. Under this *caveat*, then:) Philosophy seeks to resolve Many into One. To German philosophers the Many was the individual's world of experiences with its mystifying numerical distinctions; it was 'Nature'; whereas the One was the Ego; and their solution of the duality was simply to predicate one of the other, saying with the eastern Yogi: 'I am all that!' Coleridge's early manifested innate *imaginative* experience of the unreality of the 'subjective-objective' illusion had predisposed him to accept this solution without question, and accept it he did, as soon as he heard of it. Indeed, it would be truer to say that he *recognized* it. It was because it was in a sense something he knew already that he was able to swallow it with such surprising rapidity (winning himself a reputation for plagiarism in the process) and *yet* to assimilate it and make it thoroughly his own. He himself, therefore, was free to carry the problem of the One and the Many on to another plane. The question for him became rather, granted that the individual 'is' ultimately the Whole, to explain how more than one individual can 'be' the same Whole, yet without ceasing to be separate individuals. It was not *many phenomena = one self*, but *many selves = one Self*, which he had to explain; for his very definition of the term 'self' involved the coincident reality of other selves. Thus, with Coleridge, as with Plato, the problem of One and Many became, as his mind developed, the even more quintessential problem of Same and Other.

Now it is the second part of Coleridge's philosophy which I find most adequately elucidated in Professor Muirhead's book. The later chapters on the ethical, political and religious writings appear to me to be better than the earlier ones on Logic, Metaphysics and Nature. Nor (although I have called the second part more specifically Coleridge's own) is the defect a trivial one; for it must be remembered that Coleridge's philosophy is in very truth a rounded whole, a real *world* of thought, upon which the equator dividing its two hemispheres is merely an imaginary line drawn by myself for the convenience of cartography. Consequently, the flaw in Professor Muirhead's exposition, of which the cause appears to be as follows, spreads its baneful influence throughout the whole.

To Mr. Muirhead, Coleridge's thought is evidently valuable, less for its own intrinsic quality than as the historical anticipation, and in some degree source, of something he likes better. This something is 'modern idealism'. Thus, at the end of Chapter One, he actually defines his object in writing the book at all as having been: 'to state the broader features of nineteenth century idealism, of which more than any other he [Coleridge] was the founder.' The frequency with which he reiterates this position in the body of the book is as unnecessary as the position itself is undesirable. It is scarcely possible to read ten pages without coming on some such passage as the following:

'With regard to its general form [Coleridge's "Theological Platonism"], we may be prepared to share some of Coleridge's enthusiasm for it, if we are prepared to find in it an anticipation of the principle of which later idealists, notably Bradley,[a] have made so much, that "what is necessary and at the same time possible must be real!".'

Why? Why, in heaven's name, should our enthusiasm be allocated on such extraordinary principles? Must philosophy, too, turn antiquarian, finding nothing interesting but museum specimens of the history it already knows by heart? This choice of anticipation as a measure of value would be chilling, even were the thing anticipated more perfect than its prototype; where the later form is degenerate, it is simply disastrous. And it is the very excellence of Professor Muirhead's exposition in other respects which leaves one so completely at a loss to account for the mysterious blind spot that pre-determined him, apparently with his own full and free consent, to see just as much and no more of Coleridge's world as would fit into a framework subsequently constructed by Bradley and Bosanquet.[b]

This is in no sense intended for a gibe, nor is the present review the place for a critique of modern idealism; but, of the gulf which yawns between Coleridge's well-nigh Aristotelian wholeness and consistency of thought and the incoherent compromise and elaboration of what Mr. Muirhead himself appears to mean by 'modern idealism', no better illustration could be found than the book itself. Mr. Muirhead's idealism is one which so completely lacks the courage of its convictions as to be continually forgetting them. It is an idealism which proves to us that thought is not merely subjective —— and then, boggling at the consequence of its own doctrine, goes on to talk of it as if it were a process taking place inside the head. It puts empirical knowledge in its proper place —— and a moment afterward takes off its hat to 'science' with the abject politeness of Mr. Santayana[c] himself. It is, indeed, almost incredible that anyone, after expounding Coleridge's concept of the 'Idea' as fully and lucidly as the author of *Coleridge as Philosopher* does in his third chapter and elsewhere, should be able to write, on page 224: 'Modern Realism is not likely to accept Coleridge's characterization of mathematical objects as purely mental, and has adopted the term "subsistence" for the express purpose of indicating their essential objectivity ...' —— on the obvious assumption that 'purely mental' and 'objective' are contradictories. It is almost incredible that, after telling us with the help of quotations how Coleridge claimed to have 'unmasked the fallacy that underlies the whole Newtonian philosophy, namely, that the mind is merely a "lazy Looker-on on an external world",' nevertheless, when Professor Muirhead comes to discuss the *Theory of Life*, the fact that much of it 'would probably have been rejected by the science of his own time' (let alone by ours) is allowed to be a decisive factor in determining its untruth. As well refute an objection to the doctrine of verbal inspiration on the ground that the objector is not verbally inspired! This idealist, we are at last obliged to conclude, is unaware, even after writing it several times with his own nib, that if you *really* regard the mind as an active participant in and not 'a lazy Looker-on' on Nature, the ground is automatically knocked away beneath the whole of Newtonian science, whose theoretical constructions take their place as a myth alongside the other myths of which history has to tell. He is unaware, apparently, that, if thought is not merely subjective, it is not merely subjective.

Apropos of this, it is interesting to remark that the name of Goethe is mentioned only once throughout the book. We are, therefore, left to speculate whether the author is, or is not, aware of the existence of a Goethean science, whose method actually *assumes* from the start this participation of the mind in the production of phenomena, instead of, like the empirical method of Newtonian science, assuming its complete detachment. For Goethe's 'Urphänomen,' or the 'Ur-pflanze' of his work on the *Metamorphosis of Plants*, are simply practical working examples of Coleridge's 'Idea'. In the latter event it is to be hoped that he will remedy the defect and eradicate in the process that troublesome blind-spot. For we shall hear more in the near future both of Goethe and of Coleridge —— and the re-interpretation of the latter to a generation familiar, unlike his own, with the conception of an 'Unconscious', is a fruitful vineyard in which it would, indeed, be well to have Professor Muirhead for a labourer.

Editor's Notes

a. P. 197: Francis Herbert Bradley (1846–1924), British idealist philosopher.
b. P. 198: Bernard Bosanquet (1848–1923), British idealist philosopher.
c. P. 198: George Santayana (1863–1952), philosopher, essayist, poet, and novelist.

THE PHILOSOPHY OF SAMUEL TAYLOR COLERIDGE

first published 1932

THE SIGN UNDER which we have come together is a common interest in the overcoming of the decadence of our time through what the inaugurator of this Conference has called 'Goetheanism'. Naturally, the use of the word Goetheanism in the year 1932 not only carries our minds to this building, the Goetheanum — in order to do that the more familiar word anthroposophy or the name of Rudolf Steiner would have been sufficient — but it also takes them back to the figure of him after whom the building was named, to Goethe himself. It may well induce us to ponder over the whole relationship between anthroposophy on the one hand and on the other the legacy which Goethe bequeathed to the Western world in 1832.

It is a very, very important relationship. It is essentially a relationship of *likeness*. Only — as the subject of my lecture today, Samuel Taylor Coleridge, knew and pointed out — when two things are like one another, then, in order to become fully conscious of that likeness, it is necessary to be aware on the one hand of their *sameness*, their positive identity, and on the other hand of their *difference* from one another.

From a lecture given at the Goetheanum, Dornach, Switzerland, during the Goethe Centenary Festival, August, 1932, and slightly revised.

We may have a dim, vague perception that one thing is like another —— a confused perception, for instance, that the substance of Goethe's work is like the substance of anthroposophy. And this may well arouse our enthusiasm. But what must we do, if we want to be *fully conscious*, wide-awake and conscious, of that likeness for all that it really is? If we want to do that, we must polarise the likeness into the two contradictory tendencies of sameness and difference.

Rudolf Steiner said much, very much that was virtually *identical* with the things that Goethe had spent his life in repeating to the deaf ears of his contemporaries. As to this pole of sameness (the predominant pole) we can all rejoice with confidence in the thought that it will receive full expression here during the course of the next few weeks. Nor do I think anyone will feel a greater sense of relief and joy at this thought than those who have been obliged to observe with shame the appallingly inadequate tributes which the English periodical press has thought sufficient for the shrine of that great European genius during this centenary year.

It may not be a bad thing if what I am going to say should rather seem to emphasise the other pole, the pole of *difference*. I want to try and speak of Samuel Taylor Coleridge, and yet not of the Samuel Taylor Coleridge who is most widely known. Not of Samuel Taylor Coleridge the Romantic poet, the author of *The Ancient Mariner* and *Kubla Khan*. Not even of the lesser known, but still well-known Coleridge, the critic, the author of the *Biographia Literaria* and of the fragmentary *Lectures on*

Shakespeare. The Coleridge whom I want to present to you today is a Coleridge who is (in my country at any rate) almost entirely unread and to a very large extent unpublished. I am speaking of Coleridge the philosopher. The difficulty which he found in arranging his thoughts in an order suitable for expression and the fragmentary form which that expression too often took — some of the most important things are written on the margins of books (generally other people's books) — this difficulty has been often discussed. It has been discussed very much more often than the thoughts which he succeeded in expressing. Here, therefore, I will only say very briefly what I myself think is the arch explanation of Coleridge's failure in this respect. It is this. His whole system of *thought* resembled in character the organic *world* which Goethe revealed in his natural scientific writings. Goethe affirmed that from a single bone it ought to be possible to reconstruct the animal or type of animal to which the bone belonged. So, to Coleridge, the whole world of thought — even logic itself — was an *organic* structure. Now he himself conceived of an organism as a whole in which each part implies or contains every other part, in which each part as it were contains the whole. Thus, the moment his mind began to undertake the necessary analytical work, the splitting up into parts, which is requisite for the purpose of discursive expression, Coleridge began to feel that he was denying his own intuition. As soon as he had separated out a part of his system for the purpose of giving expression to it, he would feel with anxiety the necessity of trying to show there and then how that same part implied the whole. His extraordinarily unifying mind was too painfully aware that you cannot really say one thing correctly without saying everything. He was rightly afraid that there would not be time to say everything before going on to say the next thing, or that he would forget to do so afterwards. His incoherence of expression arose from the coherence of what he wanted to express. It was a sort of intellectual stammer.

It was this that laid him open to Carlyle's charge. Carlyle facetiously complained that Coleridge could never begin to discuss anything without first assembling round him an imposing array of "logical swim-bladders and transcendental life-preservers". Alas, by the time the transcendental life-preservers, that is the elaborate and far-reaching metaphysical arguments which were to bring the battery of the whole to bear on the little abstract fortress of the part, were complete, it sometimes happened that Coleridge had either forgotten what he began to speak of, or (more often) that his audience, being rushed too precipitately out of their depths, had lost all interest, if they had not actually left the hall.

Goethe's interest — as a knower — was directed in the first place to the world around him. It was in the ordinary sense of the word an *objective* interest. It was out of this interest in nature, and especially when it brought him into conflict with epistemological ideas widely current at the time — as happened, for example, through his intercourse with Schiller — it was out of this interest in observing Nature, and as a justification of his own *method* of observation, that he was led to develop (so far as he did so) the *theory* of knowledge which Steiner has so lovingly re-created and set in so clear a light for us. With Goethe, his method was cause, his theory of knowledge the effect.

Coleridge began from the opposite end. He was primarily interested in knowledge itself, in mind and the activity of mind. It was out of this interest, and as an application of it to a particular sphere, that his method of interpreting the phenomena of nature took shape. Theory of knowledge was cause; method was effect.

Goethe was a scientist before he was a philosopher. He tells us himself that he had "never thought about thinking". Coleridge was a philosopher (and also, in the true sense of the word, a psychologist) first; he interested himself in science only incidentally. He spent most of his life thinking about thinking.

The truth at the core of things is one and the same from whatever direction it is approached, and it is particularly interesting to observe that these two thinkers, starting from opposite poles, Goethe from the pole of Nature and Coleridge from the pole of Pure Reason or Spirit, meet. Both of them overcame (and hence the degree of misunderstanding which they have encountered) the arch fallacy of their age and our own, the fallacy that mind is exclusively *subjective*, or, to put it more crudely, that the mind is something which is shut up in a sort of box called the brain, the fallacy that the mind of man is a passive onlooker at the processes and phenomena of nature, in the creation of which it neither takes nor has taken any part, the fallacy that there are many separate minds, but no such thing as Mind.

It is this fallacy which underlies that other notion, so pathetically mistaken and yet so firmly entrenched in the world's brain today, that the inductive method, besides assisting man to control nature, may be a means of his gaining *insight* into her. That the power of controlling does not necessarily imply insight many holders of driving licences will gladly testify.

It is interesting to find both Coleridge and Goethe speaking of the same concrete entity, only by different names, characteristically different names. What Goethe *described* as the *Urphänomen* or prime phenomenon, Coleridge *defined* under the name of 'idea'. The idea, for Coleridge, is something in which all distinction between subject and object disappears. He speaks of a science "which in the Ideas that are present to the mind recognises the laws that govern in Nature if we may not say the laws that *are* Nature."

The first thing which is necessary in order to understand Coleridge is to gain some sort of grasp of what he meant by the word Reason. He insisted on a distinction in kind between Reason on the one hand and Understanding on the other. Not only in his philosophy but also in his critical writings Coleridge frequently attempted to express this distinction, to which he attached the very first importance. Yet it is at this point that the critics with one accord part company from him.

Modern criticism, as is well known, consists of anecdotes of the private lives of writers. Consequently the modern critic, when he attempts to study Coleridge and is asked to distinguish between, let us say, Imagination and Fancy or between Understanding and Reason, rightly feels that he is wasting his time. What can he do? He writes a short and snappy article on Coleridge, pointing out that the distinction between Reason and Understanding was a fiction of the fellow's opium-sodden brain, and then —— up goes the book on to the shelf for ever. Nowhere is there any understanding for the sublime truths which Coleridge, however imperfectly, has expressed.

Thus, for a lover and admirer of Coleridge it is a very great pleasure to feel that he is addressing an audience in whose hearts and minds just the very deepest and best elements in Coleridge may look to find some understanding. It is a special privilege to be permitted to address such an audience on this subject.

'Reason' for Coleridge is not something to be found manifesting in human beings; it is something *in* which human beings — and the whole of nature — are manifest. It is not merely a part or function of the individual mind. Rather it is that spiritual whole in which the individual mind — all individual minds — subsist. It is in fact as much an objective as a subjective reality. It is, to quote him, "superindividual".

The concreteness of Coleridge's conception of Reason is well brought out by the way in which he speaks of the so-called 'laws of thought'. These are, of course, the laws or rather self-evident axioms on which the possibility of logical thinking depends.[1] Coleridge describes a law of thought

---

[1] For instance—that the same thing cannot both be and not be in the same moment.

as "*a somewhat that in the mind actually exists, as any object recognised by the senses exists without us*". And he goes on to insist that these laws of thought, these objects existing in the mind, are not merely as real but actually *more* real than objects which appear to exist outside the mind. Why is this? It is because our experience of these laws is immediate. Reason is at the same time both the laws and the organ which apprehends them. Our confidence in the reality of the external objects of sense — if we examine it — is *derived* from our immediate experience of the laws of thought within us. He speaks of the mind as distinguished from all other things by being "*a subject which is also its own object*". He compares it to "*an eye which is its own mirror, beholding and self-beheld*".

You will remember how the same all-important fact of the immediacy of the mind's experience of itself is used by Rudolf Steiner in *The Philosophy of Freedom* to refute such theories as that of 'specific nervous activity' and in general theories which would limit all 'real' knowledge to knowledge of things in the sense world. This is not putting it strongly enough. It would be truer to say that the immediacy of the mind's experience of itself is the rock on which the whole of that book, and indeed the whole of Spiritual Science, is built.

This is what I meant by saying that Coleridge approached the problem of knowledge from the pole of Pure Reason or Spirit. He had *grasped in pure thought* the fact that Reason was the very substance of his mind, of his soul, of his self-consciousness. He knew that Reason was his mind and his mind was Reason. He experienced Reason as the very being of his own Ego —— and since *Being is one* everywhere and at all times; since Being is the being of all things, of nature no less than of man, Coleridge in his knowing did really approach nature from the point of view not of a creature but of a creator of nature.

On the one hand Reason is that *in* which I exist, the ocean of being by which my soul is upborn. This is true of my everyday self. But there is another point of view. Why is my soul self-conscious? Why can I say "I am"? I can only say this because through my soul or lower self there shines all the time the light of the higher Self. And of this higher Self it cannot only be said that it subsists *in* Reason or Spirit. It must also be said that it *is* Reason, that it is Spirit. So far the doctrine is one that is common to Coleridge, Kant and Rudolf Steiner. But there is something that distinguishes Coleridge's presentation of Reason from Kant's. It is true that Reason was for Coleridge, as for Kant, coextensive with nothing less than the whole of Being. But Coleridge, unlike Kant, was intensely aware of Reason — aware of it not merely as theory but in actual experience — as the *activity* of his own Ego. He felt a corresponding weight of responsibility; and his life shows that the burden proved a heavy one.

In the *Treatise on Logic* which, like so much else that Coleridge wrote or attempted, remained unfinished, he gave, I believe, the fullest expression to this philosophy of what I will call Active Reason or Active Mind. The work has never been printed, but the manuscript is fortunately in the British Museum and a great part of the material for this lecture has been drawn from it. Coleridge's logic is not a mere system of the rules of inference. On the contrary, it is characteristically enough an analysis and a representation of the *act* of thinking, yet a representation of such a kind that the reader is never allowed to lose sight of the fact that this act of thinking is the ground of Being itself, of the Being of all things. It is a logic in which one feels the presence of the Logos.

Now the essence of self-consciousness is unity, unity in multiplicity. I can say "I am" because through all the variety of my passions, sensations and experiences I am aware of a unity. Else, like the man possessed of devils, my name would be legion. My name is 'I' because I am one. I am aware of a unity. It is that unity which I call myself. Yet at the same time, said Coleridge, that unity which is myself is the unity which underlies the whole of nature. I am one, because God is one. I am one because this one God was incarnate in Man.

Thus, the higher Self, the ultimate unity of which we are made aware in experiencing the laws of thought, is not for Coleridge a transcendental Ego, in the sense that he feels he has nothing to do with it, is infinitely separated from it, takes no responsibility for it. His relation to it is not that of creature to Creator. True, it is for him as for Kant the source of the unity which underlies all external nature. But it is not a mere abstract principle like the transcendental Ego of Kant. It is an *active* unity. It is a *Productive Unity*. This is a truth which cannot, strictly speaking, be demonstrated. It can only be known by me to the extent that I experience Reason as my own activity.

I have made this attempt to enter with some precision into the metaphysical foundation of Coleridge's doctrine of Reason, because it was only when, from studying the *Logic*, I came to grasp the full implication of this conception of Reason as *Productive Unity*, that I realised the beautiful wholeness of Coleridge's system of thought.

Now the second conception of which an understanding is essential if we are to come to terms with Coleridge's philosophy, is one which constantly reappears throughout the whole of his prose-writings on all subjects. Yet very little attention has been paid to it. It is a conception which anthroposophists are specially trained to understand. It is that element in Coleridge's works which made me feel more than anything else that he was in a very special sense a forerunner of Spiritual Science. It is the conception of *the universal law of Polarity*. Elsewhere Coleridge speaks of *"the universal law of polarity or essential dualism, first promulgated by Heraclitus, 2,000 years afterwards republished and made the foundation, both of logic, physics and metaphysics, by Giordano Bruno."*

I need not spend time trying to explain the sort of thing that Coleridge meant by polarity, for you know it already. I should like, however, to try and illustrate some of the ways in which he revealed the working of this universal law.

I said that in his logic one feels the presence of the Logos. Some of the most startling, I will say the sublimest, passages in his *Treatise on Logic* are concerned with grammar and, generally, with language. I can only give a few extracts. Thus, he points out how the world of grammar subsists between the two poles of verb and noun, the one expressing activity and the other passivity, the one an action and the other a state. All the parts of speech may be so to speak polarised into these two components with one of them predominating. We may think of grammar as a sort of world revolving about an axis. Only in the axis itself do the two poles coincide. And what is this axis? It is the verb '*to be*' itself. This verb 'to be' is the only word which expresses both action and state. Only 'I am' is both verb and noun at the same time.

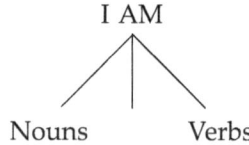

I spoke just now of the wholeness of Coleridge's system of thought. The justness of this expression will become clearer as we go on to see how the second of the two essential elements in that system arises inevitably out of the first; how the law of polarity is already implicit in the conception of Reason as *Productive Unity.*

In Coleridge's words "*the essential duality of Nature arises out of its productive unity*". Unity which is productive must strive to do two things. It must strive to reproduce itself, that is it must strive to detach from itself another being like itself and in the same act and moment it must strive to *overcome* that detachment, to overcome that individuation, thus maintaining the unity.

This is the first polarity, the polarity which underlies all life. And it is because it is based so firmly on this foundation that Coleridge's system of thought may itself be called living, organic. He himself contrasts it with the so-called 'philosophy' which was fashionable in his time and which with some unimportant trimmings is still fashionable in our own —— the Atomic Philosophy. Coleridge calls the latter a 'mechanic system' and insists that its knowledge is limited to distance and nearness, in short, to "*the relations of unproductive particles to each other*". This, he says, is the *philosophy of Death*. It holds good only of *dead* nature. Whereas all *life consists in the strife of opposites*. Water is neither oxygen nor hydrogen nor yet a mixture of both. It is no less a single body than either of its elements.

To have revealed the law of polarity as the process which underlies all life and then to be able to educe this law of polarity from productive unity, i.e. from the act of self-consciousness: to have done this even with some difficulty and obscurity is, I think, enough to justify one in saying that in Coleridge's logic one feels the presence of the Logos. The Logos is the Word, but it is also that through which all things that are have come into being. The connection between these two aspects of the Logos is not an easy one to see. We may perhaps get glimpses of it in art and poetry. The aim of this building and of the work that is carried on in it is surely to make that very connection clearer to the world. I only want to indicate in a very sketchy way how Coleridge strove to grasp in *thought* both these aspects of the Logos as well as the connection between them.

For instance, in treating of language, he points out how on the one hand the *letters* or sounds provide the elements of *sameness* (for the same letters must be used over and over again) while the *positions* of these letters (which are almost infinitely variable) provide the counter-element, or counter-pole, of *difference*. Sameness and Difference are the positive and negative aspects —— of what? Of *Likeness*.

Let us try and construct diagrammatically. It is quite appropriate to pass at this point from speech to diagram, for diagram is of the nature of geometry. And it is at this point that the creative process of Coleridge's system of thought passes into the world of space. In geometry we may catch a glimpse of the transition from pure thought to space, which is the product of thought. To hypostatise it, as we normally do, by "abstracting from the contents of an exhausted container" is, he insists, puerile. There would be no line, says Coleridge, if the mind were not capable of creating it by what he calls an 'act of length'. Mathematical points, lines and surfaces are in fact "acts of the imagination that are one with the product of those acts".

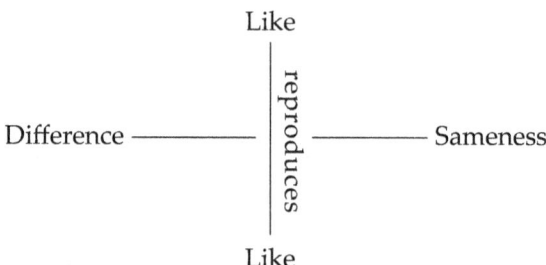

Like reproduces like in the act of productive unity. The resulting duality remains nevertheless a unity and as such may be polarised along its whole length into the two extremes of Sameness and Difference. Sameness, the eternal unity of God, is experienced by finite beings as duration in Time. Difference, His omnipresence and variety, is experienced as Space. Elsewhere Coleridge speaks more speculatively of a 'figurative space' which would have "real Being and energy and the active power of figure". The active power of figure! We see him thinking his way into the etheric. In his own words he reaches "the transition of the Dialectic into the Organic". This, he says in the *Treatise on Logic*, is the point at which Logic would cease and a 'Poetic or Formal Science' would begin.

This poetic or formal science is that science to which I have already referred. It is the realisation of what Coleridge called 'Ideas' and Goethe *Urphänomene.*

Somewhere among the unpublished works this all-important transition from the Dialectic to the Organic may yet be found, more fully worked out by Coleridge. At present the nearest thing we have to it is the *Theory of Life.* This essay is among the published works and is printed in Bohn's Library.[2] It is in many ways a most unsatisfactory production. It was originally intended as a contribution to some particular medical controversy of the day, and partly for this reason, partly owing to Coleridge's general lack of the power of arranging and controlling his material, it is extremely uneven.

There are many pages of quite insignificant matter and then, suddenly, perhaps half a page so packed with

---

[2] Also in the paperback *Selected Poetry and Prose of Coleridge*, edited by Donald A. Stauffer (*The Modern Library*, New York, 1951).

meaning that it would take four or five lectures to deal with it fully. One can however, see from it how for Coleridge *knowledge* of nature was a sort of *re-creating* of nature.

If we begin, as before, from the fundamental polarity — the I AM willing to reproduce itself or its like in self-consciousness — we may represent this as a line:

I AM
|
|

This is the polarity of Productive Unity. Coleridge also called it *'separative projection', 'the tendency at once to individuate and to connect, to detach but so as either to retain or to reproduce attachment'*. From this primary polarity Coleridge's thought generates, first Time and Space and after them the whole phenomenal world.

In order to understand it, it is necessary to remember what was said above. Each polarity, while being a duality from its own point of view, remains nevertheless a unity. Thus, while, *qua* duality, it has already been polarised, yet *qua* unity, it may again be polarised into two further contraries, and so *ad infinitum*. It is in this way that nature rises from stage to stage of complexity. This principle contains in it the concept of what is experienced empirically in the organic world as 'recapitulation'. For it has long been known from direct observation of nature that the individuals of every species, as they come to birth, recapitulate the history of the species itself. Ontogenesis repeats the stages of phylogenesis.

Diagrammatically this may be expressed, and was expressed by Coleridge, in the form of a cross. Thus, if the first polarity is represented by a line, then the two extremities of the line represent its duality. But inasmuch as it remams also the original unity, it is represented by each *point* on the line. These points can therefore again be polarised, or in other words, the original line can be polarised along the whole of its length. It thus becomes the *axis* of a new polarity. A new natural quality is produced and the production of the new quality is symbolised on the diagram by taking it into a second dimension. Throughout the whole of creation, not only as its foundation but also perceptible at each stage, the principle of *productive unity* is paramount.

It was along these lines that Coleridge sought to grasp the "transition from the Dialectic to the Organic". The 'separative projection', which gave birth to time and space, continues to work in the world of time and space which it has created. At this stage it is easily recognisable as the physical properties of Attraction and Repulsion. The tendency "to detach but so as either to retain or to reproduce attachment" is clearly, in the physical world, the polarity of Attraction and Repulsion. We have reached the concept of force, or gravitation. Polarise again and we begin to conceive the essential nature of Matter. This gives us the four co-ordinates on which the main structure of the *Theory of Life* is supported. Coleridge gives it thus:

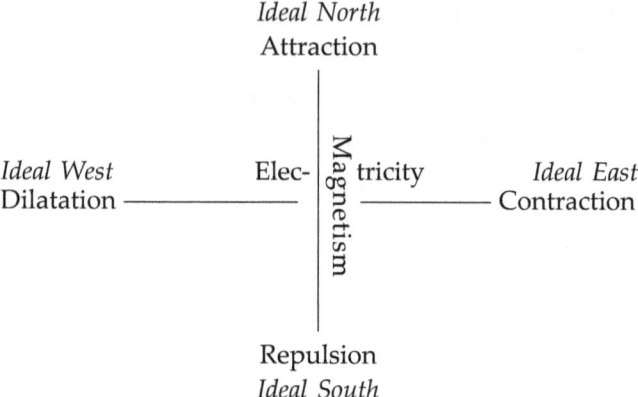

The transition from dialectic to organic must of course pass through the stage of inorganic nature. Coleridge passes from the inorganic to the organic world *via* his conception of electricity and magnetism. I only wish to give some idea of the way in which he developed everything from the original concept.

At the next stage, the organic stage, the two coordinates reappear as the principles of Reproduction (vegetables) and Irritability (insects).

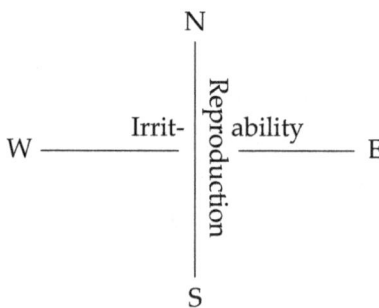

In the course of the few paragraphs which he devotes to this subject, Coleridge, emphasising the close relationship which exists between insects and flowers, throws off as a kind of poetic speculation an idea which Rudolf Steiner has since affirmed to be an historical fact. He speaks of the butterfly as a flower liberated from its stalk —— *flores liberti et libertini*.

His treatment of insects is particularly interesting. He speaks of them as nature's first attempt at consciousness. They are a sort of *externalised* version of something which is essentially *inward*, that is, of sentience. That which should be a purely inward process is here seen objectified in a materialistic spatial form. The morphology of the plant is an expression of the principle of reproduction. The irritable feeler of the insect is reproduction raised to another power. It reproduces *movement*. It imitates in its own motions the external stimulus which excited it. Yet these marvellously irritable organs are themselves only a sort of physical caricature of those far subtler motions that are proper to nature's next production —— the animal and human *soul*. Coleridge points out the startling metamorphosis of outward form which characterises nature's transition to the next stage of animal existence. The exuberant complexity of structure typical of the insect disappears altogether from the surface, having been withdrawn to the interior parts of the body. The outlines of the fish are the simplest and severest which can well be conceived. Nature sinks back exhausted from the line which she has hitherto been following and in her repose gathers strength for her newest creation —— consciousness. The insect's organ mechanically reproduces the external stimulus. The soul reproduces and retains in the form of images the impressions which come to it through the senses. This is the foundation on which later there is to be built the self-conscious life of the spirit.

Thus, at the final stage of the process of evolution, and bringing it full circle, we awake to see the whole as an expression of the original polarity. We see realised as fact that polarity which, as dialectic, was found to constitute the nature of grammar and logic —— the I AM in the act of reproducing itself. That which I AM has so long and laboriously created, itself affirms 'I am'. The Son of God awakes on earth and, awakened, names himself the Son of Man.

I will not carry this any further nor attempt to say anything of the resemblances on the one hand and the differences on the other from the *Naturphilosophie* of Schelling. I merely wanted to give a rough indication of the way in which the nature of Coleridge's thought enabled him to approach nature from *within*. The *Theory of Life* itself is no more than a sketch. What I am giving is the sketch of a sketch. Coleridge was not, in general, a close *observer* of nature, as Wordsworth and his sister were, or as Goethe was. But he was a very close observer of his own thought-processes. And this initiated him into the heart of nature. So that he was able to know nature by mentally re-creating her.

Goethe had his feet firmly planted on the earth. As a scientist, as a knower, he largely confined himself to the realm of natural science and his regular industry combined with his great genius had by the end of his life illuminated this realm with a steadily increasing flood of light. Coleridge never succeeded in finding his feet on earth at all. Look at the portrait of him in the National Portrait Gallery in London, and you will feel the full force of Wordsworth's description:

> The rapt one of the godlike *forehead*,
> The heaven-*eyed* creature

Compare the majesty of the forehead and the eyes with the pathetically weak mouth. He himself said that he had "power without strength". He was continually forming vast schemes of works to be written on every conceivable subject, or on all at once, which he never had the energy to carry out.

What does it mean to have power without strength? A flash of lightning is in many ways a very weak thing. As soon as it has come down from heaven and discharged into the earth it is diffused through the whole earth and vanishes from sight. You cannot direct it into channels. A flash of lightning will not run an electric tram. But still it is a flash of lightning.

Power is of heaven. Strength is the faculty of applying it on earth.

Goethe had strength as well as power. But Coleridge had, I think, the *kind* of power which Goethe lacked. He had the power of self-knowledge in thought and he had the strong sense of moral responsibility which self-knowledge brings.

Had I time, I should have liked to show from Coleridge's other writings how his morality, too, was derived from these two fundamental conceptions of Reason as productive unity and of polarity. Through them he arrived at a conception of the threefold consciousness of man and even of his threefold body.

In conclusion, let us remember that as followers of Rudolf Steiner we must necessarily seek to acquire this power of self-knowledge in thought and to take on this responsibility.

If we approach Coleridge's philosophy from this point of view, we shall not be oppressed with his weakness and failures as a man. Rather we shall feel a strong impulse to take into ourselves, as far as we may, and there to continue, the struggle that was his life —— the struggle to draw from the inexhaustible well of conscientious thinking the necessary feeling and the necessary strength of will.

GOETHE AND THE
TWENTIETH CENTURY
first published 1949

FEW ENGLISH PEOPLE know much of Goethe, and of that few most rather dislike him. I make this observation with some confidence because it is based on a sort of private Gallup poll which I have been desultorily conducting over the last twenty years. The dislike is not violent, but its roots are deep and it will yield neither to sincere admiration of his greatness nor to a fond love of his best lyrics. Admiration, even reverence, for a genius is one thing: the taste for a man is another. A taste for Goethe you will certainly find here and there in England, but you will find it in small circles wedded to the study of German language and literature rather than among the general reading public.

From the point of view of literary criticism this would not matter so much. What makes it important is the fact that Goethe is rarely presented to us as a writer pure and simple. We are to look on him, we are told, first and foremost as a teacher; and the lesson he teaches is the way to live. It is not a First Folio we are invited to admire, but a man. It was so that he himself wished to be regarded, and he has had his way; for it is so that he is in fact regarded by all to whom he is most dear. *Voilà un homme!* said Napoleon after meeting him. So say all true

Printed in *The Golden Blade*, 1949.

'Goetheanists'. So also said Rudolf Steiner. For it was by no means *only* the scientific work, and the all-important way of knowledge and attitude to Nature associated with it, to which Steiner attached importance. Indeed there can have been few men more deeply steeped in loving knowledge of Goethe's whole work and personality; and it is a man — not indeed a perfect, but a reverend, but emphatically an *imitable* man — who purports to be disclosed, when the author of the *Philosophy of Freedom* points (how often in his lectures!) to the author of the *Römische Elegien*.

The reasons for the distaste I have mentioned are fairly clear to me, and I shall begin by trying to state them as clearly and forcibly as I can. What then are the obstacles in the way of some twentieth-century neophyte who seeks in all humility to enter the temple of Goethe and worship at the shrine? First, we are living in very bad times. In general there are none more propitious for attaching us to the great teachers of humanity:

Who prop, thou ask'st, in these bad days my mind?...

But it must be confessed that, if it is for comfort in tribulation that we turn to the Weimar of a hundred and fifty years ago, we meet with a rather chilling reception. I do not know what sort of reading *Wilhelm Meister* may make in 1949 in a cellar in Berlin; but both the precept and the example of Goethe for the proper conduct of human life do seem to presuppose, almost as a *sine qua non*, at least three good meals a day, an adequate domestic staff to make them appear and disappear, and a comfortable sum coming in, preferably quarterly, of its own accord.

Given these together with unbroken physical health, the doctrine is plain to read and not unacceptable. If a man feels very badly indeed that he wants to go to Italy, let him go! We are to warm both hands before the fire of life, to reject no experience it offers and to profit by all. We are to have *life* — not some pale and prelatical *Ersatz* of the spirit, raised from the seed of renunciation or suffering, but good, rich, fruity human life in the ordinary sense — and we are to have it more abundantly. And then — we are to be at peace with ourselves — *beruhigt*. If that is impossible for a time, we are, it is true, to acquire strength from dispeace —— *doch stärker in der Unruhe sein*. But the last is only *obiter*. The essence of the doctrine, and all the emphasis of it, is the obligation to live a full, happy, peaceful, active life, transmuting experience — and, above all, joyful experience — gradually into wisdom. Ripeness is all.

I need not labour the obvious. The cry of one of Goethe's English admirers, Matthew Arnold, from the middle (as it seems to us) of the blue lagoon of Victorian security:

> *Strong was he, with a spirit free*
> *From mists, and sane, and clear;*
> *Clearer, how much! than ours — yet we*
> *Have a worse course to steer....*
> *But we, brought forth and rear'd in hours*
> *Of change, alarm, surprise —*
> *What shelter to grow ripe is ours?*
> *What leisure to grow wise?*

—— has, to say the least of it, lost nothing of its force today.

Disappointed, we will suppose, with the teacher, our imagined neophyte turns now to the poet. I mean the poet *as* a poet, the lyric poet pure and simple. And here he is on surer ground. "The creator of German literature" —— we are no judges of that. What we do know is, that this man sings, sings, sings. Mignon's Song, the Chorus in Heaven, and the opening scene of the second part of *Faust*, a score of *Lieder*, whose settings may well have been almost from childhood a part of the very stuff of his soul —— till he learnt German and hardly knew which was the more precious, the melodies of Schubert or the words of Goethe! But let him now, in an attempt to measure the man's true stature as a poet, advance beyond an anthology acquaintance and seek to come to grips with the whole corpus of Goethe lyric. He is likely to be bothered by the overwhelming preponderance of the erotic motive. The proportion of love-songs — adolescent in mood, though not in their intellectual and imaginal overtones — is, for a *great* poet, so enormous. "There is," said Coleridge once, "a *nimiety*, a too-much-ness about the Germans." One may — and none of these exceptionally favourable conditions is particularly common today — one may be not easily tired by regular rhymed verse, lucidly expressed; one may take a special delight in the feminine endings in which German poetry abounds; one's darling Muse may even be Erato; and *still* ... it was Max Beerbohm, parodying George Moore, who observed: "There are times, are there not, dear reader, when one is *not* thinking about girls?"

From the love-lyrics he passes — perforce, for it is a life that he has been directed to admire — to the love-affairs.

Excellent stuff here for the meticulous or the gossipy biographer, and fine, cosy reading for those who find poetry itself a little boring — if only it were Kit Marlowe or Robbie Burns they were talking of! If only it were not for the painful embarrassment of that *ecce homo*! And then, somehow or other he — or she — will have to come to terms with the whole tone of Goethe's attitude to women:

> "Pah!" said Goethe, laughing, "as if love had anything to do with the understanding! The things we love in a young woman *(Frauenzimmer)* are something quite different from understanding. We love in her beauty, youthfulness, playfulness, trustfulness, her character, her faults, her caprices, and God knows what all that is indescribable; but we do not love her understanding."[1]

I do not stop to enquire how an educated young woman of today will relish these observations of the Master. I only observe that at the point where understanding is ruled out they seem to prefer the frank appetite of Donne to the blend of cool patronage and passionate adoration, with a mild flavouring of zenana, which they will find if they apply themselves to the study of Goethe's life and writings. So, at all events, they say; and I believe they believe what they say.

Lastly, running through the whole succession of Goethe's entanglements, and indeed through his whole life, is that 'x' which it is so difficult to name without

---

[1] *Conversations with Eckermann*, 1824, January 2nd.

begging the question —— non-attachment, egotism, the will to self-development, the Renaissance or Faustian appetite for all experience, 'self-culture'. And this brings us to the gravamen of the charge against him. It is not new. It was urged, in this country, both by Carlyle's friend John Sterling and by Tennyson. It is, that at the deep heart's core there lay nothing but that refined yet ruthless egotism, that cool objectification of personal relationships as 'experiences', for which lesser men are called bounders. George Santayana, describing Faust (and therefore Goethe)[2] in his *Three Philosophical Poets*, put it clearly enough:

> He had regretted in the same way the unhappiness of Gretchen. ... He would continue, if life could last, doing things that, in some respects, he would be obliged to regret; but he would banish that regret easily, in the pursuit of some new interest, and, on the whole, he would not regret having been obliged to regret them. Otherwise, he would not have shared the whole experience of mankind, but missed the important experience of self-accusation and self-recovery.

This is a crucial passage. There are those, not overburdened with moral sense or humour, who agree that it is what Goethe practised and preached and fully approve it. I am not addressing them. We others respond rather differently. We are, for instance, willing to believe

---

[2] I am no friend to the loose practice of identifying fictitious characters with the authors who created them; but in Goethe's case it is inevitable. He himself always insisted on it, and even went so far as to tell Eckermann that poets only invent when inspiration fails. Also Santayana makes his own intention quite clear in the passage now quoted.

that, if we had the time and inclination to research into the break with Lili (for these are matters on which we prefer to form our own opinions), we should easily agree that Goethe was not to blame, or at least that his behaviour was neither mean nor unworthy. What is much harder to stomach is the sound of his voice, at Weimar later, explaining to Eckermann how important it had been for him to have the experience of being betrothed. We can swallow all the entanglements at a gulp without so much as winking. But the old man's voice, his biography festooned about with Charlottes, Kätchens, Minnas, Frederikas, Mariannes and goodness knows whom all, solemnly telling Eckermann how he had been working all his life at his own 'ennoblement' (*an meiner Veredelung*) —— this is a somewhat tougher morsel. It is not so much moral comments that spring to our lips as explosions —— of the pithy sort which Sir Toby Belch hurled from behind his hedge at the unchecked complacencies of Malvolio.

No authentic Anglo-Saxon with the right twinkle in his eye should have much difficulty in disposing of 'self-culture' —— if this is all it is. It was no Bloomsbury witling, it was not even an Englishman, it was the sedulous disciple who introduced Goethe to the world of English letters, called him hero and made his reputation here, it was, in fact, Thomas Carlyle who wrote of him in a letter: "Goethe is the greatest genius that has lived for a century, and the greatest ass that has lived for three."

We ought, however, to reflect that, whatever else 'self-culture' may have been, it was Goethe's way of dealing with a problem which faces humanity as a whole. I mean the awkward phenomenon of increasing self-consciousness. It is our problem too, this curious *malaise* of humanity; and it has grown rather worse than better since Goethe's day. It was perhaps about the eighteenth century that men first began to take more serious notice of that queer intruder on the life of the soul, the detached Onlooker present in each one of us, and half instinctively to make provision for him in their ideas and their conventions. It was then that the word *psychology* was used for the first time in its modern sense. Alongside, and a little apart from, the impulses, passions and thoughts which are the true stuff of the soul, there has come into being this nothingness, this mere awareness, which looks on and says of each: "Yes, *I* wish it, *I* feel it —— and yet this wisher and this feeler are not quite me. *I* am here, looking on all the time."

It was not always so. Formerly, if there were conflicting impulses, yet the one which prevailed was felt as the whole self in action. The whole Augustine sinned, and afterwards the whole Augustine repented. The whole Dante loved, lapsed, and loved again after a different fashion. But for us, in varying degrees, there is the sinner and the one who observes the sinner, the lover and the one who observes the lover. It is not a question of whether it is a good thing or not; it is simply a fact. The only question is, what is the right way for men to deal with it, now that it has come to stay.

Naturally it is nowhere more marked than in the sphere of the relation between men and women, for it is there that the experiencing soul behaves in the most surprising and fluctuant way. The device which the eighteenth century evolved for according recognition to the experiencing and to the observing soul in the same moment was the whole apparatus of archness and gallantry. Mark their significant use of the word 'conscious'. In contemplating Goethe's attitude to women we should always remember this. It is not simply that he accepted the conventions of his age (though we should not, either, forget that he does in fact belong to a quite remote one, having passed half his life before the French Revolution); he would instinctively feel the reason for, and the fitness of them.

Outmoded as all that apparatus is today, before we dismiss it utterly we might just ask ourselves whether our own way of meeting the problem is so very much more satisfactory; *we* detach ourselves from the little gambols of our souls by calling them 'fixations' and 'transfers'; they spoke of 'pleasing pain' and eyes that 'deal delicious death'. Which is better? You pays your money and you takes your choice! But there is no doubt what Goethe's choice would have been. He looked on the soul, as he looked on Nature, as an inexhaustibly rich gift to be accepted with joy and treated with reverence and delicacy. And as with Nature, so with the soul, the problem was to grow more and more fully conscious of it without destroying it in the process. Both our scientists and our men of letters are for the most part indifferent to the destruction, provided they can get on with the consciousness. Witness the popularity of James Joyce.

We must also take into account the *Germanity*, if I may so call it, of Goethe's own soul —— that subtle distinction of colouring and emphasis which is best felt as untranslatableness. Goethe's mother-tongue was one which can *still*, even today, employ the ineffable neuter gender, known also to the Greeks, in speaking of young females (feel the difference between "I saw her on a Sunday" and "Ich sah es an einem Sonntag") and which at the same time trails about it the faint aroma of a mystical reverence for woman that is as old as Tacitus.

He found these things, he did not make them; just as he found the social conventions of an age in which educated young women were appalled at the idea of going out unaccompanied and a society (at all events when he reached Weimar) in which adulterous *liaisons* were perhaps about as common as they are today. They were part of the air he breathed as he grew up. The only thing for which he can be accountable to praise or blame is the use he made of them. And in his hands they became that wholly untranslatable *ewig-weibliche*. Our 'eternal feminine' has acquired a facetious overtone which puts it out of court; and yet Bayard Taylor's rendering of the closing words of *Faust*:

> *The Woman-Soul leadeth us*
> *Upward and on*

is even more misleading, for it suggests the 'ennobling' influence of one of Thackeray's heroines, and I do not think that was at all what Goethe had in mind. Woman as a symbol, on the one hand of Nature and on the other of the human soul, would be much nearer the mark. Thus Santayana, in relating the words specifically to Nature, says that the *ewig-weibliche* was, for Goethe, "the ideal of something infinitely attractive and essentially inexhaustible".

I find this a little superficial, for I think there was also the underlying sense of something more than an allegorical relation, indeed of a real connection, in the foundations of the world, between Eva and the goddess Natura. Moreover, Woman (which in this kind of context always means young and attractive woman, though in the statistical nature of things there will always be one or two about who are not managing to combine both attributes) has long been apprehended by the poets and myth-makers of Christian civilisation as a symbol of the soul, and of qualities of soul. I think that the *ewig-weibliche* stood, in Goethe's imagination and feeling, first for some real woman, secondly for Nature, and thirdly for the human soul.

About Goethe's relations with women, as recorded and as a whole, there was, underlying the poetic lightness of touch, a note of earnestness and reverence that is unmistakable. It is doubtful whether any of the young ladies suffered any lasting harm, and most of them seem to have finished up by getting happily married. The passing pain was something which Goethe at least shared with them. I fancy, if I had been a *Frauenzimmer* living at about that time, I would not have run very fast to avoid a love-affair with Goethe, even if I could have known in advance how it would end. "Never," wrote

Karl Julius Schröer,[3] who was at one time Steiner's teacher, "was the relationship a frivolous one." And he pointed out that in nearly every case, after the passion had waned, it gave place to a lifelong friendship or mutual regard. Symbols they might be to his imagination, but there was always also a true personal 'meeting' and much sincere idealism. Thackeray himself could barely have improved in this last respect on some passages from the letters to Charlotte von Stein.

And then, if, as I said, the quantity of lyrics all of the same kind is at first a little overwhelming, it is the quality after all that really counts, and the only *reasonable* reflection on the matter is, that you cannot have too much of a good thing. After all, we are not obliged to read them all, however good they are. Meanwhile, one of the reasons why it would be worth while growing old and acquiring some leisure is that one would possibly have time to read the whole of the *West-Östliche Divan*, instead of merely dipping into it here and there.

We should rather look on Goethe's poetry (and I speak now of the whole of it) as one of the arsenals of the fortress of the human soul, now under attack from many different sides, and be thankful for any bit of ammunition or armoury we may find there. For the soul is the Cinderella of twentieth-century civilisation. She lives on sentiment: of which we are mortally afraid, preferring to rush out of it either to the physical extreme of violence or

---

[3] *Goethe and Marianne Willemer*, 1878. Reprinted in *Goethe und die Liebe* (Der Kommende Tag A.-G. Verlag, Stuttgart, 1922).

of appetite on the one side, or on the other to a rarefied and contentless spirituality; or perhaps to try both in turn, like Aldous Huxley. But the old man at Weimar grew wiser and wiser about all this. He knew well enough that the 'nostalgia' of which our young politico-intellectuals spend most of their time accusing each other — and which *he* would have called *Sehnsucht* — so far from being a weakness, is the most precious sacramental wine of the soul, to be used by the spirit sparingly and with reverence for the purpose of making a man.

It is Goethe's distinction, and his message to us, that he retained throughout his life *both* this reverence for the soul, which allowed him to surrender to its *varium et mutabile* without feeling an ass, *and* a deep and abiding sense of man's responsibility of self-consciousness. Only, instead of allowing the consciousness to destroy the soul, he strove to maintain it as a golden thread of self-awareness and self-control passing through all its vicissitudes and growing stronger with the lapse of time and the accumulation of experience. He was in this respect a pioneer, and it is rather our weakness than his if we allow to a few fatuities any substantial weight in the scales on which we weigh the value of 'self-culture'. No doubt he specialised somewhat in one particular brand of sentiment. What is infinitely more important is, that the mind which contained as formidable a detached Onlooker as is portrayed in Mephistopheles yet never lost its faculty for simple and reverent feeling, or its sense of the greatness of man. For it is precisely this that we are today in such great danger of losing.

But is it a danger? Might it not be rather a good thing? Do we not owe most of our miseries to this idea, promulgated at the Renaissance and confirmed with acclamation by the Romantics, that man is great? What signs precisely is he showing of it? *Si monumentum requiris circumspice* —— at Guernica, at Warsaw, at Hiroshima, or, for that matter, at almost any bookstall. Is not all this because we have forgotten that man is *not* great; that only God is great? Has man in fact any such responsibility to be fully conscious as has been suggested, or indeed any responsibility at all except to be good and obedient?

Questions of this sort are being asked with some force in the twentieth century by the sincerest and most devout Christians; they are being asked with uncompromising sincerity and often with great intellectual force; and they are being listened to. I think that any substantial revival of Christianity which may occur in the near future is likely to be one that implies this interpretation of history; one, that is to say, which rejects *in toto* as error that Renaissance affirmation of the spiritual value of experience which has been called Faustian, and as blasphemous the Romantic conception of man as a creative being. And I shall be surprised if we do not see, in the forthcoming bi-centenary year, some swingeing attacks on Goethe as the high priest of the twin heresies of pantheism and humanism.

"God", says Carlyle in one of his Essays, "or the godlike in man", he adds casually, as if the two were very much the same thing. And I doubt if Goethe would have been much more cautious. The theological writers of the twentieth century have certain advantages which he lacked. They have seen for themselves whither the postulate that God is to be found only in man may lead in art, literature and society; and in politics how easily individual self-culture degenerates into its national counterpart. And they are pretty sure that man is not the place to look for Him.

The subject is clearly not one which can be pursued here at the length it deserves. Two things, however, may be observed. First, that if it be blasphemy to conceive of God 'in' man, in the sense of being a part of his nature — some vague aspiration or higher Self — yet to conceive of Him as 'outside' man, in the same mode as objects perceived through the senses are 'outside', is idolatry. Second, that such words as 'in' and 'outside', 'pantheism' and 'humanism' are in such a context war-cries rather than instruments of thought. Through Rudolf Steiner there was revealed the process of that gradual entrusting of the Cosmic Intelligence to man, of which the Incarnation of the Word was the central event, and which is the meaning of history. At least either this was so or he was under a very strange and ingenious delusion.

The revelation must speak for itself to those who will be at pains to acquaint themselves with it. It is as remote from the vague evolutionary humanism of the Victorian intellectuals and their poet-manufactured God as it is from the precise, changeless Augustinian thearchy which is more often imagined today by the like combination of moral earnestness with intellectual integrity. None who have once been made aware of that revelation can be in any doubt about the reality of the responsibility of which I spoke earlier in this article or the sense in which it is correct to speak of man as great. Great he is, and greater he must become, for good or evil, and the only effect of his voluntarily denying his own greatness must be to make him pemissively and involuntarily great for evil —— as in the case of the Hindu stationmaster who, preferring humility to responsibility and looking always for immediate guidance, once telegraphed to his Terminus: *Man-eating tiger on up-platform stop what do?*

But to return to Goethe and our imaginary neophyte. Let him lay aside all such considerations as I have been advancing and merely proceed, undeterred by the obstacles, to a closer acquaintance with the man. At a certain point he is likely to meet with a startling experience. Those obstacles I began by stressing do not indeed disappear. But they suddenly dwindle in size; so much so as to seem quite irrelevant. The sheer *size* of Goethe's soul is suddenly impressed on him. If the water is a little brown, it is rather with sheer velocity and force and quantity than with mud. Aloof, self-contained, whole at any moment and seeming at rest in itself, on closer inspection what we were investigating under the impression that it was a brook turns out to be a roaring wall of water, a veritable Niagara.

Nor would it be easy to point to any particular source from which the impression is derived. There is no single production of Goethe's pen — not even *Faust* — which overwhelms us with an unquestioned sublimity, as do the *Divine Comedy, King Lear* or *Paradise Lost.* It is the whole man, the life, character and works taken together, which weigh upon us, the even-balanced soul weathering its own storms, the deep earnestness and reverence apparent beneath whatsoever *Leichtfertigkeiten* ("an habitual reference to interior truth" Emerson called it), the wisdom of the head untired and untiring wielded by the ever-youthful heart.

No, this is not the kind of strength which would have failed to grapple with a tragic destiny had it been called upon to do so. And, in the eye of God, may that not be perhaps the easier task? Comfort, success, prosperity and adulation need some handling. Moreover, if Goethe's external life was an easy one by our standards, we may reflect that we have no right to assume that the good life will *always* consist of that drab sacrifice punctuated by spasmodic heroism which we have learnt to accept and approve. As a teacher even of a practical way of life, he may yet speak very pertinently, if not to our children, at least to our children's children. For us, meanwhile, the lesson is, that such a man has in fact existed at all. There is strength to be drawn from the mere contact with his strength. We are reminded that the human soul has indeed the latent power and breadth and universality which are already beginning to be required of her in the discharge of responsibilities now dimly seen to be 'global' and in fact cosmic; and that, as the light of art is put out, so neither is democracy well served nor God well praised by denying her greatness.

Aloof? There is some conflict on the point. They say his friends did not find him so in the end, and his servant, according to Eckermann, adored him. Moreover he stood well with children. Schiller, after their first meeting, wrote:

> I believe, indeed, he is an egoist in an unusual degree. He has the talent of conquering men, and of binding them by small as well as great attentions: but he always knows how to hold himself free. He makes his existence benevolently felt but only like a god, without giving himself: this seems to me a consequent and well-planned conduct which is calculated to ensure the highest enjoyment of self-love....

Yet Schiller, a year or two later, loved the man this side idolatry and wrote of him as being "still more loved as a man than admired as an author". Lewes, in his *Life*, in seeking to answer the charge, admits its wide currency. "Men might," he says, "learn so much from his works had not the notion of his coldness and indifference disturbed their judgment."

It cannot be denied that, whatever it may have signified to meet Goethe in the flesh, the impression made by the record on posterity (and that is really all that the twentieth century can be concerned with) *is* very commonly one of aloofness, and of a certain chill, repelling rather than repellent. Little waterfalls make all sorts of chuckling and endearing noises, but if you listen attentively to Niagara, the predominant refrain of its thunder is *Noli me tangere!* "Goethe," said Emerson, in an essay not exactly conspicuous for lack of enthusiasm,

> can never be dear to men. His is not even the devotion to pure truth; but to truth for the sake of culture. He has no aims less large than the conquest of universal nature, of universal truth, to be his portion: a man not to be bribed, nor deceived, nor

overawed: of a stoical self-command and self-denial, and having one test for all men — *What can you teach me?*

How unobtrusively judicious is that 'to be his portion'! For the third time we touch this question of 'self-culture'. *Mein Geist... Mein Geist...* it is as easy to keep on saying as *Lord! Lord!* And yet the spirit that roared down the Niagara of Goethe's soul never did become quite 'his' spirit. For that, by virtue of the paradox at the heart of creation, only befalls those who are most vividly aware that it is *not* theirs —— that the Lord hath chosen Sion to be an habitation for himself. Then indeed it becomes theirs and, in the mysterious chemistry of the paradox, turns sweet in all the majesty of its strength. This was a consummation which Goethe never achieved. "The old Eternal Genius" (it is Emerson speaking again) "who built the world has confided himself more to this man than to any other." And yet the colossal soul was somehow not quite a sublime spirit.

That Goethe was not doctrinally a Christian is obvious enough, though his early phase of pietism was taken, as he took all else, seriously, and its influence was lifelong; though he attained to that deep respect for the Christian religion, which he expressed towards the end of *Wilhelm Meister.* What is more important for literature is a certain Christianising element in the soul, which is only partly and perhaps not necessarily dependent on doctrine at all, and which, as Arthur Clutton-Brock once pointed out in a brief essay, is detectable in a man's writings more as a kind of subtle *flavour* than anything else. Perhaps it is something to do with the soul's most secret attitude to suffering and death. Whatever it is, it is (to give an example) conspicuously absent from Milton's writings. It is lacking also from Goethe's. And this lack makes itself felt here and there in the numberless little touches which have combined to build up that impression of coldness. It would have made impossible, for instance, or must at least have modified the tone of, those unpleasing expressions of contempt for large numbers of his fellow creatures, including practically all Germans; just as, in his life, it would have ruled out the morganatic connection — domestically 'aloof' — with Christiane Vulpius.

There is one aspect of experience which the creator of Faust never really succeeded in *expressing* and that is what has been well called its 'costingness'. The recoveries are too complete; the regrets banished too easily —— so that if, in a fairly deep sense, he learned everything, we are sometimes affected with an uneasy suspicion that, in the deepest sense of all, he learned nothing. So, in the love-poems, matchless treasury as they are of pure and tender passion, there is one stop that is never opened. Nowhere has Goethe expressed that blend of earthly passion with the last selfless love of spirit for spirit which has moved not only Shakespeare, but a score of meaner talents, to music.

> *Nay, if you read this line, remember not*
> *The hand that writ it, for I love you so*
> *That I in your sweet thoughts would be forgot*
> *If thinking on me then should make you woe!*

is quite beyond his reach. When he did once move away from his lyrical métier as a singer of love-songs, namely, the expression of passion in what I have tentatively called the adolescent mood, he moved not in this direction but into the delighting, but far from venerable, pagan amorism of the *Römische Elegien*.

The two things in Goethe to which Rudolf Steiner continually drew attention were, first by a long way, his method of knowledge. Goethe's view of the limited value of purely abstract theorising about Nature was part of a conception of man's whole relation to Nature which is of religious as well as of scientific importance. Steiner himself taught that the Incarnation was an historical event which reached to the foundations not of human nature alone but of the whole earth; and that since that time the mind which, in cognition, approaches Nature with imagination and reverence, will find, not the amorphous deity of the Pantheists, but the Christ Himself in His cosmic aspect. In Goethe's attitude he found just such an approach, and it was on the positive value of this that he was concerned to dwell. For, however it may have been for Goethe himself, the importance for humanity as a whole of precisely this rare and new thing must far outweigh the question whether he had a perfect understanding of historical Christianity, of Christian doctrine, or of the Christ Himself in His personal aspect. For these we can look elsewhere.

The second thing was that transmutation of experience into wisdom and strength, which has been both admired and criticised as 'self-culture'. It is, I believe, true that there were no more passionate students of the mass of observations accumulated by the Ptolemaic astronomers than those who had themselves come to accept the Copernican system. The geocentric, but faithful and accurate, data spoke to the heliocentrically thinking reader a language unknown to those who had originally collected them. The outstanding impression which Steiner's work and personality make on those acquainted with them is his deep sense of *responsibility*, of his own responsibility to mankind and, still more, of man's responsibility to the Universe. I believe that the pain he suffered from his knowledge of the latter, combined with his actual observation of our feebleness and inadequacy, was something which it is impossible for most of us to imagine. Consequently, when he saw in Goethe the rare spectacle of a human soul at least struggling towards something like the fullness of stature that will one day be required of it, if, Christ-filled, it is to carry the burden of cosmic tensions, his thankfulness far outweighed any questions about the egocentricity of this particular soul. We must remember that he also taught reincarnation. There are remarks scattered here and there which suggest that he felt Goethe's limitations sharply enough, but they are so few and far between as to show that he also never considered it was these that mattered.

This positive attitude is clearly the only wise one; but since, if you hope to extricate people from error, you must first do justice to their truth, I have thought fit to dwell at some length on the limitations both real and supposed. Rudolf Steiner's life was neither sheltered nor leisured. It was one in which poverty played no inconsiderable part, in which selflessness was at all times paramount, which must have been, at all events in his later years, one of almost uninterrupted suffering. Yet the finger points tranquilly to that other life in Frankfurt, in Strasbourg, in Rome, in Weimar. These are bad times for a philosophy of joyous experience; yet it would be surprising indeed if we looked carefully where that finger points and found no elixir.

THE TIME-PHILOSOPHY OF
RUDOLF STEINER

first published 1955

TRUTH FOR THE medieval philosopher did not consist of the presence within the mind of man of an accurate mental copy of some purely external reality. In order that it might light up, the thought of man had first, as M. Étienne Gilson has well expressed it, to "become conformed to the being of the thing". The mind had, he says, "to be able to become all things in an intelligible manner". How different from ours then, must have been the whole picture of the relation of man to the universe, which was latent in the background of the medieval mind! When the *form* of a thing in nature lit up as *species* in his own individual intelligence, it was, for medieval man, a temporary and partial fusion of macrocosm with microcosm. Truth was nature re-forming herself in the mind of man; and this re-forming was somehow inseparable from the notion of *naming*, of the word, of speech, of utterance whether vocal or silent.

As long as thinking remained within the bosom of the word, it could go on holding *species* and *form* together. But it did not remain there. In the seventeenth century there arose the new Natural or Experimental Philosophy, as it was called, which was at first regarded as a junior

Printed in *The Golden Blade*, 1955.

and rather comic branch of philosophy. Then it began to be called Natural Science, and then just 'Science'; and by this time it had come to be regarded as a way of thought in its own right. By the middle of the nineteenth century many people had come to regard it as the *only* valid way of thought, of which academic philosophy was a junior and rather comic branch. The London Library was founded in 1841 and, until a month or two ago, if you wanted to get out a book on Philosophy, you had to go to the section marked 'Science' and walk along it until you came to the letter 'P'.

This Natural Science led to that picture of the world with which most of us have been familiar since childhood. It assumed a world consisting of 'nature' as a process going on by itself, a kind of machine, strictly governed by the laws of mechanical causality, and, set over against this, the observing mind of man. And even this observing mind was no more than an accidental flicker of consciousness hovering over the grey matter in his skull. On the one side you had nature and on the other side —— man. Only the other side was not there. Man was reduced to zero. Man *himself* was nothing more than a fleeting chain of pictures, pictures imprinted somehow on his physical brain —— very shadowy pictures of a very solid world.

Science, then, was growing and developing by confining its attention exclusively to the form and structure of nature, without seeking to know anything of the mind of man. At the same time philosophy proper, academic philosophy, began to confine its attention more and more exclusively to the mind of man, without seeking to know anything of nature. If the Greeks produced philosophies of Being, and the Middle Ages philosophies of the Word, the 'classical' philosophies (as they are beginning to be labelled) may properly be called philosophies of the Mind. The history of European philosophy, from Descartes onward, might indeed be loosely described as a steady progress, or transition, from Philosophy to Psychology. It went on concerning itself more and more exclusively with the *inside* of man's experience of the world. John Locke distinguished between the primary and secondary qualities of the objects we see, or seem to see, about us, and placed the secondary qualities such as colour, not in the objects themselves, but in the perceiving apparatus of man.

Moreover, philosophy came increasingly under the influence of the natural science which was developing, alongside of it, such theories as the molecular structure of matter and was at the same time investigating the brain and the nerves and the physical sense-organs. The microscope and the telescope were steadily improved and employed with greater and greater effect; and one may reflect how these instruments have the effect of cutting off, as it were, the microcosm from the macrocosm. The contrast between the appearance and what was believed to be the 'reality' of nature, grew sharper and sharper. Men began to talk of the 'impressions' of the senses, and before long Hume was maintaining that thoughts themselves were no more than faded sense-impressions.

Then, from the philosophy of Hume men turned again to Science and asked what it had discovered about the senses. And in its reply Science went much further than Locke had done. Locke had distinguished primary from secondary qualities, but according to the biological theory of 'specific nervous activity', or 'specific sense-energy', the quality of *all* the impressions of the senses was determined, not by the outer stimulus, not by the nature of the object perceived, but by the nature of the sense-organ itself. Finally, Kant created that structure of Transcendental Idealism which was the most widely accepted, certainly the most influential, philosophical view current in the nineteenth century. There was, it was held, a sort of Iron Curtain between nature and the human mind. On the one side of it, the reality behind the appearances of nature, the things in themselves which could never be known; and on the other side the mind and senses of man, which created, in the act of perception, that artificial world of space, and of appearances in space, by which it seems to itself to be surrounded.

It was this kind of view of the world, this Iron Curtain, which was predominant, which was almost triumphant — and above all in Central Europe — when Rudolf Steiner began to think. This —— and, in the world of science, the Darwinian theory.

In the course of the many books he wrote and lectures he gave, Steiner said many harsh things about modern natural science. He also said many very flattering things. Sometimes they may seem rather hard to reconcile. Perhaps the answer lies in this: that the *basic* response of his mind to the typical scientific and philosophical oudook of his day was not negative. It was positive. It was not, fundamentally and in its inspiration, *critical* —— but complementary. For he said this. He pointed out a consequence of the scientific doctrine of mechanical causality that had been rather overlooked. If the inwardness of nature and the inwardness of man were really united in the way that Greek, and to a lesser extent medieval, thought suggested; as long as man's motives and actions were determined from outside himself in the way that, for instance, ancient astrology envisaged; if the human microcosm was a centre, into which irradiated centripetally an unbroken influence from the macrocosm; if nature re-formed herself in man every time he thought or perceived, then man could not really experience himself as a free and undetermined being.

It was quite true that mechanical causality had reduced man himself, man the spirit, to a kind of zero. But by the very fact of doing so it had made him free. He might call himself nothing, but that nothing was free. Indeed it was free *because* — so far at least as nature was concerned — it was nothing. Or you could put it this way: If man exists *at all*, then he is free.

And now as to the doctrine of evolution, which had revolutionised biology in the latter part of the eighteenth and the early nineteenth century: Rudolf Steiner criticised very sharply, not the doctrine of evolution, but the Darwinian theory of natural selection, which is quite a different thing. For that theory is really a desperate attempt to fit into the essentially timeless framework of mechanical causality, the completely incompatible notion

THE TIME-PHILOSOPHY OF RUDOLF STEINER 251

of *metamorphosis* —— of the gradual change of one form or species into another. And to do this, Biology had to call in the aid of chance and make that the prime mover of the whole process; just as Physics is beginning to call in the aid of chance today.

Steiner, as I say, criticised the Darwinian theory, but once again this criticism is not the really essential thing. The essential thing is what he *added*. These vast vistas of time, down which not only Biology, but Geology, Astronomy, Archaeology and other sciences were inviting him to look, were a comparatively recent experience for man. When Steiner was born, most people still believed the world to be less than 6,000 years old —— though of course the fight was on. And what Steiner said to men in effect, was this: 'This new dimension, these vistas of time down which you are now for the first time gazing, this new picture in your minds of a gradual, æon-long evolution of your own body, is indeed an all-important advance in knowledge. So important that things can never be the same for you again. But you have left out half the picture —— and the more important half. You have left out the evolution of consciousness'.

It has been well said that Rudolf Steiner 'reached a different level of time-consciousness' from the ordinary man's. He certainly claimed the power to recover past events in their true time-dimension; and those who are willing to contemplate that time-dimension and allow it to work on them know how it involves a much deeper understanding of the significance of those events. We are sometimes asked to say 'in a few words' what

Anthroposophy is. It is of course impossible. But let us in this context say that the kernel of Anthroposophy is *the concept of man's self-consciousness as a process in time* —— with all that this implies. It is hopelessly inadequate, but I think it is true. How often Steiner opened a lecture by briefly depicting an older type of consciousness, a clairvoyant condition in which man and nature, or man and the spirit in nature, were still united in something the same way as animals (so some biologists and some psychologists have said) are united with the spirit in nature today; so that in the manifestations of what is called 'instinct', although the animal acts consciously, yet in a sense it is not the animal itself that is acting, but the spiritual archetype acting through it. Dr. Steiner contrasted this with man's gradual emergence into the sharp, narrow and detached self-consciousness which he enjoys today, (if 'enjoy' is the right word).

It is just this kernel, this concept of *process*, which has as yet found no real acceptance, no real understanding, anywhere outside the Anthroposophical Movement. Is it because it is really rather difficult to grasp? We shall see, later on, that there are true and important links arising here and there between the anthroposophical view and other contemporary ways of thought. But nowhere have I found any real grasp of this central fact: that self-consciousness, that *subjectivity itself*, is an historical process. There are hints of it perhaps in Jung; and sometimes some of the anthropologists — Durkheim, for instance, or Lévy-Bruhl, with his 'participation mystique' — seem to imply it. But sooner or later they drop some remark which shows that at the bottom of their imaginations they still believe that man has always, in fact, been what the Phenomenologists would call 'an embodied self in Nature' —— neither more nor less of a self than he is today. They show that they do not really believe that man's consciousness ever *was* a part of nature's any more than it is now. But only that he made a mistake and thought it was —— a very different thing.

We must now try and look for a little while at some of the things that have been happening in the realm of philosophical enquiry in our own century and especially in the second quarter of it. Quite recently there has been a sharp change of perspective, so that many people talk of all philosophy before about 1930 as a sort of closed chapter which they call 'classical' philosophy. According to this way of looking at it, the gulf between let us say the idealism of Bishop Berkeley on the one hand and the materialism of Karl Marx on the other is far less wide than the gulf that yawns between either of these two 'classical' philosophies and, say, Existentialism or Logical Positivism.

What has happened in philosophy to make people say this? It is this. Beneath all the philosophical conflicts, the Western mind, especially during the last three or four centuries, has been haunted by a certain picture of a contrast between the universe as it *is* on the one hand and, on the other, the universe as it is perceived by man. At the back of that mind, sometimes more, sometimes less fully realised and expressed, there has hovered the picture of nature as consisting of a more or less unreal tapestry of sense-perceptions hung in front of, and concealing, a reality of a quite different order. This is the background picture to the outlook of classical philosophy and science, just as the dualism of macrocosm and microcosm was the background-picture to the outlook of medieval philosophy. Previous philosophies have sought in one way or another to resolve and explain this contrast. They have wrestled each in its own way with the problem which F. H. Bradley took as the tide of his book, the problem of *Appearance and Reality*. Whereas today it is being said that there is no such problem to wrestle with. That is the difference; that is the break.

Now at first sight it may seem that, in one place at least, the break came earlier. It might, for instance, be said that dualism of appearance and reality is already excluded from the philosophy of materialism —— I mean the ordinary classical materialism, the good-old nineteenth century Rationalism, which developed into Behaviourism and of course into Marxism, the view that reality consists of matter and nothing else. It is quite true that materialism excludes any conception of a *mental* or noumenal reality, set over against the world which our senses reveal to us. But the odd thing is that classical materialism *has* retained the dualism, or a sort of spectre of it, in its own materialist form. For, thanks to that marriage between physical science and philosophy in the eighteenth and nineteenth centuries, to which I have already referred, classical materialism does picture nature as made up of a most misleading surface of solid appearances, and, secondly, beneath these, a reality of a very different order —— a reality consisting of waves, or particles, or quanta, or what you will.

Modern materialism, however, has taken a very different turn. So different that it can no longer really be called 'materialism', though it is in the same tradition. It is a kind of Metamateralism. Or we may call this line of philosophical thought — the kind that is quite uncritical of physics and physiology and starts by swallowing it whole — 'Scientism'. Medieval philosophy was a philosophy of the active word; and the typical modern Scientism — out of Wittgenstein through Russell to Ayer and Ryle — springs from a total loss of all sense of the active word. It analyses, not experience but meaning —— the meanings of words. And it finds that nearly all logical propositions are tautologies; or, to put it crudely, that logic is bunk. The conclusion is that all philosophy, or at all events, all metaphysics, is meaningless.

It is not a question, for instance, whether there is such a thing as substance, or whether the mind is distinguishable from the body. Merely to *ask* such a question is to use words in the wrong way. It is as if someone were to ask you when you said you had been to a meeting: Where was Miss X sitting? and were to add a question —— and where did *the Meeting* sit? People have imagined that there must be something called the Mind, simply because grammatically the word 'mind' is a noun. They have supposed that each person has his own private, 'inner' experience, but in actual fact he has nothing of the sort. Not even a fleeting chain of shadowy pictures or ideas —— only arrested impulses to action. Unfortunately (they add) the nature of language is such, that he can hardly avoid *talking* as though he had some sort of inner world. And therefore he has come to believe it. But it is not really so at all. The thing was very well put by Mr. C. S. Lewis in a Preface, when he pointed out that, if these thinkers are right, the whole history of human thought up to date has consisted of "almost nobody making linguistic mistakes about almost nothing". Whether it is called Logical Positivism, or Linguistic Analysis, or by some other name, the burden of its doctrine is, that man has no inside.

Metamaterialism or Scientism, then, abolishes the classical contrast between appearance and reality by affirming that words used in this way simply have no meaning. Now let us turn to the opposite extreme. We have seen philosophy proper, as distinct from Scientism, turning steadily into psychology —— dealing more and more with the inner experience of man and considering that more and more as something cut off from the outside world. And now you get a transition from classical psychology to what I will call 'meta-psychology', because I am not sure whether it ought to be called psychology, psychoanalysis or psychiatry. Freud, who was beginning to be talked of in Steiner's youth, is the best known exponent. It is rather a relief after Linguistic Analysis. Here there is no doubt at all about man having an inside. It may not be a frightfully jolly place when you get to it, but it is there all right. "Modern man," as Jung expressed it in his book. *Modern Man in Search of a Soul,* "can no longer refrain from acknowledging the might of the psychic forces within him. That distinguishes our time from all others...." The Unconscious, as Freud and Jung have conceived it, really is like a sort of *place*, an interior space where there are, shall we say, all sorts of goings-on. Philosophically, however, it has very little connection with the outside world of man's conscious experience.

And what of the realm between? What of philosophy proper? For both the extremes I have mentioned are really something else. Here and there a few philosophers *did* call a halt to the uncritical acceptance of physics and physiology as the basis of psychology; they did attempt a real criticism of science and scientism. There was, for instance, the school of Phenomenology founded by Husserl, an Austrian philosopher who was born two years before Steiner and, like him, came under the influence of Brentano.

I select this for mention because Husserl is acknowledged by the Existentialists (especially by Sartre) as one of their principal sources. Husserl pointed out that such theories as that of 'specific sense-energy', to which I referred earlier, can never really be used as the foundation for a dualism of appearance and reality. To do so is a fallacy; for it is to forget that the theory itself — the theory, that is to say, which seeks to prevent us from relying on the senses for an accurate account of the real nature of the world — is itself based on an uncritical acceptance of that very account as accurate. For it is by means of the senses that we investigate the brain and the sense-organs.

This, of course, was the very criticism which Rudolf Steiner brought to bear. I do not regard him as the unacknowledged founder of every significant movement of thought that has taken place since his day. At the same time I take note of the fact that Husserl's *Logische Untersuchungen* appeared in 1900 or 1901, some ten years after Steiner had developed the same criticism of the growing claims of Scientism in his *Truth and Science*. (He afterwards repeated it in the better known *Philosophy of Freedom*.)

The point of the 'phenomenological reduction', as this critical approach to science has been called, is that it rules out the rationalist-Marxist attempt to project a man's own self and to see it as placed *within* the system of causality. At the same time it claims to destroy the tapestry image — the cleft between appearance and reality — and with this it takes away, apart from faith or revelation — or something else — the last hope of some ideal and inward unity of man with the Absolute *behind* the curtain of the senses. A little earlier I remarked that the system of mechanical causality implies that "if man exists at all, he is free". Well, *ex-sistere* means in Latin to 'stand outside', and Existentialism points out that man's existence as a conscious being consists precisely in this standing outside the world of nature and causality. For if he attempts to conceive himself as a part of that machinery, or indeed a part of anything, then, whether he likes it or not, the self which is *doing the conceiving* remains as much aloof as ever.

Between the very moment of consciousness and all else whatsoever, including any number of remembered or empirical selves, there exists for Sartre, "an irreducible gulf of Non-being". Man does exist, then, and he is free. But this fact of his existence gives him no content, no inside. Man's existence is not anything which can be effectively analysed or discussed. It can only be *lived*. It is behaviour that counts. For 'man is only what he is doing'.

Aquinas said that in God existence and essence, or being, were one and the same. For Existentialism, man is a being for whom existence precedes essence. There are no values, unless he makes them; and he himself has no being, until he makes it with his own will and the actions that proceed from it. It is like old times to find the Existentialists — particularly Heidegger — grappling once more, like any Socrates, with the old problem of Being and Not-being. Sartre, by a kind of audacious philosophical *coup*, actually *equates* human consciousness with Not-being. As in science, so in philosophy, the classical 'model' of a detached mind observing a pre-established world has been shaken. For the observer finds his own volition inextricably involved with the phenomenon —— only not now as part of it, but rather as its complement or cause. We seem to have been passing from philosophies of the Mind to philosophies of Behaviour, Will and Being.

Broadly speaking, then — and I am speaking throughout very broadly indeed, not expounding or refuting anything, but only *describing* in very broad strokes — broadly speaking, in Existentialism you have the acutest possible awareness of that zero-point of its own being to which humanity began reducing itself when it first began to think of the 'laws of nature'. And, what is more important, an equally acute awareness of the practical and moral consequences. Existentialism has made a sort of virtue of the zero-point. It is frankly apprehensive of that 'gulf of Non-being' —— and, even more so, of the liberty which results from it. Its key-word is *Angst* or *angoisse* —— 'dread', as it is usually translated. Thus, Karl Jaspers writes of "the dizzy consciousness of myself in liberty". And Sartre, going further still, describes man as a being who is "*condemned* to freedom".

There is not space here to contrast the Christian Existentialism of Kierkegaard and Marcel with the non-Christian or atheist variety best known from the work of Sartre. What is common to them both is a quality hard to convey descriptively, though it is at once felt on impact. I mean a weighty, almost crushing, sense of *responsibility* in face of the universe. Wherever he looks, the Existentialist sees a poster inscribed with the words, "It all depends on me". And he takes the words to heart. Read a few pages of Kierkegaard, and you are suddenly brought up with an almost horrifying shock: "Good heavens — this man really means what he says!" And then, just possibly, you may feel rather ashamed of yourself.

It is out of this *feeling* of responsibility, and not from any categorical imperative, that Marcel develops the striking paragraphs on fidelity in his book. *Being and Having*; pointing out that, in a changing personality, fidelity is a function of freedom and a condition of self-development, and not (as is widely and erroneously assumed today), a clog on both.

I think Existentialism may well owe some of its flavour to the lonely experiences undergone by so many responsible and trusty human beings in Resistance Movements in the days when torture was a daily occurrence. Sartre has suggested as much in a moving passage. And I suspect that Existentialism appeals, as it would have done to no other, to a generation uneasily aware that man is not only free and independent enough, but now also probably powerful enough, to destroy the earth, if he chooses.

I am convinced also that it appeals to young people because of its bracing contrast with all that 'depersonification' of man, by which they are surrounded alike in the intellectual and in the social sphere. They grow up in a world where man is treated more and more as 'a thing among things'. And then Existentialism comes to them —— not pleadingly, cap and hand, and saying: "Perhaps after all man is not merely a thing among things." Not a bit of it. Existentialism says very brusquely indeed: "Man is *not* a thing among things." It says: "Only the deuce of a lot of very muddled thinking could ever have supposed man to be a thing among things." It even says: "On the contrary, it is only because man is *not* a thing among things, that the things themselves have any existence."

If we try to illuminate the three streams of contemporary speculative thought, which I have sought to distinguish, with the light of Anthroposophy, this is much the same as trying to see them in the new time-dimension. They are Metamaterialism (exemplified in Linguistic Analysis), Existentialism and Metapsychology.

In the case of Linguistic Analysis, the time-dimension is already there in the true nature of language itself. That is, of course, for anyone with the slightest feeling for language. If you look at all closely at the *history* of the meanings of words, and then reflect on the part which the active, image-forming faculty has played in it —— well, that is the end of Linguistic Analysis. I am told its exponents affirm that 'they are not interested in etymology'. And I am not surprised to hear it. I do not suppose a Crystal Palace is much interested in dynamite.

I think nevetherless that, as the twentieth century grows older, there will be more and more people of this way of thinking. And I cannot help wondering if the increasing phenomenon of 'word-blindness' in children (which appears to prevent them from 'reading' a word, as distinct from seeing a number of letters) is a hint to us that more and more human beings are being born to whom such an outlook will make a quick and easy appeal. Is not this connected with the loss or absence of just that symbolising, image-making faculty that is present in 'the active word'? Well, I suggested that the decline of medieval philosophy indicated a sort of 'falling out of the word'. It seems that it is possible to fall *right* out of it! And here one begins to understand the enormous importance Rudolf Steiner attached to Eurythmy and Speech Formation.

In language, if it is felt historically, in the history of meaning, we see the time-process of self-consciousness most intimately displayed. For the history of meaning is the inner surface of the history of thought. In language, as it develops and changes through the course of its history, we can watch a cosmic intelligence gradually descending and incarnating as human intelligence. We behold the microcosm emerging from the macrocosm —— and seeking now to return thither on its own wings. And from this it is not such a very long leap of the understanding to feel, at work beneath the history of meaning, as it emerges from the past into the present and future, something that is not often referred to nowadays —— I mean the true *substance*. What then is substance? Rudolf Steiner, with his highly developed faculty for recovering past events in their time-dimension, was able to reveal that it is none other than the Spiritual Hierarchies and their interweaving activity in the world of nature, in history, in the individual soul. The Spiritual Hierarchies are the inner side of the inner surface of the history of thought. Their activities and relations have been displayed by Steiner in many books and lectures, but nowhere perhaps so fully and yet so succinctly as in the series of *Leading Thoughts*, which were about the last thing he wrote before his death in 1925.

There are many currents of contemporary thought from which it is not such a very long leap to conceive the Spiritual Hierarchies as active in all three spheres of nature, history, and the individual soul. Read, for instance, that profound and original book by Douglas Harding, published in 1952, *The Hierarchy of Heaven and Earth*. Today it is a far shorter leap — for all sorts of people — than it must have been 30, 40, or 50 years ago. Or consider the third sphere —— the life of the individual soul: thanks to the growth in popularity of Metapsychology, numberless otherwise sceptical minds are conditioned to accept, with a complaisance which I often find surprising, this notion of 'the Unconscious' as an integral and positive part — a sort of new dimension — of the human being. I wonder what John Stuart Mill would have said to anyone who had used the term 'the Unconscious' as the subject of a verb implying sentience. "The Unconscious longs ... the Unconscious strives ..." and so forth. We have seen something of how the Jungian school of psychology has passed *through*, so to speak, those merely physical echoes — the spectral secretions and excretions which originally made up the Freudian Unconscious — into their non-physical sources, the archetypes in a so-called 'Collective Unconscious'. We have seen, perhaps, something of the renewal of the human faculty of creating and apprehending symbols, which is associated with that school. Read a little of Groddeck if you want to experience this in its most luxuriant form. We have heard the habitation of those archetypes referred to as 'the spiritual world or the Collective Unconscious —— whichever you prefer'. You may have wondered if this was justified. For does it not imply that what the lecturing biologist called 'the spiritual world' is merely a metaphor; that he was not talking about an objective reality, but of some kind of purely subjective goings on within the self of man?

Let us hear what Rudolf Steiner has to say in a brief extract from those same *Leading Thoughts*:

> To ordinary self-observation, the inner world of man reveals only a portion of that, in the midst of which it stands. Intensified experience in consciousness shows it to be contained within a living spiritual Reality.

The experiences of the human soul reveal not only a Self but a world of the Spirit, which the Self can know by deeper spiritual knowledge as a world united with its own being.

This brings us to the paradox — or, to use a word which has become popular in modern theology, the 'tension' — at the core of Anthroposophy. It is the thing that makes it so difficult to explain to a newcomer without giving him the impression that one is quibbling or compromising. "Nature," says Dr. Steiner elsewhere in the *Leading Thoughts*, "will indeed exist in man; but it will be an echo in human experience of the Divine relation to the Cosmos which prevailed in the earlier stages of cosmic evolution." Are we talking about a Spiritual World, or about the 'echo' of a Spiritual World?

Descartes called man a 'thinking substance'. Today, when physical science, ignoring the time-dimension, resolves 'things' into empty space (empty, that is, of what classical Science called 'matter'), and when philosophy, ignoring the time-dimension, reduces the mind and self of man to not-being, we may well ask of both man and nature: "What is your substance, whereof you are made?" Is it the same substance that underlies both thought and things?

Merely to answer 'yes' to this question — leaving out the time-dimension — is no truer than to answer 'no'. For our thoughts — at all events those that can be expressed in words — are *in* the time-dimension and cannot apprehend the true nature of Being in abstraction from it. Such is the teaching of Anthroposophy, which leads us, in Steiner's words, "to overcome the idea of an undefined Spirituality, pantheistically conceived as holding sway at the root of all things". For substance is none other than the Spiritual Hierarchies and their activities and relations. "We are led," he says, "to a conception that is definite and real, capable of clear ideas about the Spiritual Beings of the Hierarchies. For the reality is everywhere a reality of Being. Whatsoever in it is not Being, is the activity that proceeds in the relation of one Being to another."

It is these Beings, then, and their activities and relations that we shall seek to descry behind nature, behind history and in the life of the individual.

To be an anthroposophist and to accept the spiritual Hierarchies as a fact does not mean believing in a sort of external divine staircase, like the one at the end of the second act of the opera *Hansel and Gretel*. But neither does it mean accepting them as a poetic or allegorical symbol for the subjective workings of the human mind. If you say, Well, it must mean one or the other, the answer is, No. The answer is, that you have left out the time-dimension. In the time-dimension, and only there, can we understand how the Hierarchies are truly hierarchies *and yet how, today, their life is the substance of our own wills. For the mind and the senses, the world is their finished work, from which they have withdrawn their being. In the individual human will they have their present existence.*

I have spoken of the burden, the sense of responsibility felt by the Existentialists, for whom the unsupported, personal will carries the whole weight of the Universe. If we really accepted with our hearts as well as our minds that *the substance of our wills is the lower Spiritual*

Hierarchies — just as 'matter' is the deepest sacrifice of the highest Beings of all — should we feel the weight of that responsibility *more*, or *less*, than they do? Should we feel more or less 'dread' than Sartre does when he reflects on the liberty to which he is 'condemned'; when he is appalled by the thought that 'his choice could be otherwise'?

But even when we have grasped this, when we have overcome the contradiction of the being and not-being of the Hierarchies by taking the time-dimension into ourselves, there remains another paradox at the heart of the paradox we have just surmounted. For the whole burden of this article has been that the first half of the historical process of man's self-consciousness involves its complete severance, not only from the world of nature but also, and along with that, from the Divine World which gave him birth. For this, as we saw, was the condition and the price of his freedom. But this involves reducing man, as man, to an absolute zero. But how can a zero exist? How — and we may ask the Existentialists this — can it exist even as naked will or as a bare potentiality of being, called 'consciousness'? Their answer, as far as I can make out, is that it cannot really, and yet it does. And that the whole affair is a merciless and a cracking strain; the final words of Sartre's principal book are: "Man is a useless passion."

All the same, we should not underrate the Existentialists. For, if we are, or if we wish to become, truly anthroposophists and not mere snappers-up of unconsidered esoterical trifles, we shall know, and we shall feel, that there *is* really a gulf of Not-being to be leaped across, that there is really a zero-point to be turned, and to be turned not by just making pretty patterns with our thoughts, but by will, by action, by trusty behaviour, by the 'fidelity' of which Gabriel Marcel has written so movingly, by the courage to which Rudolf Steiner again and again exhorted his followers. And if we ask whether there is any resolution to *this* paradox, and whether there is any Being to whom we can look for help in this cosmic dilemma, the answers which Anthroposophy gives are, that in the time-dimension there is one spiritual link between the 'existing' microcosm and the living macrocosm of the remote past, out of which it sprang. One link remains unbroken; namely the rhythm of man's repeated lives on earth. Man's life on earth is a link which supports his existence, without infringing his freedom, because (and after all we cannot quite avoid a paradox) it *is* broken from time to time —— by death. And that there is one Being of the Hierarchies, to whom he can look for help, and yet remain free, because that Being's help is given by way of gesture and example rather than by way of interference (if one may use the term with reverence). Lastly, that there is Another greater than he, beyond all the Hierarchies, whose help is of a different order, because He offers us His Substance; because He offers us the substance of the macrocosm, and bids us make it our own. In No. 54 of the *Leading Thoughts*, Rudolf Steiner wrote:

> 1. In ideation man lives not in Being, but in Picture-being — in a realm of Non-being — with his conscious Spiritual Soul. Thus is he freed from living and experiencing with the Cosmos. Pictures do not compel; Being alone has power to

compel. And if man does direct himself according to the pictures, his doing so is independent of them; it is in freedom from the Universe.

2. In the moment of such ideation man is joined to the Being of the Universe by that alone which he has become through his own past: through his former lives on Earth, and lives between death and new birth.

3. Only through Michael's activity and the Christ-Impulse, can man achieve this leap across the gulf of Non-Being in relation to the Cosmos.

THE FALL IN MAN AND NATURE
first published 1959

IT IS A TRUISM that the historical event which is now commonly referred to as the 'Scientific Revolution', involved a violent change in men's ideas about the world and their own place in it. Very soon the new outlook began to affect also man's picture of his own past and future. Nowhere indeed is the contrast greater than it is here between the notions that prevailed before and after the Scientific Revolution. For here it amounted to a complete reversal.

If we examine all the ideas and assumptions that now cluster round such words as 'progress' and 'progressive', we shall be astonished to find that none of them had been heard of before the seventeenth century. Things have been getting better and will get better still; so it was argued in the seventeenth and eighteenth centuries, mainly by French writers, who said that the sum of human happiness must inevitably increase, as Reason took more and more effective control of human affairs. Men have been getting better (morally) and will get better still; so it was argued, more now perhaps by English writers, in the eighteenth and nineteenth centuries. Man is naturally good and both can and will grow perfect. People differed about the steps to be taken to that end. Shelley, for instance, and his teacher Godwin, supposed that all that was required was to overcome the oppression of tyrants.

Printed in *Anthroposophical Quarterly*, Winter 1959.

Rousseau would have man return to a 'State of Nature', where his natural goodness would work unhampered. But, as time went on, more and more people agreed about the general principle of 'progress'. There followed the doctrine of biological evolution which, if it was incompatible with Rousseau's fantasy of the Noble Savage, nevertheless gave an enormous fillip to the idea of progress as being the very stuff of which history is made. The story of man, it was (and very largely still is) taught to every child in school, is the story of the *rise* of man.

But before the Scientific Revolution precisely the opposite was believed and taught. Things have been getting worse and will get worse still. Milton doubted whether it was not already too late for the human race to produce another great poem; perhaps its degeneration had gone too far already. History must be the narrative not of the rise, but of the *fall* of man, beginning with his expulsion from paradise and continuing into the foreseeable future. Man is naturally wicked.

The conviction that man is neither good nor innocent by nature, owing to the original sin implanted in his heredity, culminated just before the Scientific Revolution in the religious movement inaugurated by Calvin. For Calvin 'natural' man was not simply not good, he had no goodness at all in him. Calvin spoke of the 'total depravity' of unregenerate man. All his righteousness was as filthy rags. His natural impulses, however seemingly beneficent, were morally worthless; real goodness, and such as alone could lead to his salvation, could only be bestowed on him by Grace. It could only arise from the working in him of the Holy Spirit in despite of Nature.

This conception of an absolute conflict between Nature and Grace was however not confined to the followers of Calvin. It has been, in the course of history, the deep conviction of innumerable souls, and it is still the leading thought of no small number. One thinks in this connection of the theology associated with the name of Karl Barth, or with that of Reinhold Niebuhr. It has perhaps rarely been put more succinctly than it was by that wonderful personality, Simone Weil, in an essay published posthumously in *The Twentieth Century* for June, 1959:

> In all the crucial problems of human existence the only choice is between supernatural Good on the one hand and Evil on the other.

The other view — that man is naturally good — has also been, although over a shorter period, and is still the deepest and sincerest conviction of many human souls. It is, for example, the mainspring of 'humanism'. Is it possible, one asks — and anxiously, when one thinks of the deep and sincere conviction which either doctrine is capable of arousing — that they can both be true? Could we, for instance, reconcile them by supposing an original evolutionary 'rise' of man, with the help of Nature and with natural goodness innate in him, followed by a 'fall', from which he can only be rescued by Grace? It would seem not —— not, that is, if we really understand what is and always has been meant by the Fall of Man.

THE FALL IN MAN AND NATURE

Milton in the IXth Book of *Paradise Lost* describes as follows the moment when Eve plucked the apple:

> So saying, her rash hand in evil hour,
> Forth reaching for the fruit, she pluck'd, she eat:
> Earth felt the wound, and Nature from her seat
> Sighing through all her works gave signs of woe
> That all was lost.

Man did not fall *from* Nature, or a state of nature, but Nature fell *with* him. I believe it is the case that all the known forms of the Paradise Myth represent Nature as implicated in the fall of man from his paradisal state. They all contain or imply a kind of magical sympathy between Man and Nature, which made this inevitable.

Now it is an essential part of the task of Anthroposophy to re-state the old Myth-wisdom in conceptual form and, in so doing, to bring out its historical truth. And it follows from what has been said that, if we seek to contemplate the story of man's fall from paradise in the light of Anthroposophy, we must first endeavour to understand the truth that underlies this 'magical' link between Man and Nature, on which its whole character depends.

The fourth lecture of the cycle *Building Stones for an Understanding of the Mystery of Golgotha*, deals briefly with it in particular relation to the Fall; but in a wider sense this link between Man and Nature was of course a subject to which Rudolf Steiner addressed himself at the start of his life and to which he returned over and over again right up to the end. We find it in the *Philosophy of Freedom*, as we find it in the *Leading Thoughts*. From this enormous mass of material I want here to refer to only two passages.

In No. 25 of the *Michael Letters* (those introductory Essays to the later Leading Thoughts), which is entitled: *The Relation of Man's Perceiving and Thinking Organisation to the World*, he describes how Imaginative Cognition shows us that:

> Fundamentally man has not united himself at all intensively with his sense-system. Properly speaking, it is not he who lives in this system of the senses, but the surrounding world. This has built itself and its existence (*Wesen*) into his sense-organisation.

Built 'itself'; not 'a copy of itself'. In other words it is really an illusion to locate the break, or gap, between ourselves on the one hand and nature on the other — as we normally do — at the surface of our skins. It is set much deeper inside us; and what we look on as the 'outside' world is in fact in a large measure the working of our own sense-organisation, in which the outside world 'lives'. This is also implicit in the argument of the *Philosophy of Freedom*, but in the *Leading Thoughts* it is put in a more startling way, and one which forces us to consider what it would be like, not merely to accept the 'link' as a belief, but also to experience it in actual perception.

We shall find that some of the consequences are puzzling, not only for the ordinary man who is quite confident that 'he' is here inside his skin, and nature is over there outside him, but also for the student of Anthroposophy. Perhaps *more* puzzling for the latter. We had been brought up — most of us — in the conviction that natural science long ago established that nature is a process governed by impersonal laws and that it is merely fanciful (a 'pathetic fallacy') to attribute to her any sort of underlying spirit or consciousness of her own. Poets may project into her workings the image of their joys and sorrows, but all this has no reality. It was just from Rudolf Steiner that we learned, or seemed to learn — and with what relief! — that this dry conception of nature was after all untrue. One has only to think of the very title of such a lecture-cycle as *The Spiritual Beings in the Heavenly Bodies and in the Kingdoms of Nature*; or again, of all that Steiner has said — for example in the cycle *Man as Symphony of the Creative Word* — about the Elemental Beings. We learn there, and we learn in all manner of detail, of the part played in the processes of nature by salamanders, sylphs and undines and of how, even in the mineral world — which it is perhaps easiest for us to conceive of as devoid of life or spirit of any sort — the gnomes are active. If we fix our attention on all this, we may be excused for feeling that it is almost a fundamental tenet of Anthroposophy that nature has indeed a spiritual life, a spiritual substance of her own, which she preserves quite independently of man.

Independently? We shall find that, in all this connection, we have to pick our words very carefully indeed. And this brings me to the second of the two passages bearing on the link between man and nature, to which I wish particularly to refer. It is a passage, towards the end of the third lecture of the cycle just mentioned (*The Spiritual Beings in the Heavenly Bodies and in the Kingdoms of Nature*), in which Steiner endeavours to convey to us some idea of the activity of the Third Hierarchy. These beings, he tells us, are concerned with human consciousness; he goes so far as to say that they "really only live in the process of man's culture". But then he adds that, just as a plant puts forth seed, so do these Beings of the Third Hierarchy bring forth other beings from themselves. And what are these other beings? They are none other than the Elemental Beings! The Elemental Beings, whose task it is to sustain the world of Nature, are nevertheless the 'offspring' of the Third Hierarchy. They "descend from the environment of man into the Kingdoms of Nature".

Thus a deeper study of Anthroposophy — a careful consideration even of the Elemental Beings themselves — can only lead us to feel that (no matter whether we think of nature as spirit-filled or devoid of spirit) it is an illusion to think, as we do all the time, of Man over here and of Nature over there 'going on by itself'. We must think of a different kind of duality altogether; not of Man and Nature, but of something more like Outer Man and Inner Man, or Waking Man and Sleeping Man. By 'Sleeping Man' I mean of course not only man when actually slumbering, but all that realm of his limbs and his will, which continues asleep even during the waking day. Then we begin to see our way through another difficulty. It is a very real difficulty indeed; and it confronted us as soon as we tried to realise in all seriousness the Leading

THE FALL IN MAN AND NATURE

Thought referred to above. For if we conceive of the gap between Man and Nature as ceasing on the hither side of our senses, if we think of Nature as being virtually a part of our sense organism, then we inevitably find ourselves asking, with some dismay: But what happens to Nature when it is not being perceived by me or by anyone else? What happens to Helvellyn in winter time when there are no tourists about —— or at all times in the unvisited depths of the sea?

That it is an illusion to imagine Nature unperceived as being or remaining 'the same thing' as Nature perceived is a truth about which Anthroposophy and modern Physics agree. Modern Physics assumes for its purposes that Nature unperceived consists of some kind of network of waves or particles. What does Anthroposophy assume? That Nature unperceived is the unconscious, sleeping being of humanity; just as Nature perceived is the self-reflection of waking humanity.

We may also point out that the converse is true, and that the waking consciousness of man depends precisely on that perceiving, on that reflection. But when we do so, we must again distinguish very carefully. Certainly the waking consciousness of man — that peculiar awareness of an inner and an outer world — depends on his experience in perceiving nature. But this *need not* necessarily have involved that sense of complete detachment from the outer world of nature, which is our normal experience today. There is another way of having an outer and an inner world, from the one we know. Elsewhere in that same lecture cycle (*The Spiritual Beings in the Heavenly*

Bodies and in the Kingdoms of Nature) Steiner endeavours to portray, not now the function, but the *experience* — the type of consciousness — of the Third Hierarchy. He does so by contrasting it with that of human beings. *We* are aware of our inner world, consisting of private thoughts and feelings, and, over against that, of an outer world consisting of independent objects or, in a word, of 'nature'. What have the Beings of the Third Hierarchy to correspond with this? When *they* experience an outer world, he says, they experience the outer manifestation of their own being; and when they turn away from this to an inner world, the experience he describes for them is that of being filled with the spirit —— of being filled with other and higher spiritual beings.

I believe it is along these lines that we must try to think, if we seek to understand the sort of consciousness man would have had today if he had never fallen. It must have been this angelic type of consciousness which he enjoyed in some measure in 'paradise'. Had he never fallen, then, as his evolution proceeded, he would have gone on experiencing this 'being filled with Spirit-beings' ever more and more intensely; but at the same time he would have grown to experience it more and more wakefully as constituting somehow his own experience, his own Ego; and in doing so, he would have grown into experiencing the outer world (which he would have called 'nature') more and more powerfully as the manifestation of that spirit-filled Ego.

Instead of that, how does fallen man in fact experience himself and nature? He finds himself confronted by —

within — emptiness; and — without — a 'nature', which is not, it seems, his own manifestation at all; which 'goes on by itself', like a machine; which, if it ever was the work of the Gods, is only a 'finished work', from which they have long withdrawn. In the third lecture of the course on *The World of the Senses and the World of the Spirit*[1] Rudolf Steiner speaks of the effect on our sense-organs of a certain maladjustment between man's etheric and his physical body. We shall understand the full meaning of that lecture — and at the same time the meaning of the passages in the *Leading Thoughts* which refer to nature as a 'finished work' devoid of spirit — only if we can come to think that, not only our sense organs but the whole world around us — the whole of what *we* call 'nature' — is actually the product of that maladjustment.

It is characteristic, then, of what I have called 'angelic' consciousness, that it does not develop a separate, hidden, inner world of private thoughts and feelings. These Beings reflect, or pass on, the light they receive from above; and that *is* their inner life. Or we can put it that they do indeed have an inner life, but do not feel it as being exclusively their own. It is their own, inasmuch as it is 'inner', but not in the sense of being at their disposal. They are aware of possessing it only as trustees are aware of possessing trust property, that is, on such terms that the possibility of their using it for their own

---

[1] This was one of two lecture-cycles on which the conference where this lecture was delivered was especially based.

benefit simply does not arise. It could only arise in the case of fraud or treachery.

On the occasion of the Fall, all this was changed by the intervention of Lucifer. Lucifer induced man to begin hiding and hoarding his inner life, and to take pride in it — as 'a room of one's own' — making it into something separate and detached alike from its own outward manifestation (nature) and from the inner world of spirit-beings. In the inner life: instead of the old 'being filled with Spirit-beings' —— Egotism. In the outer life: instead of the old experiencing nature as one's own manifestation —— a complete falling apart of Man and Nature. Man is now started on the long road which ends in his present normal relation to nature, wherein nature is not merely his own outward manifestation, nor that of the higher Spiritual Beings who shine through him; wherein nature is not a manifestation at all, but an object —— a finished work. It is easy to see how it is this new relation to nature that has made possible lying, deceit and error —— none of which are possible for beings whose outer world always and immediately corresponds with their inner experience.

Now we begin to see how the Fall in Man and Nature, which is my subject, includes — how it really *is* — that falling apart of Man and Nature which I have tried to characterise in greater detail. Natural Science is the study of fallen nature carried on by fallen man. But, besides natural science, as it is taught today, there is another kind of knowledge of the world —— a kind which is at the same time knowledge of self. And that is what we call

Higher Knowledge. When we labour towards the attainment of higher knowledge, it is not done in order to satisfy curiosity, or for the sake of attaining power over nature. Rather we are seeking the repair of that 'falling-apart'; we are labouring for the re-union of man and nature and, through that, the redemption of Nature herself. It is at quite an early stage on the path to self-knowledge — as we learn from the cycle, *The World of the Senses and the World of the Spirit* — that man "grows together with the objects with his physical body, that is with his senses, in the active, ruling Will". That is to say, he begins once more to experience the objects in nature as his own manifestation, as the manifestation of his own will, which 'swims' in the active, ruling will.

But it is obvious from all that has been said that this overcoming of the separateness of man and nature — Lucifer's gift — cannot be achieved without overcoming Lucifer's concomitant and inseparable gift of Egotism. What does it signify — when we are thinking in terms of higher knowledge — to overcome Egotism? Rudolf Steiner has several times given us the answer. For instance, in the Introductory lecture to the *Excursus on St. Mark's Gospel*:

> The thing of greatest importance when we begin to approach the spiritual world is, that we learn to regard *ourselves* absolutely with the same indifference with which we regard the outer world.

Here is the usual absence of emphasis —— the seemingly casual understatement: we are 'beginning' to 'approach' the spiritual world and already we must regard ourselves 'absolutely' with the same indifference with which we regard the outer world. Pause on it: think it through. What are we to make of such a hard saying? What sort of a human being am I being asked to become? Would it not be better to turn back before it is too late? How can I be indifferent to myself? I *am* myself! Who then is this 'I' which is to do the being indifferent?

The answer can only be that it is not yet born. That it is at most beginning to struggle out of the womb into existence. This is the being who was "born of water and the spirit", when the early Christians were baptised into Grace by the early Church. It is not surprising that we are told in the *Inner Realities of Evolution*,[2] and elsewhere, that Higher Knowledge, too, can only be the gift of Grace. It is not something we can claim as of right, whatever our efforts may have been towards it.

Thus the opening of the gulf between man and nature, and the egotism of man, are really the same thing, seen from two different sides. Those Christians who condemn as Manichean heresy the view that the Fall was a Fall into matter fail to realise this. Yet, like many rather startling truths, it is obvious when we come to reflect on it. Only if we experience our own feelings as *no more* a part of us than the outside world, can we also experience the outside world as *as much* a part of us as our own feelings —— and, thus, as our own 'manifestation'. It is as simple as that. That is to say, the *theory* is simple. But if

---

[2] The second of the two cycles on which the conference was based.

THE FALL IN MAN AND NATURE 283

Euclid is to be believed, behind a theory or theorem there usually lies a problem. We turn from the theorem to the problem; because we know now why we must struggle on through the centuries to begin acquiring the enormous will-power which is obviously required to overcome egotism in this 'absolute' sense.

Will-power is of no interest to us in itself, but because, as it grows, it is transformed into an actual organ of perception —— the only one that will answer.

To turn from the theorem to the problem is like the change from reading, in the well-lit cabin of a comfortable liner, a book about tempests and natation, to struggling in the Atlantic waves in the middle of a stormy night. At once we are made aware that for years, for centuries, for incarnations, we have been seeking our own pleasure; or if not pleasure, at least comfort; or if not comfort, at least exemption from grievous pain; and to all this we are now — somehow — to become 'indifferent'! So inveterate is the bad habit into which we have slipped that it has come to seem the obvious, indeed the only possible, way of behaving. The moment we try to shift it, we feel its crushing weight. Every effort to put it off reminds us of our slavery. (We may even feel that *we* are the most contemptible slaves of all —— for ever babbling about 'freedom' but never taking any really resolute step to achieve it.) We begin, in short, to experience the Fall from within —— to realise it as *our* Fall.

At the same time another very old concept becomes more than a concept to us. 'Sin', too, may be approached either objectively or subjectively. As an extreme instance of the purely objective approach it is related of the late President Coolidge (whose habit of thought was political rather than religious) that he once broke a long habit by attending a service in church. Questioned by his family afterwards about the sermon, he replied: "He preached about sin." And when he was asked what the preacher said about sin, he replied: "He was against it." There you have the purely objective approach. As anthroposophists we can stop short at this approach only if we are insufficiently aware of that 'complementarity' of the two sides of the Fall, of which I have spoken —— on the one hand our detachment from the world of nature, and on the other —— egotism. Much could be said about the whole relation of the Threshold to that 'finished work' aspect of nature —— and indeed to the difficulty of understanding it. Nature, drained, so to speak, of the spirit, *is* from one point of view the Threshold. That is why humanity as a whole is approaching it in our time. Where is the Spirit which has been drained away from nature? Within ourselves. At the Threshold we must experience the whole of the Spiritual World as in a manner our Spirit, the whole of past time as *our* past —— and in the same instant we must see what we have made of it with Lucifer's help. Then, if we really *meet* the Guardian and do not try to slip past him, we shall feel ourselves as what we are — weaklings who have hopelessly failed in a great responsibility placed on our shoulders, deceivers who have miserably betrayed our trust. The sense of sin is the chilling touch of one of the Guardian's fingers on our heart. As soon as we feel that touch, we shall know what the word 'sin' can mean, not to President Coolidge and his family (if the story is true) and to the objective school, but to a broken and a contrite heart.

We have tried up to now to see something of what lies behind the great Myth of Man's and Nature's Fall —— and their redemption through Grace. What of that other myth (for it *is* a myth) of 'progress' and the natural goodness of man? Must we simply reject it? Or has that, too, any basis of truth? We have seen how deeply it has taken hold of the minds and hearts of some men —— the poet Shelley, to take one example. Let us ask again, as we did at the start: Is there any sense in which both can be true?

This reminds us of the other question which has been touched on, and which many of us find some difficulty in answering: How can it be true, *both* that Nature is the 'finished work' of the spirit *and* that Nature is filled with living spirit —— working, for example, through the Elemental Beings?

I believe the two questions are closely connected, and that it is no accident that the second myth (of 'progress' and the like) took shape so late in man's history, when his experience of nature as 'finished' was already so far advanced. I shall try to throw some light on them by referring to two more passages from Rudolf Steiner's lectures.

It is common to contrast the Old and New Testaments on the lines that the former presents the religion of the Father and the latter the religion of the Son. In thinking so, we tend to dwell on the emphasis placed by the Gospels on the child in man, and especially on the child Jesus in the Gospel of St. Luke. It may therefore come with a shock of surprise when we find that Steiner relates precisely the Nathan Jesus of the Luke Gospel with the Father forces. This he does in the third of the lectures collected in the volume called *Christmas*, when he is speaking of the change in the date of the Christmas festival from January 6th to December 25th. He points out that the new date was the day following the one assigned in the Church's calendar to Adam and Eve (December 24th) and he tells us that in the Nathan Jesus we find above all the Father force, the preserved residue as it were of man's original divine heritage, his original innocence before his Fall. And on another occasion, in a single lecture entitled *The Son of God and the Son of Man*, he describes how in many respects the child under three years may be compared with this Nathan Jesus being.

If we follow up these lines of thought, we are led to conclude that there is indeed a speck of *natural* goodness surviving in man, apart from the operation of Grace, and that it is an error to postulate his total depravity. It seems that he is allowed to carry with him this preserved remainder of his original innocence as a kind of viaticum on the long journey through sin and woe. Further, that we cannot truly grasp the relation between Nature and Grace without some understanding of the relation between Jesus and Christ.

More abstractly, we may perhaps say that the mystery of the two pairs of apparently contradictory truths with which we have been concerned resolves itself into the mystery of Time. Contradictory propositions cannot both be true *at the same time*. But what is time? There seems no doubt that today we have too literal and quantitative a conception of it, just as we have of space. Perhaps what is wanted in the Movement is for someone to arise who will work out ways of helping us to transcend the 'classical' conception of time, as Mr. George Adams has been helping us to begin the task of transcending the classical conception of space. It will involve a study of astrality; for just as we grasp the true nature of space only to the extent that we are at home in the etheric world, so we grasp the true nature of time only to the extent that we are at home in the astral world.

Instead of bringing my observations to a proper close, as a good lecturer should, I am impelled to end this lecture by throwing out a number of suggestions. The first is, that special attention might be paid to that very difficult Michael Letter which immediately precedes the one I have quoted from. It is number XXIV in my edition and is entitled 'Man in his Macrocosmic Essence (*Wesenheit*)'.[3] In this letter Rudolf Steiner describes how etheric forces flow into the earth from the surrounding universe, and with them "the world-impulses which are active in the astral body of man". But while, in the case of plants, this present influx or influence is all we need to grasp, in the case of both men and animals it is otherwise.

---

[3] But see also for a much more discursive treatment of 'astral time', Lecture V in the book *Anthroposophy, an Introduction*.

In their case there are two different kinds of astrality —— the inflowing impulses already mentioned and the astrality already 'in' or 'streaming through' the earth, and these represent a present which is also past (*die im gegenwärtigen Irdischen aus der Vorzeit bewahrten Astralkräfte*). But this second kind of astrality is in turn connected, not with sun-forces flowing in from the universe, but with Old Sun, which in some way is to be thought of as still there in our present Earth. Perhaps we may think that, just as Earth in addition to that influence from the sun, and to the working of the Sun-spirit who united himself with Earth at the Mystery of Golgotha, has the Old Sun (its own past incarnation) in some way still present within it, so in addition to what may be bestowed on us by Grace, we retain in some way and to some extent and as part of our nature our 'original' innocence. Here at all events are deep mysteries which point to the need for a new imagination of Time before they can be properly understood.

If we think of Nature, as we experience her with our senses, as the outer waking Man, and of all that in Nature which remains unexperienced as the inner, sleeping Man, then clearly we must relate very closely the invisible Spirit upholding and sustaining Nature with this sleeping, unconscious pole in Man. This is also perhaps the "Spiritual Earth" occasionally referred to by Steiner in the *Michael Letters*. And we are likely to find that time is something quite different for this sleeping Man from what it is for waking humanity, and that it is only by the latter that time is experienced as a tidy, quantitative sequence of moments and events. The threefold being of

Man, with its sleeping and its waking poles, is itself derived from the interweaving of the three spiritual Hierarchies. Is it only the Third and lowest Hierarchy (who "only live in the process of man's culture") that is to be thought of as living in time, as we understand and experience it? With the advent of rhythm, mere sequence becomes qualitative as well as quantitative; rhythm depends on a co-existence, on some plane, of the before and after. We may perhaps approach in this way the relation of the Second Hierarchy to time. And we may do well to think of the First Hierarchy as transcending our time altogether —— or *containing* it. We may think of the sublime Beings of the First Hierarchy as containing in their bosom at once the 'finished work' phase of nature and that spirit-filled phase which *we* can also truthfully describe as 'past' —— at once the original Innocence from which we fell and the Grace towards which we are striving.

MAN, THOUGHT AND NATURE
first published 1962

IT IS FAIRLY generally believed by those whose acquaintance with Rudolf Steiner and his work is limited to hearsay, that he was trying in some way to put the clock back. This is especially the case, it is thought, in the account which he gave of the being of nature. When a man speaks with confidence, for example, of Hierarchies of Spiritual Beings, then — as long as all this is brought forward only in connection with the human soul — people are prepared to concede that he may be exploring, in his own way, the subjective world of the human Unconscious. Has not C. G. Jung done something of the kind? But when he goes on to affirm that the same Beings also stand behind what we call the laws of nature —— then, surely, he is asking us to restore an old way of thinking — an 'animistic' way — which, in the light of modern science, we have long rightly abandoned.

I do not wish to concern myself with the question, how far older ways of interpreting nature, which disappeared in the course of the scientific revolution, were justified, and how far they were confused and inaccurate. But I do wish to ask —— and, so far as I am able, to answer, the general question: Whether it is true to say that the Spiritual Science, or Anthroposophy, of Rudolf Steiner

Printed in *Anthroposophical Quarterly*, 1962.

seeks to restore an old relation of thought between man and nature.

Now it is not possible to understand Steiner's own way of interpreting nature without some understanding of what he meant by two very common words —— words we all use many times every day, but which meant something quite different to him from what they did to nearly all his contemporaries, and from what they still do mean to the great majority of people. These words are 'thinking' and 'thought'.

If you look at a list of the publications, or read his autobiography, you will find that this question — What is the true nature of thought and what happens when we think? — was also the first one he set himself to answer. One might even say that he was, first and foremost, a man who thought about thinking, and that everything else followed from that.

Of course others have also thought about thinking, and some of them have arrived at conclusions which in important respects resembled his own. The difference is that these others, once they have proved the point to their satisfaction, commonly forget all about it. They do not get on to thinking in a different way about the Creation because of the conclusions they have arrived at about the nature of thinking itself. Steiner did. He took his own conclusions so seriously that he at once began to act on them and continued to do so throughout his life. They became part of his whole being and behaviour. That is why I ventured to suggest as I did just now —— not so much that he formed a theory about the nature of thinking, but that — for himself to begin with — he altered the meaning of the word 'Thinking'.

Let me try to describe, in the broadest possible way, the sort of consequences which would follow, if the meaning of such words as 'Thought' and 'Thinking' should be altered in the same way for the world in general. And here an analogy may perhaps help. It so happens that there are two other quite different words, which have changed their meanings — in the course of the last two or three hundred years — in an equally striking (and in some respects a rather similar) manner. I am referring to the words Gravity and Gravitation.

What does the word Gravity mean to us today? What sort of picture, or idea, do we have in our minds when we use it in phrases like 'the force of gravity'? It is an idea of something which, in a greater or less degree, pervades the whole of space. Invisible, inaudible, impalpable, we have to conceive of it as a sort of web of delicately adjusted and complicatedly interacting lines, or fields, of force which is somehow present in space from the centre of the earth to the farthest limits of our solar system, and beyond that to the world of the stars.

That is what Gravity means today. But what did the word mean yesterday? What did it mean before the time of Kepler and Newton? In those days it meant simply … 'gravitas' … heaviness or weight.

Now weight is something that is limited to the earth. And, if we try to take ourselves back in imagination to a time when Gravity meant no more than weight, we have, as it were, to empty our idea of space of what it contains in the way of these invisible forces. And we have to let Gravity mean something wholly confined to the earth, something that has no meaning outside the earth and its immediate vicinity.

And then —— into the vacuum which we have created we have to watch the modern concept of Gravity flooding back and filling it, almost as the rising tide fills a hollow in the rocks. In this way we may come to understand, and to feel, what happened in the seventeenth century —— how something, which was formerly thought of as narrowly confined to the earth — (and it really involved the whole Aristotelian conception of the earth as the centre of the universe) — how this expanded, in the picture men formed of it, rose up from the earth and became instead, something that filled the wide spaces of the universe — something in which the earth did indeed participate — but only as one among many heavenly bodies —— no longer as its exclusive container.

When we think about the word Thinking today, we ordinarily mean by it something which is confined within our skins or, if you like, in a corner of our brains. But I am asking you to imagine it coming to mean something very different. Just as we look back to a time before Kepler and Newton, when Gravity had such a cramped and parochial meaning — quite other than the spacious one we now attach to it — so, I am persuaded that our descendants will look back, perhaps with amusement, to a time when Thinking and Thought had the strangely cramped and parochial meaning which we attach to them today. Because, for them, Thinking will be something as to which one simply takes it for granted that it permeates the whole world of nature and indeed the whole universe.

The title of this lecture is "Man, Thought and Nature". Thought does indeed stand between man and nature; it is the most important of all the links between them. Why is the nature of Thinking such an important issue? Because it is the medium in which there comes about that special relation between man and nature, which we call knowledge. It is true that, since the scientific revolution, Western man, at all events, has come to feel more and more strongly that all reliable knowledge comes to him through the senses; but that does not make what I said any less true.

The operative word, after all, is 'through'. We know the world through the senses; but we only do so by relating more and more Thought with the rudimentary impressions, which are all that the unaided senses can furnish. It is only because of the Thinking that we do, and have done in the past, from childhood on, that, when we look around us, we do not stare uncomprehendingly at a chaos of unrelated impressions, but perceive an ordered — a coherent world of beings, objects and events — a world which, to some extent at least, we can already say we know.

Almost everyone who thinks about such matters at all agrees that this is so, including even those who identify the mind with the brain and try to gain knowledge of it by using the analogy of machines which the brain has itself constructed. But what is so very singular about the epistemological outlook of our generation is: that on the one hand they have the idea that the whole configuration, colour, appearance and cohesion of nature depends on Thinking and yet, on the other, they have the idea that this Thinking is no more than a kind of a flicker going on in a corner of the brain.

Now this is really a very strange marriage of ideas indeed ... and has led to all sorts of matrimonial jars, all sorts of difficulties, all sorts of uneasy metaphysical arguments about what (if anything) is actually there outside of us and what is not really there, but is only a kind of appearance, or deception. All sorts of lyrical backchat about Juniper trees when there is no one about in the Quad!

If the concept of Gravitation was startling, when it first appeared, it was not because it was any sort of fantastic and far-fetched paradox; but rather because it was so extremely simple and even so obvious. In the same way, Steiner's insistence — and Goethe's before him — that the Thinking on which our experience of nature depends, really is *in* — objectively in — nature —— and is not a kind of searchlight-beam proceeding from a magic-lantern in the human skull, may be startling at first encounter; but it is really much simpler and more obvious, a much less tortured and artificial notion than the received assumptions of physics, physiology and psychology.

One word, however, of warning: for the special purpose of emphasising a change of meaning that might come about I have been comparing the concept of Thinking with the concept of Gravitation. In many other respects it is a bad comparison —— almost a comparison between two opposites. Really a better comparison would be with Light, which also permeates the space of our solar system, and all space in a greater or less degree. "The mind," as Steiner himself once put it, "is related to thought, as the eye is to light." Everyone accepts the very special relation that exists between the eye and light; but no one suggests that light is simply something that goes on in the eye.

Yet —— when it is a case of Thinking, rather than of Light, then the idea of it as a process, in which the mind of man directly participates, but which nevertheless goes on outside his body — or (so far as it has a spatial co-efficient) both outside and within his body — this idea certainly does take us back to older ideas of the nature of man and his relation to the world around him —— ideas that have long been discarded. That is to say, they have been discarded in the West, though they remain a *sine qua non* of most oriental philosophy and religion. As a matter of history, therefore, there is also this difference between the case of the word Thought, and the case of the word Gravity, from which I drew my analogy. I spoke as if both words alike had begun with a cabined and confined meaning. But, in the case of Thought and Thinking, language did not *start* with the confined meaning. That is itself the end-product of a previous inward process of contraction —— contraction, if you like, to the brain.

Without going back to the age of Myth-Consciousness, a sensitive reading of, for example, Greek philosophy can make us feel very vividly how thinking was, in former days, not merely theoretically supposed to be, but actually experienced as a kind of natural process going on in a man's environment, in which his own mind participated. I do not think it possible really to understand Greek philosophy without realising this — really to understand, for instance, what Aristotle meant by his Passive and Active Intelligence, or the cosmogony of Plato's *Timaeus*. It is not a thing one can prove. It is a question of a certain sensitiveness to language and a refusal to read into words, when they were uttered more than, say, 1,000 years ago, meanings that have only developed long since. Granted this, there are all sorts of delicate symptoms of what I am saying. For instance, the delightful passage in one of Plato's Dialogues (I cannot recall which), where the group of speakers are trying to 'chase', as we might still say, an elusive idea, which they cannot quite succeed in formulating. Only for them — it becomes obvious, as you read — the experience really was like a chase! It reads rather as if they were a bunch of cricketers at fielding-practice ... or more as if they had a small, slippery animal in their midst. You can feel, in the whole way it is presented, how Thinking was experienced more as a kind of participation in an objective process.

Is Rudolf Steiner, then — I revert to the question with which I began — advocating a return to these ancient ways? No. He certainly is not. It could never be so, for the simple reason that the whole of his teaching is based on an evolution of human consciousness. This contraction of Thinking, inwards to the brain, of which I have been speaking, was, for him, an absolutely essential stage in that evolution and only a stage. But — now — why was it so essential? Because it was this that finally detached man from nature, of which he formerly felt himself to be a part and only a part. Originally he felt himself — spiritually as well as physically — a functioning member of the natural world, somewhat as the finger is a member of the physical body.

Once this detachment has been accepted positively and experienced to the full, then, the relation between man and nature — however mystical or 'supersensible' it may be — can never be the same as it was before.

At the same time — and this is how the misunderstanding about putting the clock back may have arisen — evolution for Steiner was not quite the simple, one-way affair which it is too often supposed to be, and especially by biologists. For him, all evolution — one could almost say all development of any sort — was not simply an ascent of the material towards ever greater complexity of organisation; it was also a descent, an involution of the Spirit into the Material, which it, the Spirit, organises and transforms, and through which it acquires a new intensity, a new level of self-awareness.

If you want to represent the process of evolution diagrammatically, you must think, not as the evolutionary Humanists do, of a straight line sloping on and on and on and up and up and up; but rather of a curve like a capital 'U'. Now, if you move down the left-hand side, or limb, of a letter 'U', round the curve at the bottom and up the right-hand limb, you will keep on reaching points on the right side, which are at the same level as corresponding points on the left; and these levels you certainly did pass on your way down. The journey on will, by its nature — to that extent — involve a journey back, or a return ... Oddly enough it is very much the same with a clock. It is not only when you move the hands backwards that you bring them back to where they were before; you also do it when you move them forwards.

The history of Paganism is the history of the human Spirit slowly emerging from the Spirit of nature, and still dreamingly aware of its former union. We are becoming more and more alive to this, as a fact of history. Besides throwing fresh light on the process — and in all manner of detail — Steiner went further. He forecast the further evolutionary ascent of the human Spirit ... shall I say? — up the right-hand limb of the 'U' — that is, a re-union of the free Spirit of man with the Spirit of Nature, but without loss of its own sovereign identity. And it is the very heart of his finding that this re-ascent was made possible by the Incarnation and Death of the Divine Man (whom he also called "The Representative of Humanity") in Palestine 2,000 years ago.

You may ask: Are there any indications of this, beyond his bare assertion? Is it just an *ipse dixit*? There are a great many indications. Coming events cast their shadows before. The more one studies the history of Western thought and Western culture generally — if he really studies it in depth — the less likely he is to feel, about Anthroposophy, that it is a brand new set of ideas delivered at the door by Rudolf Steiner in a neat brown-paper parcel. It begins to look much more like a coming-to-the-surface at last, and out into the clear light of day, of something that has long been at work in the dark —— or nearly in the dark ... half-hidden, always trying to reach the surface, and occasionally succeeding in doing so —— for a brief period, and perhaps in an unexpected form ... then vanishing again into obscurity.

I cannot do much more than throw out a hint or two of the sort of thing I mean. Coming events cast their shadows before; and long before the process of detachment of which I have spoken reached its culmination, but when it was already much farther advanced than in Plato's time, you may hear premonitory notes of an altogether new relation between man and nature, which this detachment was to render possible.

You may, for instance, trace out the working of that stream of thought, which first became articulate about the third century of our era —— and which is often loosely classified as Neo-Platonism... As Thought, this Neo-Platonism is only cultivated by small groups here and there. It is really like a stream running underground. One thinks of the Greek tale of the Nymph Arethusa —— or perhaps of Ruskin's charming story of *The King of the Golden River*. You hear it working on from the third into the fourth and fifth centuries; then, scarcely again until the fourteenth and fifteenth centuries, for instance, in the circle known as the Florentine Academy —— and so on.

Mostly, you hear it underground, and when its waters do thrust up for a moment, to sparkle in the sunlight, it is because they have taken hold more of the Feeling life and appear, transformed, as artistic or poetic inspiration. The Florentine Academy was one of the channels through which this occurred. Read Professor Wind's excellent book *Pagan Mysteries in the Renaissance*, read especially the footnotes, and you will see how much of this Neo-Platonic stream is there, bubbling to the surface, in Florentine painting ... for example, in that astoundingly beautiful group of the three Graces, on the left-centre of Botticelli's picture called the *Primavera*.

You will, if you listen, hear the noise of the subterranean waters again in the little-read writings of our Cambridge Platonists in the seventeenth century ... Men like Cudworth and Henry More. And then, after a shorter interval this time, you see it enjoying the open air and sunshine of a wider appeal in that great movement in art and literature which dominated the aesthetic experience of the late eighteenth and early nineteenth centuries —— in the so-called Romantic Movement. One thinks, in our own country, of names like Blake, Wordsworth, Coleridge and others. Nor has the Golden River altogether vanished underground again since then. It enjoys the light of day in the work of a few of our living poets, in whose verses one feels moving the breath of the Creative Word, the breath of the Logos, and of a deep human response to the Logos, the breath that is alone the true breath of poetry. Of these poets Kathleen Raine[1] is an outstanding example.

---

[1] This lecture was delivered at Rudolf Steiner House, London, as part of a programme celebrating the centenary of Rudolf Steiner's birth. Kathleen Raine was in the chair.

The Greek philosophers, as the Greek spirit emerged from that more thoroughgoing intermingling with the Spirit — or Spirits — of nature, which gave rise to the rich Imaginations of their Mythology —— the Greeks evolved their doctrine of the Logos ... the creative Word, which informs both man and nature. The nature-poetry of the Romantic tradition does indeed reflect this older tradition in many ways; but it is also very different from it.

There is little, if any, evidence that the Greeks were moved by the beauty of nature, or, more precisely, little evidence that they were ever moved in such a way as to be aware of themselves as moved by it.

Yet that is the very essence of the Romantic Inspiration in the aspect of its response to nature. It imports a *reciprocal* relation between the spirit of man and the spirit of nature, which the Greek, and later the Roman, exponents of the Logos could never have understood.

It is rather as if a musical instrument, which was being played on ... an Aeolian harp perhaps, played on by nature herself ... fell silent for a while. And then, after an interval, when it began to sound again, it was no longer merely an instrument, but had become aware of itself as such ... and could itself take part in the playing of itself.

Now — for the first time — we have a relation between man and nature in which the Twoness is as important as the Oneness. It is even already becoming the kind of relation that made possible such a definition of Anthroposophy as Rudolf Steiner gave in the last few weeks of his life, when he called it "A path of Knowledge to guide the Spiritual in the Human Being to the Spiritual in the Universe".

There is a remarkable apostrophe to nature in one of Shaftesbury's essays which he wrote under the inspiration of the Cambridge Platonists, and which made a considerable stir, when it appeared at the beginning of the eighteenth century, especially among the leaders of the Romantic Movement in Germany ... Herder, Lessing, Schiller and Goethe. Here is only a sentence or two from it:

"O Mighty Genius," he begins, "sole-animating and inspiring Power. Author and Subject of these thoughts! ..." And when later he turns to the nature of thought itself, he speaks of how, in thinking, we are in a manner "conscious of that original and eternally existent Thought, whence we derive our own". It is through Thought, he says that "Nature communicates herself more immediately to us, so as in some manner to inhabit within our souls."

"Author — and Subject — of these thoughts!" This reciprocal relation between man and nature, which was at the same time a union, was beginning to change from a philosophical into a concrete, a poetic experience. And nowhere did this happen more intensively than in the spirit of Goethe. Those who know anything of the whole feel of the Goethean approach to nature will readily understand why he appreciated Shaftesbury. When he writes poetry, Goethe insists, he feels that nature herself is expressing herself in him. And all the more so, he adds significantly, when nature is also the subject of the poem. Author and Subject. For Goethe, when the poet contemplates Nature, it is nothing less than Nature herself contemplating herself, and rejoicing in what she sees.

We are approaching the point where the course of the river no longer lies in the past and the question arises: what the stream is going to do in the future. For, with the coming of Goethe — who was a scientist no less than a poet — something like a possible transition began from embodiment of the new experience in literature and art to its embodiment also in that more sharply defined relation of knowledge which we call 'Science'.

The Centenary Exhibition emphasises the part played by Goethe's scientific writings in the development of Steiner's thought. He owed them a debt which he never tired of acknowledging (though Steiner never, I think, actually borrowed an idea from anyone. He was an Initiate, who got at his Thinking direct). For Goethe's scientific method did really involve an actual participation in the Thinking that is present and active in the world of nature.

And it is just this controlled participation which was carried infinitely further by Steiner. In his writings of a more philosophical nature he also used such words as 'Thinking', 'Thoughts', 'Concepts'. But in the great body of his later work he more frequently alluded to the Spirit — in so far as it is active and formative in the world of nature — as the 'Etheric' or 'Ethereal'. Mr. Adams, in his lecture, showed how these ethereal forms and forces — which are the source both of our Thinking and of our Life — enter into space, not in the first place as physical, earth-centred forces, like those of Gravity, but as forces working, in opposition to Gravity, from the periphery of the universe.

Within them, at the same time united with and detached from them, the human being has his own etheric body. One may think of it, using a metaphor, as a kind of cell, with something like a membrane between it and the rest of the etheric world ... a pervious and infinitely elastic membrane. It is this that makes possible (for this 'Membrane', as I have called it, can be strengthened by exercises in concentration and other kinds of self-discipline) those detailed investigations, which Rudolf Steiner himself was able to carry out, and the results of which he has bequeathed to us in such rich profusion.

For, besides enunciating the method with far greater clarity than had previously been achieved, he was himself a pioneer in that process of knowledge wherein the Spirit of man is both united with, and detached from, the Spirit of nature — united with it and thus experiencing it from within — and at the same time contemplating it, as the ordinary scientist contemplates his subject-matter, from outside.

Yet Spiritual Science, while it must aim at the exactness and precision that accompanies the mode of observation from without, is also very much more than mere observation, or contemplation.

There is one old conception of the relation between man and the universe — abandoned in the course of the scientific revolution — which Steiner certainly has restored:

> Whereas God contains in Him all things, because He is their source, Man contains in him all things, because he is their centre.

Those are the words of the Florentine Pico della Mirandola; but what they express was never a recondite notion known only to small circles of Platonists or Neo-Platonists. It would be nearer the mark to say that it was taken for granted all over the place ... Sir Toby Belch and Sir Andrew Aguecheek, for example, were both familiar with it. I mean the conception of man as a microcosm within the macrocosm —— a miniature world, linked with the great one by numberless immaterial threads.

Such a conception is indeed almost implicit in much that has been said. But here again there is a striking difference. This conception, in its old form, was embryonic. In it, the microcosm was essentially passive, depending from the macrocosm, somewhat as a puppet that is dangled on strings. And this older, embryonic relation in fact still largely subsists — to strengthen and uphold him — in the instinctive life of man, in sleep and after death, until he is reborn in a physical body. Yet, for Anthroposophy, what is essential is the *activity* of this microcosm.

Steiner found that there has been going forward, throughout history, a real process of withdrawal ... ex-carnation ... of the life of the Spirit from its original home in the macrocosm, and thus from the world of nature. Nature, he said, is in fact becoming more and more a mere product, a 'finished work' of the Gods, more and more the lifeless machine, going on by itself, of its own momentum —— which the nineteenth century imagined it to be. Nature is really dying!

It was in this light that he interpreted that process of contraction of human experience in thinking, from the wide spaces of the universe into its sharp little focus in the brain.

If we do not immediately see the connection between the two it is because we are apt to distinguish sharply between our consciousness of nature and nature herself. But such a distinction is not wholly valid —— and is not valid at all in the crude way we commonly assume. Thus, the contraction of thinking is simply another aspect of the dying process, or rather it is the dying process, experienced from within. And what we today distinguish sharply from ourselves, and coldly investigate, as 'Nature', is itself the end-product of that process.

The Spirit of man was, thus, for Steiner not only a microcosm; it was a microcosm into which a dying natural world had long been slowly withering. And he gave all the energy of his own life to the task of proclaiming that this withering process can only be arrested and reversed by the energy of the microcosm —— of man himself! Thus, the Spirit of man was, for him, really a seed or germ, out of which the dying Spirit of nature seeks to be reborn.

The exertion of the purified human will —— the strengthening of the human etheric body and, with that, the carrying of will-forces into his thinking —— all these are entailed by the 'higher knowledge' of which he wrote. And all these betoken something more than the knowledge that comes of observation from without. They are not even the concern of man alone. They are really the first step in an age-long process of cosmic rebirth.

Man has not only to know nature; he has to re-awaken her. But this he can only do by knowing her — truly knowing her — knowing her in depth. And this re-awakening, which began when the conscious gaze of poets and artists first rested on her sleeping form in admiration and rapture —— this will continue, he said, until she stirs, and opens her eyes, and arises again in strength, in the strength of the Spirit of man, to walk hand in hand with science now, as well as with art.

It may be objected that this whole conception is impossibly anthropocentric and implies a megalomaniac overestimate by man of his own importance. But before such an objection is raised, there are two things it is well to remember. In the first place, we Human Beings have already, in the further pursuit of physical science, been fixed with the responsibility of *not destroying* the earth. Is it in fact such a very very long step from this to our finding, through Spiritual Science, that we also have the responsibility of preserving her life and renewing her Spirit?

For the second thing, we must go back to the analogy with which we began... and as we do so, it becomes rather more than an analogy. When space began to fill up with those forces of Gravity, which had hitherto been so peculiarly earth's own, and which man could actually suffer and feel in his own little body, it might have been thought that that would lead to megalomania. Under the old system the earth had indeed been the centre —— yes, but in Aristotelian physics, it was also the *sump* of the universe —— a sort of rock-bottom into which all that was gross and unspiritual everywhere in the universe was precipitated by its Gravitas in the old sense. And now — hey presto! — all that was changed! The earth was floated free in space and actually became herself a 'Heavenly Body'. It might well have been thought that this earth would now become invested with a new and overweening importance!

Instead, something quite different happened. When the meaning of the word 'Gravity' changed, the centre of gravity shifted at the same time. It was the sun which henceforth occupied the central position, at first of the universe as a whole, and still today of the solar system. For Copernicus himself and some of the other scientists of the day, this change from a geocentric to a heliocentric system was much more than an astronomical re-adjustment. They rejoiced, in all humility, that the royal dignity of the source of life and light had at last been accorded its proper place in the scheme of things.

Rudolf Steiner described his Theory of Knowledge as "a Pauline Theory". He never tired of quoting St Paul's words from the Epistle to the Galatians: "Not I live, but the Christ liveth in me." And he made it very clear that it is only on these terms that his path of knowledge can be followed. His Spiritual Science in fact is not anthropocentric but Christocentric. And it follows from this that the end of the path can never be reached by one or two men here and there, but only by all men in fellowship and communion. In the end, it is not this or that man, but only man himself, in whom the Spirit of nature can fully rise again into life.

RUDOLF STEINER'S CONCEPT OF MIND
first published 1961

THE TRUE NATURE of human thought is a matter of concern to everyone, whether he knows it or not Everyone is concerned, therefore, with Rudolf Steiner's concept of mind; but not everyone will wish to acquaint himself with the framework on which the exposition of that concept was first stretched and displayed, for not everyone is interested in the history of philosophy in the nineteenth century. Here, then, in the short space available, the attempt will be made to say what it was that Steiner thought about thinking, so far as the writer understands it, and without much reference to the framework within which it was originally presented.

It is founded on two axioms. Steiner himself does not call them axioms, or place them at the beginning of his exposition. He does, however, draw very special attention to them, pointing out that, though both are commonly overlooked, both are self-evident to reflection.

In the first place, *a concept as such is not one of a series of perfect replicas; it is numerically identical in all the individual minds that think it.* This proposition is not really even open to argument, because on it depends the very possibility of arguing. Yet, as Steiner himself points out in his major philosophical work, *Die Philosophie der Freiheit*[1] it:

---

[1] Translated into English under the title: *The Philosophy of Freedom* (Rudolf Steiner Press, London, 1949).

"conflicts with a common prejudice which is very hard to overcome. The victims of this prejudice are unable to see that the concept of a triangle which my head grasps is the same as the concept which my neighbour's head grasps..."

It is easy to see how this prejudice comes about. The naïve man believes himself — with some excuse, as we shall see when we come to the second axiom — to be the creator of his thoughts and he is led by this to assume that each person has his detached private concepts. Nevertheless, hard as it may be,

> It is a fundamental demand of philosophic thinking to overcome this prejudice. The one uniform concept of 'triangle' does not split up into a multiplicity because it is thought by many persons. For the thinking of the many is itself a unity.

Or, as Steiner put it elsewhere metaphorically: "The mind is related to thought as the eye is to light."

The second axiom is this: that *thinking is our own activity*. This, again, is a matter of direct experience. Our thoughts cannot be thrust on us, as our sensations are, from without. They demand our co-operation, our own activity before we can be said to have thought them —— before they can *be* our thoughts. Opinions, confessions, etc., brought about by modern techniques of persuasion, whether physiological or otherwise, are at most the exception which proves this rule. They are felt to be monstrous, precisely because they seek to *compel* that which bears upon it the very signature of the victim's own free act.

For the same reason — because the thought-process is so intimately and entirely *our own act* — it is impossible to observe it in its actual occurrence. We do not notice it, because we cannot contemplate what we ourselves effect while we are in the article of effecting it. This is Alexander's distinction between 'enjoyment' and 'contemplation'.[2] Steiner puts it as follows:

> There are two things which are incompatible with one another: productive activity and the contemplation of that activity. This is recognised even in the First Book of Moses. It represents God as creating the world in the first six days, and only after its completion is any contemplation of the world possible: 'And God saw everything that he had made and, behold, it was very good.' The same applies to our thinking. It must be there first, if we would observe it.

But although we do not, and cannot, both think and observe ourselves thinking in the same moment, we never (while we remain sane) have any doubt that the thoughts in our minds are in fact 'ours'. So much so that, as already pointed out, we commonly — though erroneously — regard them as a sort of private world lodged within us. There is thus an important distinction to be made between *thinking* as an act, albeit an unnoticed act, and thought as the *concept*, which results from the act, and which we both notice and appropriate. Steiner emphasised that he made *thinking* his starting-point and not concepts and ideas, which are first gained by means of thinking:

---

[2] See the opening pages of S. W. Alexander's well-known 1916–18 Gifford Lectures, published as the book, *Space, Time and Deity* (Macmillan, 1920).

My remarks regarding the self-dependent, self-sufficient character of thinking cannot, therefore, be simply transferred to concepts. (I make special mention of this, because it is here that I differ from Hegel, who regards the concept as something primary and ultimate.)

It is this, indeed, which distinguishes Steiner's Objective Idealism from the Subjective Idealism which, in one form or another, was predominant both in Germany and in England at the time when he was writing.

It was Rudolf Steiner's view that many philosophical errors have arisen from the fact that philosophers have been too ready to enquire what we can know and what we cannot know, without first enquiring what we mean by 'knowing'. This was, above all, the omssion which he sought to rectify and it may be said that his own philosophy is primarily an epistemology, a theory of knowledge. Why is it so important that we should grasp the true nature of thinking? Because thinking is the 'instrument of knowledge'. A philosopher starting out to construct a true theory of knowledge must start, if he is faithful to his calling, from the very beginning. If we start from any assumptions at all — astronomical or historical assumptions, for instance, or assumptions about the part played by the brain and the nerves or sense-organs in the process of knowledge — we are clearly not starting from zero. We are starting from something on which cognitive activity has already been expended. The same remark applies if we start from the 'ego', or 'consciousness', or 'the mind', or by raising the question whether there is such an entity as the mind, or from the experience of a 'normal observer'. Only if we start from thinking itself, no such objection can be made. For thinking is the very first possible move we can make in the direction from ignorance towards knowledge. We cannot think about the world, or about anything at all, without thinking.

Thus, by way of example, it follows from the former of the two axioms that thinking is anterior even to the elementary distinction between subject and object. Thinking

> produces these two concepts just as it produces all others. When, therefore, I, as thinking subject, refer a concept to an object, we must not regard this reference as something purely subjective. It is not the subject, but thinking, which makes the reference. The subject does not think because it is a subject, rather it conceives itself to be a subject because it can think. The activity performed by man as a thinking being is thus not merely subjective. Rather it is neither subjective nor objective; it transcends both these concepts. I ought never to say that I, as an individual subject, think, but rather that I, as subject, exist myself by the grace of thinking. Thinking is thus an element which leads me beyond myself and relates me to objects. At the same time it separates me from them, inasmuch as it sets me, as subject, over against them.
>
> It is just this which constitutes the double nature of man. His thinking embraces himself and the rest of the world. But by this same act of thinking he determines himself also as an individual, in contrast with the objective world.

If, however, I owe my separate existence, as subject, to 'the grace of thinking', yet something else besides thinking is required to bring this separate existence about. This brings us to the other primary element with which any theory of knowledge must deal, namely perception. Unlike my thoughts, my perceptions are private and personal to me, inasmuch as they depend on my point of observation and my separate physical organism. It is the perceptual element in the totality of my experience which thinking makes use of, as the means, to bring about my subjectivity —— that is, my separate existence apart from nature and apart from my fellow human beings.

This important, and from one point of view startling, proposition requires a little further consideration. It is startling because we are accustomed to accept precisely the *perceptual* element in our experience — the evidence, as we say, of our senses — as constituting the 'public' world that is common to all mankind; while we contrast with this the 'private', inner world of our thoughts. This is justifiable enough in the ordinary loose use of language, but how carefully we must distinguish under the strict discipline of an epistemological enquiry! It is just here that the difference between 'thought' (as the product of the act) and 'thinking', the act itself, is relevant. For if it is *pure* thinking, disentangled from all perception, to which we are directing our attention, then, as we have seen, it is precisely this which *is not* private and personal to ourselves. And again, if it is pure perception, disentangled from all thinking, to which we are directing our attention, then it is precisely this which *is* private and personal to ourselves. Thus, it is not perception alone which can ever put us in touch with the solid, public, objective world, but only the percept mixed with thinking.

'Disentangled from all thinking', 'pure perception' —— we are of course going too fast; and it is impossible to avoid doing so in the brief space at our disposal. Concepts and percepts are, for Steiner, the bricks out of which the whole edifice of human knowledge is constructed; and the *pure* concept and the *pure* percept are accordingly the only elements on which an adequate *theory* of knowledge can be based.

> The moment a percept appears in my field of observation, thinking, too, becomes active through me. A member of my thought-system, a definite intuition, a concept, connects itself with the percept.

The terminology which Steiner employs to denote this important act of union between percept and corresponding concept may profitably be compared with the 'presentational symbolism' of Susanne Langer.[3] It is these conceptually determined percepts (he calls them *Vorstellungen* —— representations) which make up the public world of our actual, everyday experience.

A good deal has been said already of the nature of the concept. We must now ask what Steiner meant by 'percept'. But let it first be made clear (in view of what has just been said on the topic of 'subjectivity') what he did *not* mean. He did not mean anything in the nature of a subjective representation; he did not mean the same thing as perception. *Esse est percipi* was no part of his

---

[3] Professor Langer's books, *Feeling and Form* (Routledge and Kegan Paul, 1953) and *Problems of Art* (Routledge and Kegan Paul, 1957), are gaining increasing recognition on this side of the Atlantic among those who are interested in symbols and symbolism. Her most intensive treatment of the aspect here considered will be found in the earlier *Philosophy in a New Key* (Routledge and Kegan Paul, 1951).

doctrine. 'It is not,' he writes, 'the process of perception, but the object of this process, which I call the "percept".' And again: '"objective" means that which, for perception, presents itself as external to the perceiving subject.' What *are* subjective, on the other hand, are the after-images of those determined percepts, which remain in the mind when actual perception has ceased. These he called *Ideen* —— ideas; and it is these which are the principal source of error and illusion, and the cause why the 'public' world-picture is by no means necessarily also an 'objective' one. The pure concept of a triangle is one and the same in your mind and mine —— not so the perceptual trappings, which may have stuck, as it were, to the concept, left there by particular representations of triangles on particular blackboards.

Just as the concept unavoidably presents itself to us as the product of our own activity, so the percept unavoidably presents itself as *not* the product of our own activity. Indeed, that is almost its definition. The percept is all *that* in the totality of our experience which is *not* the product of our activity. It may, for that reason and to that extent, be properly described as 'given':

> What then is a percept? This question, asked in this general way, is absurd. A percept occurs always as a perfectly determinate, concrete content. This content is immediately given and is completely contained in the given. The only question we can ask concerning the given content is, what it is apart from perception, that is, what it is for thinking. The question concerning the 'what' of a percept can, therefore, only refer to the conceptual intuition which corresponds to the percept.

Here it will be necessary to say something of Steiner's concept of 'the Given', which plays such an important part in his epistemology. We find that he uses the word in two different ways. William James, writing on man's experience of time, adopted from E. R. Clay that useful term 'the specious present'. By analogy with this use — once more introducing a piece of terminology not employed by Steiner himself — we will call his 'given', in the first sense, 'the specious Given'.[4] It is simply what we actually find, of any description whatever, when we look around us in the world. What we find, that is, at the point in our lives when we first decide to tackle the problem of knowledge (not, therefore, at the breast or in the cradle). We have made up our minds about the true nature of the instrument called thought. The next step is to apply our thinking for the general purpose of acquiring knowledge. And clearly we must start where we actually find ourselves. We have no right to start with assumptions of any sort. We have certainly no right to pretend that we start from some imaginary state of mind, such as a man might have who had perceptions but as yet no thoughts —— the 'blooming, buzzing confusion' of which William James also wrote. Whatever preceded the starting-point must, *to begin with*, be taken for granted. What we are actually surrounded by is a world of phenomena, both outer and inner — trees, houses, books, theories, pains, pleasures, dreams, hallucinations and what you will —

---

[4] The initial capital is intended merely to indicate that the adjective is used substantively.

some parts of which present themselves as connected or related wholes, while others are as yet unconnected and unrelated.

How, asked Steiner in his doctoral thesis *Wahrheit und Wissenschaft*,[5] do we start out upon the business of *knowing* about all this? We have to discover a bridge that leads from the picture of the world as given to the picture of it which our cognitive activity unfolds:

> Somewhere in the Given, we must discover the spot where we can get to work, where something homogeneous to cognition meets us ... If there is to be knowledge, everything depends on there being, somewhere within the Given, a field in which our cognitive activity does not merely presuppose the Given, but is at work in the very heart of the Given itself.

This spot, or field, is the activity of thinking. At all points and at every moment it keeps inserting us, as it were, into the very texture of the Given. Out for a walk, we hear a sudden whirring noise, which 'means' nothing to us; a moment later a partridge rises from the hedge near at hand. The concept of cause and effect arises in us to unite the two percepts and at once becomes part of the Given. Next time we heard the whirring noise, it carries its meaning within it.

And now, what proved such a disadvantage when our problem was to *notice* the act of thinking, to be *aware* of it — namely, the fact that we 'enjoy' thinking and do not

---

[5] Translated into English under the title: "Truth and Science" (in *The Philosophy of Spiritual Activity*, G. P. Putnam & Sons, London and New York, 1922).

'contemplate' it, *because thinking is so much our own activity (so much our very self in action)* — now this becomes the very stamp upon its passport to utility. For the problem of knowledge is always how to relate the knower to the known. What has the phenomenal world got to *do* with me, the observing outsider? Why should there, and how can there, be a link between them called truth, or knowledge? Well, it seems there is one point where the two incompatibles coalesce; one point where 'the object of observation is qualitatively identical with the activity directed upon it.' And that point is, precisely, the activity of thinking.

Now if we reason back a little from the example of the whirring noise and the partridge, we at once have it brought home to us that the specious Given is positively full of such conceptual determinations. This applies even to that part of the specious Given which we call 'sense-data'. We owe it to our concepts that we perceive a world of shapes, forms, 'things' at all. 'The picture of the world with which we begin philosophical reflection,' wrote Steiner in *Truth and Science,*

> is already qualified by predicates which are the results solely of the act of knowing. We have no right to accept these predicates without question. On the contrary, we must carefully extract them from out of the world-picture, in order that it may appear in its purity without any admixture due to the process of cognition.

This brings us to his other use of the term 'given' — according to which it coincides with the pure percept, prior to all conceptual determinations whatsoever — to that element in experience which is *wholly* perceptual. Let us call it here the 'net Given'. It is important to be clear that the Given is never actually experienced 'net'. Thus, the net Given is something which a philosopher is concerned with, not as knower, but as epistemologist. This is a distinction Positivism fails to observe. Certainly we are not entitled to build up a picture of the world by starting from James's 'blooming, buzzing confusion' —— a thing we never experience. But that is not to say that we *are* entitled to treat the specious Given (i.e. the world as normally experienced) as though it were the same as the net Given. We arrive at the concept of the net Given, not empirically, but by analysis. We may say of it (as James said of what he called the 'real', in contrast to the 'specious', present): 'Reflection leads us to the conclusion that it must exist, but that it *does* exist can never be a part of our immediate experience.'

To seek to limit the *theory* of knowledge by applying to it, for instance, the principle of verification is like seeking to use a well-cooked meal, not for eating, but as material for making pots and pans; or like hunting for your spectacles with the help of those very spectacles which are already (you have forgotten) lodged on your nose.

Steiner declared at the beginning of the introduction to the original edition of *Truth and Science*, that his aim was 'to reduce the act of cognition, by analysis, to its ultimate elements'. He showed that, if we analyse it, the sense-experience from which we take our start, discloses itself to be no such ultimate element. It may be a 'public', but it is nevertheless a highly subjective, picture of the world and one which is 'overcome' in the process of knowledge itself. Positivism (and — in so far as it is based on an uncritical acceptance of positivist doctrine — this is true of modern science also) treats this initial experience — the specious Given — as constituting also the *ultimately* given starting-point for all reliable knowledge. This was where Steiner differed from them both.

We start, he said — as we must — from the Given; but in the course of the adventure our epistemological analysis itself establishes that that starting-point was not, after all, 'given' in the absolute sense we had supposed. On the contrary, it is and was saturated at all points with the activity of thinking, past and present. Only unfortunately we cannot *experience* separately — the one divided from the other — either the thinking activity or the net Given which is independent of it. Two courses are therefore open to us. We can reject the analysis — on the ground perhaps that it raises questions which 'cannot be asked' — and go on pretending to ourselves that the specious Given is as independent of thinking as the net Given. We shall then conclude that the only thing to do is to learn all we can 'about' the specious Given, with the help of precision instruments and mathematical generalisation, on the footing that our observing minds are mere onlookers, quite detached from it. Or we can, as Steiner did, deem illegitimate the refusal to distinguish because we cannot divide. In that case we shall conclude, with him, that an edifice of knowledge or science erected on the specious

Given is incomplete and unreliable — for we know that the latter already includes the results of thinking — and may well, therefore, be tainted with subjectivity and error. We shall then be obliged to abandon the common assumption that all thinking and knowing is thinking 'about', and knowing 'about', and that truth is an ideal reproduction of some given object. We shall conclude, instead, with Gabriel Marcel, that 'all knowledge is contingent on a participation in being, for which it cannot account because it continually presupposes it.'

With this we really reach the end of our exposition of Steiner's concept of mind and are already beginning to survey its consequences and application. These are the province of the other contributors to this volume.[6] But the following should perhaps be added before we close.

If we are determined to eliminate all subjectivity and to be uncompromisingly empirical, if we insist on verifying from experience at all points, from the very start onwards, our only course is to find some way of penetrating with full consciousness into that unconscious no-man's-land (or should one say 'every-man's-land'?) which lies between the net Given and the specious Given. This is the realm where thinking performs the function of Coleridge's 'primary imagination', or what Susanne Langer calls

---

[6] See Introduction to the 1966 edition, p. 16.

'formulation'. It is, incidentally, the realm where language is born.[7]

It is obvious that this penetration cannot be effected with only the techniques and disciplines which science has so far developed. Instrument after instrument of ever greater precision and power is invented and applied, but, for our purpose, *the mind itself* must be treated as an instrument and *its* precision and power systematically augmented.[8] It follows from all that has been said of the relation between thinking and perceiving that the strengthened thinking to which the discipline inculcated by Steiner is directed, must also result in widening the field of *perception* or *observation* themselves (as those words are ordinarily understood). This aspect he deals with in his Introductions to Goethe's scientific writings and in his short treatise *Grundlinien einer Erkenntnistheorie der Goetheschen Weltanschauung*[9] which, together with the two books previously referred to in this article, contain

---

[7] In this connection it is interesting to consider the work of the late Ernst Cassirer, whose *Philosophy of Symbolic Forms* (*Philosophie der Symbolischen Formen*, tr. R. Mannheim, Yale and Oxford University Presses, 1953) appeared two or three years before Steiner's death and was first translated into English during the 1950s. For it is on the basis of an historical approach to language, looked at in this way, that Cassirer builds up his own theory of knowledge as mental activity.

[8] The impotence of ordinary, unstrengthened thinking to deal effectively with any subject-matter *except* the specious Given has been more than sufficiently elaborated by the linguistic variants of positivist doctrine which have been developed in the West since Steiner's death.

[9] Translated into English under the title: *Goethe's Conception of the World* (Rudolf Steiner Press, London and Anthroposophic Press, New York City, 1928).

the fundamental principles underlying Rudolf Steiner's concept of mind.

Moreover, since thinking is at one and the same time the activity of man himself *and* his only guarantee of objectivity, we have no right to assume that sense-perception is the indispensable witness to reality. Thinking is — and strengthened thinking will be aware of itself as being — that factor in man 'through which he inserts himself spiritually into reality'. It will make direct contact with reality somewhat in the manner we normally attribute to perception and if, on the one hand, it is 'an active process taking place in the human mind', on the other hand it will be 'a perception mediated by no sense-organ ... a perception in which the percipient is himself active, and a self-activity which is at the same time perceived.'[10]

It is with the detailed results, both of that enhanced faculty of observation and of these purely spiritual perceptions, that so large a part of Steiner's books and lectures are concerned. But long before he began to bring them before the public, he had laid, in purely philosophical form, the epistemological foundation on which his investigations were based, and it is this foundation we have briefly tried to sketch here.

---

[10] *Goethe's Conception of the World.*

SELECTED WORKS BY OWEN BARFIELD

First published

Books by Owen Barfield

The Silver Trumpet	1925
History in English Words	1926
Poetic Diction: A Study in Meaning	1928
Romanticism Comes of Age	1944
This Ever Diverse Pair	1950
Saving the Appearances: A Study in Idolatry	1957
Worlds Apart: A Dialogue of the 1960's	1963
Unancestral Voice	1965
Speaker's Meaning	1967
What Coleridge Thought	1971
The Rediscovery of Meaning, and Other Essays	1977
History, Guilt and Habit	1979
Orpheus: A Poetic Drama	1983 (written 1937)
Owen Barfield on C. S. Lewis	1989
Night Operation	2008 (written 1975)
Eager Spring	2008 (written 1988)
The Rose on the Ash-Heap	2009 (written 1929)

Translations and edited works of Rudolf Steiner

World Economy: The Formation of a Science of World-Economics (trans. with T. Gordon-Jones)	1936
Anthroposophy: An Introduction	1961
The Case for Anthroposophy	1970
Guidance in Esoteric Training (trans. with Charles Davy)	1972
The Year Participated: being Rudolf Steiner's *Calendar of the Soul* translated and paraphrased for an English ear	1985

Edited works by other authors

Man and Animal: Their Essential Differences, by Hermann Poppelbaum	1960
The Voice of Cecil Harwood	1979

www.ingramcontent.com/pod-product-compliance
Lightning Source LLC
Chambersburg PA
CBHW031308150426
43191CB00005B/124